The Heart of
EMERSON'S JOURNALS

EDITED BY
BLISS PERRY

DOVER PUBLICATIONS, INC.
NEW YORK

Published in Canada by General Publishing Company, Ltd., 30
Lesmill Road, Don Mills, Toronto, Ontario.
Published in the United Kingdom by Constable and Company,
Ltd., 3 The Lanchesters, 162–164 Fulham Palace Road, London
W6 9ER.

Bibliographical Note

This Dover edition, first published in 1995, is an unaltered and
unabridged republication of the 1958 Dover edition which was an
unabridged reprint of the 1926 Houghton Mifflin edition. The
Dover edition is published through special arrangement with
Houghton Mifflin.

Library of Congress Cataloging-in-Publication Data

Emerson, Ralph Waldo, 1803–1882.
    The heart of Emerson's journals / edited by Bliss Perry.
       p.   cm.
    "An unaltered and unabridged republication of the 1958
Dover edition which was an unabridged reprint of the 1926
Houghton Mifflin edition"—T.p. verso.
    Includes index.
    ISBN 0-486-28508-1 (pbk.)
    1. Emerson, Ralph Waldo, 1803–1882—Diaries.
2. Authors, American—19th century—Diaries I. Perry,
Bliss, 1860–1954. II. Title.
PS1631.A3   1995
818'.303—dc20
[B]   95-11703
                                   CIP

Manufactured in the United States of America
Dover Publications, Inc., 31 East 2nd Street, Mineola, N.Y. 11501

PREFACE

THE richness of the unprinted material in Emerson's diaries has been known to the reading public ever since Elliot Cabot drew upon it for his *Memoir* of Emerson. Dr. Edward W. Emerson quoted from it freely in his *Emerson in Concord*, and in his notes to the twelve volumes of the Centenary Edition of his father's works, published in 1903. Lovers of Emerson were finally gratified by the publication of his *Journals* in their entirety. They appeared in ten volumes, under the joint editorship of Dr. Emerson and Waldo Emerson Forbes, in 1909–14. Their extraordinary interest was at once recognized by students, but to the general reading public these ten stout volumes seemed somewhat formidable. Professor Michaud promptly issued, in French, a condensation in two volumes, but hitherto no Selection from the *Journals* has been attempted for Emerson's countrymen. It has been undertaken by the present editor, with the consent of Emerson's surviving children and with the coöperation of his publishers, in the belief that a single volume edition of the *Journals* will now be welcomed by the ever-widening circle of readers of our most distinguished American writer.

It is not known when Emerson first began to keep a journal, but there are fairly full records from 1820, when he was seventeen, to 1875, when he was seventy-two. The famous diaries of John Wesley and of John Quincy Adams cover only a slightly longer period of time. The

range of topics and of moods, in these fifty-five years, is
very wide. The historian will find Emerson's *Journals*
quite as typical of New England in the nineteenth century as are the diaries of John Winthrop, of Cotton
Mather, and of Samuel Sewall in earlier epochs. Emerson's record of local and provincial fact is often as racy as
Thoreau's, and his notation of seasons and birds and
flowers quite as enthusiastic, if not so meticulously accurate. He makes shrewd judgments upon his contemporaries. He narrates his walks with Ellery Channing,
Hawthorne, and Thoreau, and his talks with Alcott and
Margaret Fuller. He gives the frankest personal impression of national figures like Webster and Everett, John
Brown and Lincoln. More significant still are the records
of his reading, of his thoughts, of material for future
poems or essays, of solitary ecstasies in the presence of
beauty, of valiant voyages of an exploring soul. Emerson
here reveals religious moods as deep and tender as those of
George Fox or St. Augustine, philosophical questionings
as poignant as those penned by Joubert or Amiel. Nor
has his master Montaigne more of the sharp tang of
reality, of endless, unsatisfied human curiosity about
oneself.

Emerson once described his diaries as his 'Savings
Bank.' Here he jotted down poetical or rhetorical phrases
for future use; he garnered his thoughts, — gleaned from
saunterings in the woods or by Walden Pond, — knowing
that some day he should need them for a book or for a
lecture. He indexed his long row of manuscript volumes
carefully. From them he drew the material of his addresses and the addresses in turn served as material for

the finished *Essays.* Singularly interesting are the first
prose drafts of some of his famous poems, like 'Each and
All,' 'The Two Rivers,' and 'Days.' But whether the
first sketches were prose or verse, meditations upon
human life or analyses of himself, they all went into the
'Savings Bank' as reserve capital for the hour of need.

There is a certain freshness and charm in these original
jottings that is sometimes lost in the smoothly finished
paragraphs of the published *Essays.* The *Journals,* for
the most part, are highly felicitous in style. That lack of
unity and coherence and sustained logic which has so
frequently been charged against Emerson as a writer of
prose is naturally less perceptible upon the random pages
of the 'Savings Bank.' Here is one golden coin after
another, — hundreds and hundreds of them,   and no
one wants them fused into an ingot. In the ten volumes
from which the contents of this single volume have been
selected there is no doubt some diffuseness, some over-
writing of spiritual experience. In a single volume these
defects are scarcely noticeable; and there is a gain in in-
cisiveness and in that sheer brilliance of tone which char-
acterizes the great passages of the *Essays.*

In literary quality, then, and still more in autobio-
graphic interest, the present volume is believed to challenge comparison with any book that Emerson published
in his life-time. Some of the most famous utterances of
the Phi Beta Kappa oration, of the Divinity School
Address, and of Emerson's best-known essays, are here to
be found in their original phrasing. It is possible to trace
also the whole story of Emerson's revolt against a con-
ventionalized conception of Christianity, in spite of many

a note of affectionate loyalty to the old order of things in Puritan New England. Here, too, are Emerson's offhand or inveterate impressions of books and authors, some of them penetrating and some of them shallow but all of them charmingly expressed. There is the magic of poetic moods recorded before the rapture has grown dim; but in general there is less transcendentalism in the *Journals* than one might expect from reading the *Essays* and the *Poems*. And there is likewise far less provincialism of mind and of experience than many twentieth-century readers have been assured that they would discover in the Concord rhapsodist. The entries in his *Journals* emphasize better than any of the biographies the significance of his travels. In early life he made two long sojourns in the South. Three times he visited Europe for extended periods. One would scarcely have expected to meet the sedate citizen of Concord in the Revolutionary clubs of Paris in 1848. Nor does one commonly associate him with crossing the Mississippi River again and again on the winter ice in order to keep his annual lecture engagements in the West. Those Western experiences were of priceless value to Emerson in helping him to perceive the character of his countrymen.

Finally, the reader of this volume should be reminded that Emerson put his deposits in the 'Savings Bank' when he felt like it, without any compulsion of the calendar. For weeks or months at a time he made no entries whatever; then his thoughts seemed to swarm, and there will be many apparently unrelated paragraphs set down on the same day, perhaps at different hours. Sometimes he used loose sheets of paper for journalizing, and

not even the painstaking skill of his son and grandson
has been equal to the task of determining the precise date
of various passages. It makes little difference, after all,
but the reader must not be perplexed at finding two or
more entries assigned to the same date. Whenever Emerson gave the subject of an entry, it has been retained.
The place of writing — like 'London,' 'St. Augustine,'
'Paris' — is also indicated if known, but after 1835 the
place may be understood to be Concord, unless otherwise
stated.

In arranging the volume for the press, it has been
thought advisable to follow as closely as possible the
grouping of the years of Emerson's life as it is preserved
in the complete edition of the *Journals*. The years 1820–
24, for instance, corresponding to Volume I of the complete *Journals*, are here represented by a single group of
passages, and each group throughout Emerson's life is
prefixed by a brief editorial note explaining the events or
circumstances to which Emerson makes allusion. In
this way footnotes have been avoided. A few proper
names written merely in initials by Emerson are here
printed in full, enclosed in brackets. Lovers of the
Journals in their entirety may miss here and there a
favorite passage, but their remedy is easy. They have
only to turn to the complete edition, with such book-
lover's charity as they can command for another book-
lover who has performed the fascinating but difficult task
of making this arbitrary choice from what Dryden would
call 'God's plenty' of treasure.

BLISS PERRY

Cambridge, 1926

CHRONOLOGICAL TABLE

1803. Emerson born, in Boston, May 25.

1813–17. At the Boston Latin School.

1817–21. At Harvard College.

1821–28. Teaching school and studying Divinity at Harvard.

1829. Pastor of Second Church of Boston. Married, Sept., to Ellen Louisa Tucker.

1831. Death of his wife (February).

1832. Resigned his pastorate (September). Sailed for Europe (December).

1833. Returned from Europe (October).

1834. Death of Edward Emerson in Porto Rico.

1835. Married to Lydia Jackson (September).

1836. Charles Emerson died (May). *Nature* published (September). Emerson's son Waldo born (October).

1837. *Phi Beta Kappa Address* (*The American Scholar;* August 31).

1838. *Divinity School Address* (July 15).

1841. *Essays. First Series.*

1842. His son Waldo died (January). Editor of *Dial* (1842–44).

1844. *Essays. Second Series.*

1847. *Poems.* Second visit to Europe.

1850. *Representative Men.*

1856. *English Traits.*

1860. *Conduct of Life.*

1867. *May Day* (poems). Received degree of LL.D. from Harvard, and was elected an Overseer of the University.

1870. *Society and Solitude.*

1872. House burned; third visit to Europe.

1875. *Letters and Social Aims.*

1882. Died at Concord, April 27.

The Heart of
EMERSON'S JOURNALS

THE HEART OF
EMERSON'S JOURNALS

1820–24

[THE first journals kept by Emerson have disappeared. The earliest that has survived is marked No. XVII, and dates from the beginning of the year 1820, when he was in his Junior year at Harvard. Sometimes he entered his intermittent diary in what he called his 'Blotting-Book.' At other times he gave the diary the fanciful title of the 'Wide World.' It also served as a common-place book into which he copied such prose and verse as pleased him, together with drafts of college essays, lists of poetical phrases, and copies of the letters he was writing, particularly to his aunt Mary Moody Emerson. There are some fragments of original verse, a few pages of imaginative romance, and long disquisitions on ethical and literary subjects, written in frank imitation of the style of Chateaubriand, of Edward Everett and other authors, – for the youthful Emerson, like Stevenson fifty years later, loved for a while to 'play the sedulous ape.'

This miscellaneous matter decreases rapidly, however, after his graduation in 1821. For the last half of that year he seems to have kept no journal at all. He was teaching in his older brother William's school for young ladies, in his mother's home at Boston. In the spring of 1823, his mother moved to Canterbury, a region in Roxbury which

is now included in Franklin Park. In August of that year
the young school-master made a solitary walking trip to
the Connecticut River, and visited the new college at
Amherst. In the spring of 1824, as the long passage of
self-assessment written in April 18 indicates, he decided
definitely to enter the ministry.]

Cambridge, Jan. 25, 1820

These pages are intended at their commencement to
contain a record of new thoughts (when they occur); for a
receptacle of all the old ideas that partial but peculiar
peepings at antiquity can furnish or furbish; for tablet to
save the wear and tear of weak Memory, and, in short,
for all the various purposes and utility, real or imaginary,
which are usually comprehended under that comprehensive title *Common Place book.*

Cambridge, February 7

Mr. K., a lawyer of Boston, gave a fine character of a
distinguished individual in private conversation, which
in part I shall set down. 'Webster is a rather large man,
about five feet, seven, or nine, in height, and thirty-nine
or forty years old — he has a long head, very large black
eyes, bushy eyebrows, a commanding expression, — and
his hair is coal-black, and coarse as a crow's nest. His
voice is sepulchral — there is not the least variety or the
least harmony of tone — it commands, it fills, it echoes,
but is harsh and discordant. — He possesses an admirable
readiness, a fine memory and a faculty of perfect abstrac-
tion, an unparallelled impudence and a tremendous power
of concentration — he brings all that he has ever heard,

read or seen to bear on the case in question. He growls along the bar to see who will run, and if nobody runs he WILL fight. He knows his strength, has a perfect confidence in his own powers, and is distinguished by a spirit of fixed determination; he marks his path out, and will cut off fifty heads rather than turn out of it; but is generous and free from malice, and will never move a step to make a severe remark. His genius is such that, if he descends to be pathetic, he becomes ridiculous. He has no wit and never laughs, though he is very shrewd and sarcastic, and sometimes sets the whole court in a roar by the singularity or pointedness of a remark. His imagination is what the light of a furnace is to its heat, a necessary attendant — nothing sparkling or agreeable, but dreadful and gloomy.' This is the finest character I have ever heard pourtrayed, and very truly drawn, with little or no exaggeration.

Cambridge, March 11

Thus long I have been in Cambridge this term (three or four weeks) and have not before this moment paid my devoirs to the Gnomes to whom I dedicated this quaint and heterogeneous manuscript. Is it because matter has been wanting? — no — I have written much elsewhere in prose, poetry, and miscellany — let me put the most favourable construction on the case and say that I have been better employed. Beside considerable attention, however unsuccessful, to college studies, I have finished Bisset's life of Burke, as well as Burke's 'Regicide Peace,' together with considerable variety of desultory reading, generally speaking, highly entertaining and instructive.

The Pythologian poem does not proceed very rapidly, though I have experienced some poetic moments. Could I seat myself in the alcove of one of those public libraries which human pride and literary rivalship have made costly, splendid and magnificent, it would indeed be an enviable situation. I would plunge into the classic lore of chivalrous story and of the fairy-land bards, and unclosing the ponderous volumes of the firmest believers in magic and in the potency of consecrated crosier or elfin ring, I would let my soul sail away delighted into their wildest phantasies.

Cambridge, April 2

Spring has returned and has begun to unfold her beautiful array, to throw herself on wild-flower couches, to walk abroad on the hills and summon her songsters to do her sweet homage. The Muses have issued from the library and costly winter dwelling of their votaries, and are gone up to build their bowers on Parnassus, and to melt their ice-bound fountains. Castalia is flowing rapturously and lifting her foam on high. The hunter and the shepherd are abroad on the rock and the vallies echo to the merry, merry horn. The Poet, of course, is wandering, while Nature's thousand melodies are warbling to him. This soft bewitching luxury of vernal gales and accompanying beauty overwhelms. It produces a lassitude which is full of mental enjoyment and which we would not exchange for more vigorous pleasure. Although so long as the spell endures, little or nothing is accomplished, nevertheless, I believe it operates to divest the mind of old and worn-out contemplations and bestows new fresh, ness upon life, and leaves behind it imaginations of enchantment for the mind to mould into splendid forms and gorgeous fancies which shall long continue to fascinate, after the physical phenomena which woke them have ceased to create delight.

Cambridge, April 4

Judging from opportunity enjoyed, I ought to have this evening a flow of thought, rich, abundant and deep; after having heard Mr. Everett deliver his Introductory Lecture, in length one and one half hour, having read much and profitably in the *Quarterly Review*, and lastly having heard Dr. Warren's introductory lecture to anatomy, — all in the compass of a day — and the mind possessing a temperament well adapted to receive with calm attention what was offered.

Cambridge, April 4

I here make a resolution to make myself acquainted with the Greek language and antiquities and history with long and serious attention and study; (always with the assistance of circumstances.)

Cambridge, June 7

Have been of late reading patches of Barrow and Ben Jonson; and what the object — not curiosity? no — nor expectation of edification intellectual or moral — but merely because they are authors where vigorous phrases and quaint, peculiar words and expressions may be sought and found, the better 'to rattle out the battle of my thoughts.'

Cambridge, August 8

I have been reading the *Novum Organum*. Lord Bacon is indeed a wonderful writer; he condenses an unrivaled degree of matter in one paragraph. He never suffers himself 'to swerve from the direct forthright,' or to babble or speak unguardedly on his proper topic, and withal writes with more melody and rich cadence than any writer (I had almost said, of England) on a similar subject.

Cambridge, Aug. 8

There is a strange face in the Freshman class whom I should like to know very much. He has a great deal of character in his features and should be a fast friend or bitter enemy. His name is ——. I shall endeavour to become acquainted with him and wish, if possible, that I might be able to recall at a future period the singular sensations which his presence produced at this.

Cambridge, August 23

To-morrow finishes the Junior year. As it is time to close our accounts, we will conclude likewise this book which has been formed from the meditations and fancies which have sprinkled the miscellany-corner of my mind for two terms past. It was begun in the winter vacation. I think it has been an improving employment decidedly. It has not encroached upon other occupations and has afforded seasonable aid at various times to enlarge or enliven scanty themes, etc. Nor has it monopolized the energies of composition for literary exercises. Whilst I have written in it, I have begun and completed my Pythologian Poem of 260 lines, — and my Dissertation on the Character of Socrates.   It has prevented the *ennui* of many an idle moment and has perhaps enriched my stock of language for future exertions.   Much of it has been written with a view to their preservation, as hints for a peculiar pursuit at the distance of years.   Little or none of it was elaborate — its office was to be a hasty, sketchy composition, containing at times elements of graver order.

DRAMA

Cambridge, September

Campbell, the poet, said to Professor Everett that the only chance which America has for a truly national literature is to be found in the Drama; we are bound to reverence such high authority, and at least to examine the correctness of the position.

Cambridge, October

I have determined to grant a new charter to my pen, having finished my commonplace book, which I commenced in January, and with as much success as I was ambitious of — whose whole aim was the small utility of being the exchequer to the accumulating store of organized verbs, nouns and substantives, to wit, sentences.   It has been a source of entertainment, and accomplished its end, and on this account has induced me to repeat or rather continue the experiment.   Wherefore, On!

Cambridge, October 15

Different mortals improve resources of happiness which are entirely different.   This I find more apparent in the

familiar instances obvious at college recitations. My
more fortunate neighbours exult in the display of mathematical study, while I, after feeling the humiliating sense
of dependence and inferiority, which, like the goading,
soul-sickening sense of extreme poverty, palsies effort,
esteem myself abundantly compensated, if with my pen,
I can marshal whole catalogues of nouns and verbs, to
express to the life the imbecility I felt. . . .

Cambridge, October 25

I find myself often idle, vagrant, stupid and hollow.
This is somewhat appalling and, if I do not discipline
myself with diligent care, I shall suffer severely from remorse and the sense of inferiority hereafter. All around
me are industrious and will be great, I am indolent and
shall be insignificant. Avert it, heaven! avert it, virtue!
I need excitement.

Cambridge, December 15

I claim and clasp a moment's respite from this irksome
school to saunter in the fields of my own wayward thought.
The afternoon was gloomy and preparing to snow, —
dull, ugly weather. But when I came out from the hot,
steaming, stoved, stinking, dirty, A-B spelling-school-
room, I almost soared and mounted the atmosphere at
breathing the free magnificent air, the noble breath of life.
It was a delightful exhilaration; but it soon passed off.

Cambridge, March 14 [1821]

I am reading Price, on Morals, and intend to read it
with care and commentary. I shall set down here what

remarks occur to me upon the matter or manner of his
argument. On the 56th page, Dr. Price says that right
and wrong are not determined by any reasoning or deduction, but by the ultimate perception of the human
mind. It is to be desired that this were capable of satisfactory proof, but, as it is in direct opposition to the scep-
tical philosophy, it cannot stand unsupported by strong
and sufficient evidence. I will however read more and see
if it is proved or no. —

Cambridge, Sabbath, March 25

I am sick — if I should die what would become of me?
We forget ourselves and our destinies in health, and the
chief use of temporary sickness is to remind us of these
concerns. I must improve my time better. I must prepare myself for the great profession I have purposed to
undertake.

Cambridge, April 1

It is Sabbath again, and I am for the most part recovered. Is it a wise dispensation that we can never know
what influence our own prayers have in restoring the
health we have prayed God to restore?

Boston, January 12, 1822

After a considerable interval I am still willing to think
that these commonplace books are very useful and harm-
less things, — at least sufficiently so, to warrant another
trial.

Boston, February

I have not much cause, I sometimes think, to wish my Alma Mater well, personally; I was not often highly flattered by success, and was every day mortified by my own ill fate or ill conduct. Still, when I went today to the ground where I had had the brightest thoughts of my little life and filled up the little measure of my knowledge, and had felt sentimental for a time, and poetical for a time, and had seen many fine faces, and traversed many fine walks, and enjoyed much pleasant, learned, or friendly society, — I felt a crowd of pleasant thoughts, as I went posting about from place to place, and room to chapel.

Boston, May 13

In twelve days I shall be nineteen years old; which I count a miserable thing. Has any other educated person lived so many years and lost so many days? I do not say acquired so little, for by an ease of thought and certain looseness of mind I have perhaps been the subject of as many ideas as many of mine age. But mine approaching maturity is attended with a goading sense of emptiness and wasted capacity. . . .

Look next from the history of my intellect to the history of my heart. A blank, my lord. I have not the kind affections of a pigeon. Ungenerous and selfish, cautious and cold, I yet wish to be romantic; have not sufficient feeling to speak a natural, hearty welcome to a friend or stranger, and yet send abroad wishes and fancies of a friendship with a man I never knew. There is not in the whole wide Universe of God (my relations to Himself I do not understand) one being to whom I am attached with warm and entire devotion, — not a being to whom I have joined fate for weal or wo, not one whose interests I have nearly and dearly at heart; — and this I say at the most susceptible age of man. Perhaps at the distance of a score of years, if I then inhabit this world, or still more, if I do not, these will appear frightful confessions; they may or may not, — it is a true picture of a barren and desolate soul.

DEDICATION

Boston, July 11

I dedicate my book to the Spirit of America.

Boston, November 29

The ardour of my college friendship for —— is nearly extinct, and it is with difficulty that I can now recall those sensations of vivid pleasure which his presence was wont to waken spontaneously for a period of more than two years. To be so agreeably excited by the features of an individual personally unknown to me, and for so long a time, was surely a curious incident in the history of so cold a being, and well worth a second thought.

MORAL SENSE

Boston, January 11, 1823

. . . There is one distinction amid these fading phenomena — one decided distinction which is real and eternal and which will survive nature — I mean the distinction of Right and Wrong. Your opinions upon all other topics, and your feelings with regard to this world, in childhood, youth, and age, perpetually change. Your perceptions of right and wrong never change.

TIME

Boston, March 18

After two moons I shall have fulfilled twenty years. Amid the fleeting generations of the human race and in the abyss of years I lift my solitary voice unheeded and unknown, and complain unto inexorable Time: — 'Stop, Destroyer, overwhelmer, stop one brief moment this uncontrollable career. Ravisher of the creation, suffer me a little space, that I may pluck some spoils, as I pass onward, to be the fruits and monuments of the scenes through which I have travelled.' Fool! you implore the deaf torrent to relax the speed of its cataract,

'At ille
Labitur et labetur in omne volubilis aevum.'

Boston, Sunday Evening, March 23, 1823

. . . One youth among the multitudes of mankind, one grain of sand on the seashore, unknown in the midst of my contemporaries, I am hastening to put on the manly robe. From childhood the names of the great have ever resounded in my ear, and it is impossible that I should be indifferent to the rank which I must take in the innumerable assembly of men, or that I should shut my eyes upon the huge interval which separates me from the minds which I am wont to venerate.

Boston, April

. . . There is no waste, no period to the Moral universe. An antiquity that is without beginning, and a futurity that is without end, is its history. A principle of life and truth in itself which it is impossible to conceive of as liable to death or suspension, or as less than infinite in the extent of its rule, binding God and man in its irreversible decree, — is coexistent with Deity. . . .

Worcester; August 22 evening, 8 *o'clock*

I reached Worcester one half hour ago, having walked forty miles without difficulty. Every time I traverse a turnpike I find it harder to conceive how they are supported; I met but three or four travellers between Roxbury and Worcester. . . .

Belchertown, August 25

After passing through West Brookfield, I breakfasted among some right worshipful waggoners at the pleasant town of Western, and then passed through a part of Palmer (I believe) and Ware to this place. I count that road pleasant and that air good, which forces me to smile from mere animal pleasure, albeit I may be a smiling man; so I am free to commend the road from Cutler's Tavern in Western, as far as Babcock's in Ware, to any youthful traveller, who walks upon a cloudless August morning. Let me not forget to record here the benevolent landlady of Ware who offered me her liquors and crackers upon the precarious credit of my return, rather than exchange my bills.

Amherst, August 28

In the afternoon I went to the College. The infant college is an infant Hercules. Never was so much striving, outstretching, and advancing in a literary cause as is exhibited here. . . .

The students are all divided into thriving opposition societies, which gather libraries, laboratories, mineral cabinets, etc., with an indefatigable spirit, which nothing but rivalry could inspire. Upon this impulse, they write, speak, and study in a sort of fury, which, I think, promises a harvest of attainments. The Commencement was plainly that of a young college, but had strength and eloquence mixed with the apparent '*vestigia ruris,*' and the scholar who gained the prize for declamation, the evening before, would have a first prize at any Cambridge competition.

The College is supposed to be worth net 85,000 dollars.

Canterbury, September, 1823

I have often found cause to complain that my thoughts have an ebb and flow. Whether any laws fix them, and what the laws are, I cannot ascertain. I have quoted a thousand times the memory of Milton and tried to bind my thinking season to one part of the year, or to one sort of weather; to the sweet influence of the Pleiades, or to the summer reign of Lyra. The worst is, that the ebb is certain, long and frequent, while the flow comes transiently and seldom. . . .

The dreams of my childhood are all fading away and giving place to some very sober and very disgusting views of a quiet mediocrity of talents and condition — nor does it appear to me that any application of which I am capable, any efforts, any sacrifices, could at this moment restore any reasonableness to the familiar expectations of my earlier youth.

SELF-ESTEEM
Canterbury, December 14

I see no reason why I should bow my head to man, or cringe in my demeanour.

Canterbury, January, 1824

No man would consent to live in society if he was obliged to admit everybody to his house that chose to come.

BEGINNINGS
Canterbury, undated

It is excellent advice both in writing and in action to avoid a too great elevation at first. Let one's beginnings be temperate and unpretending, and the more elevated parts will rise from these with a just and full effect. We were not made to breathe oxygen, or to talk poetry, or to be always wise.

Canterbury, undated

What can the reason be why a priest of whatever god, under whatever form, should in every clime and age be open to such liberal abuse, and to ineradicable suspicion? Is the reason to be found in Ecclesiastical History? Questionless this has been very bad. The pious professors have been outrageous rogues in a thousand temples from Memphis to Boston. Or is its origin deeper fixed in the nature of the profession? . . .

MORAL BEAUTY

Canterbury, February 20

Material beauty perishes or palls. Intellectual beauty limits admiration to seasons and ages; hath its ebbs and flows of delight. . . . But moral beauty is lovely, imperishable, perfect. It is dear to the child and to the patriarch, to Heaven, Angel, Man. . . . None that can understand Milton's *Comus* can read it without warming to the holy emotions it panegyrizes.

I would freely give all I ever hoped to be, even when my air-blown hopes were brilliant and glorious, — not as now — to have given down that sweet strain to posterity to do good in a golden way. . . .

Canterbury, undated

They say there is a tune which is forbidden to be played in the European armies because it makes the Swiss desert, since it reminds them so forcibly of their hills and home. I have heard many *Swiss tunes* played in college. Balancing between getting and not getting a hard lesson, a breath of fragrant air from the fields coming in at the window would serve as a Swiss tune and make me desert to the glens from which it came. Nor is that vagabond inclination wholly gone yet. And many a sultry afternoon, last summer, I left my Latin and my English to go with my gun and see the rabbits and squirrels and robins in the woods. Goodbye, Sir. Stop a moment. I have heard a clergyman of Maine say that in his Parish are the Penobscot Indians, and that when any one of them in summer has been absent for some weeks a-hunting, he comes back among them a different person and altogether unlike any of the rest, with an eagle's eye, a wild look, and commanding carriage and gesture; but after a few weeks it wears off again into the indolent dronelike apathy which all exhibit. Good day, Sir.

Canterbury, March 21

In metaphysics, 'the gymnastics of the soul,' what has reason done since Plato's day but rend and tear his gorgeous fabric. And how are we the wiser? Instead of the unmeasurable theatre which we deemed was here opened to the range of the understanding, we are now reduced to a little circle of definitions and logic round which we may humbly run. And how has Faith fared? Why, the Reformer's axe has hewed down idol after idol, and corruption and imperfection, until Faith is bare and very cold. And they have not done stripping yet, but must reach the bone. The old fable said Truth was by gods or men made naked. I wish the gods would help her to a garment or make her fairer. From Eden to America the apples of the tree of knowledge are but bitter fruit in the end.

MYSELF
Canterbury, Sunday, April 18, 1824

'Nil fuit unquam sic dispar sibi.'
HORACE

I am beginning my professional studies. In a month I shall be legally a man. And I deliberately dedicate my time, my talents, and my hopes to the Church. Man is an animal that looks before and after; and I should be loth to reflect at a remote period that I took so solemn a step in my existence without some careful examination of my past and present life. Since I cannot alter, I would not repent the resolution I have made, and this page must be witness to the latest year of my life whether I have good grounds to warrant my determination.

I cannot dissemble that my abilities are below my ambition. And I find that I judged by a false criterion when I measured my powers by my ability to understand and to criticize the intellectual character of another. For men graduate their respect, not by the secret wealth, but by the outward use; not by the power to understand, but by the power to act. I have, or had, a strong imagination, and consequently a keen relish for the beauties of poetry. The exercise which the practice of composition gives to this faculty is the cause of my immoderate fondness for writing, which has swelled these pages to a voluminous extent. My reasoning faculty is proportionably weak, nor can I ever hope to write a Butler's Analogy or an Essay of Hume. Nor is it strange that with this confession I should choose theology, which is from everlasting to everlasting 'debateable ground.' For, the highest species of reasoning upon divine subjects is rather the fruit of a sort of moral imagination, than of the 'Reasoning Machines,' such as Locke and Clarke and David Hume. Dr. Channing's Dudleian Lecture is the model of what I mean, and the faculty which produced this is akin to the higher flights of the fancy. I may add that the preaching most in vogue at the present day depends chiefly on imagination for its success, and asks those accomplishments which I believe are most within my grasp. I have set down little which can gratify my vanity, and I must further say that every comparison of myself with my mates that six or seven, perhaps sixteen or seventeen, years have made, has convinced me that there exists a signal defect of character which neutralizes in great part the just influence my talents ought to have. Whether that defect be in the *address*, in the fault of good forms, — which, Queen Isabella said, were like perpetual letters-commendatory — or deeper seated in an absence of common *sympathies*, or even in a levity of the understanding, I cannot tell. But its bitter fruits are a sore uneasiness in the company of most men and women, a frigid fear of offending and jealousy of disrespect, an inability to lead and an unwillingness to follow the current conversation, which contrive to make me second with all those among whom chiefly I wish to be first.

Hence my bearing in the world is the direct opposite of that good-humoured independence and self-esteem which should mark the gentleman. Be it here remembered that there is a decent pride which is conspicuous in the perfect model of a Christian man. I am unfortunate also, as was Rienzi, in a propensity to laugh, or rather, snicker. I am ill at ease, therefore, among men. I criticize with hardness; I lavishly applaud; I weakly argue; and I wonder with a 'foolish face of praise.'

Now the profession of law demands a good deal of personal address, an impregnable confidence in one's own powers, upon all occasions expected and unexpected, and a logical mode of thinking and speaking — which I do not possess, and may not reasonably hope to obtain. Medicine also makes large demands on the practitioner for a seducing mannerism. And I have no taste for the pestle and mortar, for Bell on the bones, or Hunter, or Celsus.

But in Divinity I hope to thrive. I inherit from my sire a formality of manner and speech, but I derive from him, or his patriotic parent, a passionate love for the strains of eloquence. I burn after the '*aliquid immensum infinitum-que*' which Cicero desired. What we ardently love we learn to imitate. My understanding venerates and my heart loves that cause which is dear to God and man — the laws of morals, the Revelations which sanction, and the blood of martyrs and triumphant suffering of the saints which seal them. In my better hours, I am the believer (if not the dupe) of brilliant promises, and can respect myself as the possessor of those powers which command the reason and passions of the multitude. The office of a clergyman is twofold: public preaching and private influence. Entire success in the first is the lot of few, but this I am encouraged to expect. If, however, the individual himself lack that moral worth which is to secure the last, his studies upon the first are idly spent. The most prodigious genius, a seraph's eloquence, will shamefully defeat its own end, if it has not first won the heart of the defender to the cause he defends. But the coolest reason cannot censure my choice when I oblige myself *professionally* to a life which all wise men freely and advisedly adopt. I put no great restraint on myself, and can therefore claim little merit in a manner of life which chimes with inclination and habit. But I would learn to love virtue for her own sake. I would have my pen so guided as was Milton's when a deep and enthusiastic love of goodness and of God dictated the *Comus*

to the bard, or that prose rhapsody in the Third Book of
Prelaty. I would sacrifice inclination to the interest of
mind and soul. I would remember that

'Spare Fast oft with Gods doth diet,'

that Justinian devoted but one out of twenty-four hours
to sleep, and this week (for instance) I will remember to
curtail my dinner and supper sensibly and rise from table
each day with an appetite, till Tuesday evening next, and
so see if it be a fact that I can understand more clearly.

I have mentioned a defect of character; perhaps it is
not one, but many. Every wise man aims at an entire
conquest of himself. We applaud, as possessed of extraordinary good sense, one who never makes the slightest
mistake in speech or action; one in whom not only every
important step of life, but every passage of conversation,
every duty of the day, even every movement of every
muscle — hands, feet, and tongue, are measured and dictated by deliberate reason. I am not assuredly that excellent creature. A score of words and deeds issue from
me daily, of which I am not the master. They are begot-
ten of weakness and born of shame. I cannot assume the
elevation I ought, — but lose the influence I should exert
among those of meaner or younger understanding, for
want of sufficient *bottom* in my nature, for want of that
confidence of manner which springs from an erect mind
which is without fear and without reproach. In my frequent humiliation, even before women and children, I am
compelled to remember the poor boy who cried, 'I told
you, Father, they would find me out.' Even those feelings
which are counted noble and generous take in me the

taint of frailty. For my strong propensity to friendship, instead of working out its manly ends, degenerates to a fondness for particular casts of feature, perchance not unlike the doting of old King James. Stateliness and silence hang very like Mokannah's suspicious silver veil, only concealing what is best not shewn. What is called a warm heart, I have not.

The stern accuser Conscience cries that the catalogue of confessions is not yet full. I am a lover of indolence, and of the belly. And the good have a right to ask the neophyte who wears this garment of scarlet sin, why he comes where all are apparelled in white? Dares he hope that some patches of pure and generous feeling, some bright fragments of lofty thought, it may be of divine poesy, shall charm the eye away from all the parti-coloured shades of his character? And when he is clothed in the vestments of the priest, and has inscribed on his forehead 'Holiness to the Lord,' and wears on his breast the breastplate of the tribes, then can the Ethiopian change his skin, and the unclean be pure? Or how shall I strenuously enforce on men the duties and habits to which I am a stranger? Physician, heal thyself; I need not go far for an answer to so natural a question. I am young in my everlasting existence. I already discern the deep dye of elementary errors, which threaten to colour its infinity of duration. And I judge that if I devote my nights and days *in form*, to the service of God and the War against Sin, I shall soon be prepared to do the same *in substance*.

I cannot accurately estimate my chances of success, in my profession, and in life. Were it just to judge the future

from the past, they would be very low. In my case, I
think it is not. I have never expected success in my present employment. My scholars are carefully instructed,
my money is faithfully earned, but the instructor is little
wiser, and the duties were never congenial with my disposition. Thus far the dupe of Hope, I have trudged on
with my bundle at my back, and my eye fixed on the distant hill where my burden would fall. It may be I shall
write *dupe* a long time to come, and the end of life shall
intervene betwixt me and the release. My trust is that
my profession shall be my regeneration of mind, manners,
inward and outward estate; or rather my starting-point,
for I have hoped to put on eloquence as a robe, and by
goodness and zeal and the awfulness of Virtue to press
and prevail over the false judgments, the rebel passions
and corrupt habits of men. We blame the past, we mag-
nify and gild the future, and are not wiser for the multitude of days. Spin on, ye of the adamantine spindle, spin
on, my fragile thread.

Canterbury, undated

... There is another sort of book which appears now
and then in the world, once in two or three centuries perhaps, and which soon or late gets a foothold in popular
esteem. I allude to those books which collect and embody
the wisdom of their times, and so mark the stages of
human improvement. Such are the Proverbs of Solomon,
the Essays of Montaigne, and eminently the Essays of
Bacon. Such also (though in my judgment in far less degree) is the proper merit of Mr. Pope's judicious poems,
the Moral Essays and Essay on Man, which, without

originality, seize upon all the popular speculations float-
ing among sensible men and give them in a compact
graceful form to the following age. I should like to add
another volume to this valuable work. I am not so fool-
hardy as to write *Sequel to Bacon* on my title-page; and
there are some reasons that induce me to suppose that
the undertaking of this enterprise does not imply any
censurable arrogance. . . .

Canterbury, undated

Why has my motley diary no jokes? Because it is a
soliloquy and every man is grave alone.

Canterbury, December 1

I may digress, where all is digression, to utter a wish
not altogether fruitless, that there might be an order introduced into the mass of reading that occupies or im-
pends over me. It was a reasonable advice that a scholar
gave me to *build* in the studies of a day; to begin with
solid labour at Hebrew and Greek; theological criticism,
moral philosophy and laborious writing should succeed;
then history; then elegant letters — that species of books
which is at once the most elevated amusement and the
most productive suggester of thought, of which the instant
specimens are the bulk of Johnson's works, as Lives of
Poets, Rambler, etc., Pope's Moral Essays, and conspicuously Montaigne's Essays. Thus much for the day.
But what arrangement in priority of subjects? When
shall I read Greek, when Roman, when Austrian, when
Ecclesiastical, when American history? Whilst we deliberate, time escapes. A poor plan is better than none, as

a poor law. I propose, therefore, every morning before breakfast to read a chapter in Greek Testament with its Commentary. Afterwards, if time serve, *Le Clerc;* or my reading and writing for dissertations; then Mitford (all history is Ecclesiastical, and all reasonings go back to Greece), and the day end with Milton, Shakspere, Cicero or Everett, Burke, Mackintosh, Playfair, Stewart, Scott, Pope, Dryden. . . .

Canterbury, December 10

I confess I am a little cynical on some topics, and when a whole nation is roaring Patriotism at the top of its voice, I am fain to explore the cleanness of its hands and purity of its heart. I have generally found the gravest and most useful citizens are not the easiest provoked to swell the noise, though they may be punctual at the polls.

1825-28

[EMERSON entered the Harvard Divinity School in February, 1825, but his health failed rapidly and his eyes gave out. A change was essential, and in the spring he worked on his uncle's farm in Newton. During the summer he was strong enough to take some private pupils, and in the autumn he taught school at Chelmsford. Early in 1826, he taught at Roxbury, and from April 5 to the end of the summer he had pupils in a house which his mother had now taken in Cambridge. He wrote but little in his journal during this period.

On October 10, 1826, in spite of his very brief and broken sojourn at the Divinity school, he was 'approbated to preach' by the Middlesex Association of Ministers, who were aware of his high character and gift of expression, and remembered, doubtless, the fame of his father and grandfather as pulpit orators. 'If they had examined me,' Emerson said later, 'they never would have passed me.'

But within a month he was threatened with consumption, — a malady fatal to many of the Emersons, — and was obliged to sail for South Carolina for the winter. On his way back, in May and June, 1827, he preached in Washington, Philadelphia, and New York, but feeling still too infirm to accept a regular pulpit, he settled down once more in Divinity Hall, Cambridge. In December of this year he met, at Concord, N.H., Ellen Louisa Tucker, and promptly fell in love.

There are few entries in the journal during 1828. He was still at Divinity Hall. The mental condition of his brilliant younger brother Edward gave ground for serious alarm. Waldo's formal engagement to Miss Tucker took place in December. He had already been invited to become associated with the Reverend Henry Ware, Jr., in the pastorate of the Second Church of Boston.]

Roxbury, January 4, 1825

I have closed my school. I have begun a new year. I have begun my studies, and this day a moment of indolence engendered in me phantasms and feelings that struggled to find vent in rhyme. I thought of the passage of my years, of their even and eventless tenor, and of the crisis which is but a little way before, when a month will determine the dark or bright dye they must assume forever. I turn now to my lamp and my tomes. I have nothing to do with society. My unpleasing boyhood is past, my youth wanes into the age of man, and what are the unsuppressed glee, the cheering games, the golden hair and shining eyes of youth unto me? I withdraw myself from their spell. A solemn voice commands me to retire. And if in those scenes my blood and brow have been cold, if my tongue has stammered where fashion and gaiety were voluble, and I have had no grace amid the influences of Beauty and the festivities of Grandeur, I shall not hastily conclude my soul ignobly born and its horoscope fully cast. I will not yet believe that because it has lain so tranquil, great argument could not make it stir. I will not believe because I cannot unite dignity, as many can, to folly, that I am not born to fill the eye of great

expectation, to speak when the people listen, nor to cast
my mite into the great treasury of morals and intellect.
I will not quite despair, nor quench my flambeau in the
dust of 'Easy live and quiet die.'

Canterbury, undated

It is my own humor to despise pedigree. I was educated
to prize it. The kind Aunt whose cares instructed my
youth (and whom may God reward), told me oft the
virtues of her and mine ancestors. They have been
clergymen for many generations, and the piety of all and
the eloquence of many is yet praised in the Churches.
But the dead sleep in their moonless night; my business
is with the living.

REFLECTIONS

Roxbury, February 8

It is the evening of February eighth, which was never
renowned that I know. But, be that as it may, 'tis the
last evening I spend in Canterbury. I go to my College
Chamber to-morrow a little changed for better or worse
since I left it in 1821. I have learned a few more names
and dates, additional facility of expression, the gauge of
my own ignorance, its sounding-places and bottomless
depths. I have inverted my inquiries two or three times
on myself, and have learned what a sinner and a saint I
am. My cardinal vice of intellectual dissipation — sinful
strolling from book to book, from care to idleness — is
my cardinal vice still; is a malady that belongs to the
chapter of Incurables. I have written two or three hundred pages that will be of use to me. I have earned two

or three thousand dollars which have paid my debts and obligated my neighbors, so that I thank Heaven I can say none of my house is the worse for me. In short, I have grown older and have seen something of the vanity and something of the value of existence, have seen what shallow things men are, and how independent of external circumstances may be the states of mind called good and ill.

Cambridge, February

I have a mind to try if my muse hath not lost a whit of her nimbleness; if the damps of this new region, its prescribed and formal study, haven't chilled a little her prurient and prolific heat. I would boldly take down a topic and enter the lists, were there not reason to remember and fear the old Orthodoxy concerning Fortune (and I think I have heard it whispered of fairies too and of wit even), that, when the humoursome, jealous coquette is presumed on, she withdraweth straight her smiles, and leaves the audacious votary to curse his self-conceit in the dark. . . .

Cambridge, January 8, 1826

I come with mended eyes to my ancient friend and consoler. Has the interval of silence made the writer wiser? Does his mind teem with well weighed judgments? The moral and intellectual universe has not halted because the eye of the observer was closed. Compensation has been woven to want, loss to gain, good to evil, and good to good, with the same industry, and the same concealment of an intelligent cause. And in my joy to write and read again I will not pester my imagination with what is done unseen, with the burden that is put in the contrary scale, with the sowing of the death-seed in the place of the nettle that was rooted up. I am a more cheerful philosopher, and am rather anxious to thank Oromasdes than to fear Ahriman.

Since I wrote before, I know something more of the grounds of hope and fear of what is to come. But if my knowledge is greater, so is my courage. I know that I *know* next to nothing, but I know too that the amount of probabilities is vast, both in mind and in morals. It is not certain that God exists, but that he does not is a most bewildering and improbable chimæra.

COMPENSATION

Cambridge, undated

All things are double one against another, said Solomon. The whole of what we know is a system of compensations. Every defect in one manner is made up in another. Every suffering is rewarded; every sacrifice is made up; every debt is paid.

SLAVE TRADE

Cambridge, undated

To stop the slave traffic the nations should league themselves in indissoluble bands, should link the thunderbolts of national power to demolish this debtor to all Justice human and divine.

Cambridge, March 27

My years are passing away. Infirmities are already stealing on me that may be the deadly enemies that are to dissolve me to dirt, and little is yet done to establish my consideration among my contemporaries, and less to get a memory when I am gone. I confess the foolish ambition to be valued, with qualification. I do not want to be known by them that know me not, but where my name is mentioned I would have it respected. My recollections of early life are not very pleasant.

PUBLIC PRAYER

Cambridge, April 12

Most men, who have given their attention to the prayers publicly offered in a Christian congregation, have felt in the institution an unsuitableness to their feelings. . . .

That it is right to ask God's blessing on us is certainly reasonable. That it is right to enumerate our wants, our sins, even our sentiments, in addresses to this unseen Idea, seems just and natural. And it may probably be averred with safety that there has been no man who never prayed. That persons whom like circumstances and like feelings assimilate, that a family, that a picked society of friends, should unite in this service, does not, I conceive, violate any precept of just reason. It certainly is a question of more difficult solution whether a promiscuous assemblage, such as is contained in houses of public worship, and collected by such motives, can unite with propriety to advantage in any petition such as is usually offered by one man.

PROGRESS OF AN INDIVIDUAL IN KNOWLEDGE

Cambridge, April

Every cultivated man observes, in his past years, intervals of mentality — and is accustomed to consider the present state of his mind as the result rather of many periods of singular intenseness of thought and feeling than of a perpetual and equable expansion. Corn grows by jumps. The ordinary growth of mind, especially till the old age of man, depends on aliment procured from without. But this aliment for which we search the bosoms of other men, or their books, or the face of external nature, will be got in larger or less amounts according to circumstances quite as often without as within our controul.

Whoever explores his recollection of those periods, will find that by some casualty or some study he had arrived at one of those general ideas which not only epitomize whole trains of thought, but cast a flood of new light upon things inscrutable before; after waiting mostly in the vestibule, had picked up unawares the Master Key, whose wards and springs open every door, and the surprised adventurer goes on astonished from cell to cell, from chamber to chamber, gratified, but overawed at the unexplored extent and opulence of his own possessions.

Cambridge, August 3

Yesterday I attended the funeral solemnities in Faneuil Hall in honour of John Adams and Thomas Jefferson. The oration of Mr. Webster was worthy of his fame, and what is much more, was worthy of the august occasion. Never, I think, were the awful charms of person, manners

and voice outdone. For though in the beginning un-
promising, and in other parts imperfect, in what was
truly grand he fully realized the boldest conception of
eloquence.

Cambridge, September 10

The days blow me onward into the desarts of Eternity;
I live a few strong moments, in the course, perhaps, of
each day; I observe a little the ways of man, and in them
accumulated, the ways of God. I act a little. I shape my
fortunes, as it seems to me, not at all.

Cambridge, September 23

Health, action, happiness. How they ebb from me!
Poor Sisyphus saw his stone stop once, at least, when
Orpheus chaunted. I must roll mine up and up and up
how high a hill!

Cambridge, September 28

I was born cold. My bodily habit is cold. I shiver in
and out; don't heat to the good purposes called enthusiasm a quarter so quick and kindly as my neighbours.

Cambridge, November

I find in Burke almost the same thought I had entertained as an original remark three years ago: that nothing but the moral quality of actions can penetrate
through vast intervals of time.

At Sea; Sunday, December 3, 1826

'Tis a nine days' wonder to me, this voyage of mine.
Here I have been rolling through the weary leagues of

salt water, musing much on myself and on man, with some new but incoherent thinking. . . .

After a day or two, I found I could live as comfortably in this tent, tossed on the ocean, as if it were pitched on the mountains ashore. But it is the irresistible sentiment of the first day, whilst your philosophy is sea-sick, to fancy man is violating the order of nature in coming out here where he assuredly has no business; and that, in virtue of this trespass on his part, the wind has a right to his canvass and the shark to his body. Whilst his philosophy is distempered, so is his imagination. The whole music of the sea is desolate and monitory. The wave and the cloud and the wind suggest power more than beauty to the ear and eye. But the recovery is rapid, and the terrible soon subsides into the sublime.

Charleston, South Carolina, December 13

I have for a fortnight past writ nothing. My bosom's lord sits somewhat drowsily on his throne. It is because I think not at all that I write not at all. There is to me something alarming in these *periods* of mentality. One day I am a doctor, and the next I am a dunce, that is, so far as relates to my own resources. . . .

No man has travelled in the United States from the North to the South without observing the change and amelioration of manners. In this city, it is most observable, the use of the conventions of address among the lowest classes, which are coarsely neglected by the labouring classes at the North. Two negroes recognize each other in the street, though both in rags, and both, it may be, balancing a burden on their heads, with the same

graduated advances of salutation that well-bred men who
are strangers to each other would use in Boston. They do
not part before they have shaken hands and bid good-bye
with an inclination of the head. There is a grace and perfection too about these courtesies which could not be
imitated by a Northern labourer where he designed to be
extremely civil. Indeed I have never seen an awkward
Carolinian.

Charleston, S.C., January 4, 1827

A new year has opened its bitter cold eye upon me, here
where I sought warm weather. A new year has opened on
me and found my best hopes set aside, my projects all
suspended. A new year has found me perchance no more
fit to live and no more fit to die than the last. But the
eye of the mind has at least grown richer in its hoard of
observations. It has detected some more of the darkling
lines that connect past events to the present, and the
present to the future; that run unheeded, uncommented,
in a thousand mazes wherever society subsists, and are
the moral cords of men by which the Deity is manifested
to the vigilant, or, more truly, to the illuminated observer.

St. Augustine, February 16

If a man carefully examine his thoughts he will be surprised to find how much he lives in the future. His well being is always ahead. Such a creature is probably immortal.

St. Augustine, February

Much of what we learn, and to the highest purposes, of
life is caught in moments, and rather by a sublime instinct
than by modes which can be explained in detail.

St. Augustine, February 25

I attended mass in the Catholic Church. The mass is
in Latin and the sermon in English, and the audience,
who are Spaniards, understand neither. The services
have been recently interrupted by the imprisonment of
the (clergyman) worthy father for debt in the Castle of
St. Marks.

St. Augustine, February 27

A fortnight since I attended a meeting of the Bible
Society. The Treasurer of this institution is Marshal of
the district, and by a somewhat unfortunate arrangement
had appointed a special meeting of the Society, and a
slave-auction, at the same time and place, one being in the
Government house, and the other in the adjoining yard.
One ear therefore heard the glad tidings of great joy,
whilst the other was regaled with 'Going, gentlemen,
going!' And almost without changing our position we
might aid in sending the Scriptures into Africa, or bid for
'four children without the mother' who had been kid-
napped therefrom.

Charleston, April 6

A new event is added to the quiet history of my life. I
have connected myself by friendship to a man [Achille
Murat] who with as ardent a love of truth as that which
animates me, with a mind surpassing mine in the variety
of its research, and sharpened and strengthened to an
energy for *action* to which I have no pretension, by advantages of birth and practical connexion with mankind
beyond almost all men in the world, — is, yet, that which

I had ever supposed only a creature of the imagination —
a consistent Atheist, — and a disbeliever in the existence,
and, of course, in the immortality of the soul. My faith in
these points is strong and I trust, as I live, indestructible.
Meantime I love and honour this intrepid doubter. His
soul is noble, and his virtue, as the virtue of a Sadducee
must always be, is sublime.

Charleston, S. C., April 17

Let the glory of the world go where it will, the mind has
its own glory. What it doth, endures. No man can serve
many masters. And often the choice is not given you between greatness in the world and greatness of soul, which
you will choose, but both advantages are not compatible.
The night is fine; the stars shed down their severe influences upon me, and I feel a joy in my solitude that the
merriment of vulgar society can never communicate.
There is a pleasure in the thought that the particular tone
of my mind at this moment may be new in the universe;
that the emotions of this hour may be peculiar and un-
exampled in the whole eternity of moral being. I lead a
new life. I occupy new ground in the world of spirits, un-
tenanted before. I commence a career of thought and
action which is expanding before me into a distant and
dazzling infinity. Strange thoughts start up like angels
in my way and beckon me onward. I doubt not I tread
on the highway that leads to the Divinity.

Alexandria, Va., May 15 [to Miss Emerson]

I am writing here in pleasant durance till the sun will
let me go home. . . . I am not sure I am a jot better or

worse than when I left home . . . only in this, that I
preached Sunday morning in Washington without any
pain or inconvenience. . . . I have not lost my courage or
the possession of my thoughts. . . . It seems to me lately
that we have many capacities which we lack time and
occasion to improve. If I read the *Bride of Lammermoor*,
a thousand imperfect suggestions arise in my mind, to
which could I give heed, I should be a novelist. When I
chance to light on a verse of genuine poetry, it may be in
a corner of a newspaper, a forcible sympathy awakens
a legion of little goblins in the recesses of the soul, and if
I had leisure to attend to the fine tiny rabble, I should
straightway become a poet. In my day dreams, I so often
hunger and thirst to be a painter, beside all the spasmodic
attachments I indulge to each of the sciences and each
province of letters. They all in turn play the coquette
with my imagination, and it may be I shall die at the last
a forlorn bachelor jilted of them all.

THE PRESIDENT

Alexandria, May 19

Mr. Adams went out a swimming the other day into
the Potomac, and went near to a boat which was coming
down the river. Some rude blackguards were in it, who,
not knowing the character of the swimmer, amused themselves with laughing at his bald head as it poppled up and
down in the water, and, as they drew nearer, threatened
to crack open his round pate if he came nigh them. The
President of the United States was, I believe, compelled
to waive the point of honour and seek a more retired
bathing-place.

Boston, August 24 [to Miss Emerson]

When I attended church, and the man in the pulpit was all clay and not of tuneable metal, I thought that if men would avoid that general language and general manner in which they strive to hide all that is peculiar, and would say only what was uppermost in their own minds, after their own individual manner, every man would be interesting.

Cambridge, undated, 1828

We are very apt to over-rate the importance of our actions. Men of a very religious turn of mind are apt to think (at least their language gives this impression) that the designs of God in the world are very much affected [by], if not dependent upon what shall be done or determined by themselves, or their society, or their country. . . .

The true way to consider things is this: Truth says, Give yourself no manner of anxiety about events, about the consequences of actions. They are really of no importance to us. They have another Director, controller, guide. The whole object of the universe to us is the formation of character. If you think you came into being for the purpose of taking an important part in the administration of events, to guard a province of the moral creation from ruin, and that its salvation hangs on the success of your single arm, you have wholly mistaken your business.

Cambridge, Divinity Hall, July 10, 1828

I am always made uneasy when the conversation turns in my presence upon popular ignorance and the duty of

adapting our public harangues and writings to the mind
of the people. 'Tis all pedantry and ignorance. The
people know as much and reason as well as we do. None
so quick as they to discern brilliant genius or solid
parts. And I observe that all those who use this cant
most, are such as do not rise above mediocrity of understanding.

Cambridge, undated

I am not so enamoured of liberty as to love to be idle.
But the only evil I find in idleness is unhappiness. I love
to be my own master, when my spirits are prompt, when
my brain is vegete and apt for thought. If I were richer,
I should lead a better life than I do; that is, better divided
and more able. I should ride on horseback a good deal;
I should bowl, and create an appetite for my studies by
intermixing some heat and labour in affairs. The chief
advantage I should propose myself in wealth would be
the independence of manner and conversation it would
bestow and which I eagerly covet and seldom quite attain, and in some companies never.

It is a peculiarity (I find by observation upon others)
of humour in me, my strong propensity for strolling. I
deliberately shut up my books in a cloudy July noon, put
on my old clothes and old hat and slink away to the
whortleberry bushes and slip with the greatest satisfaction into a little cowpath where I am sure I can defy
observation. This point gained, I solace myself for hours
with picking blueberries and other trash of the woods, far
from fame, behind the birch-trees. I seldom enjoy hours
as I do these. I remember them in winter; I expect them

in spring. I do not know a creature that I think has the same humour, or would think it respectable. . . .

When I consider the constitutional calamity of my family, which, in its falling upon Edward, has buried at once so many towering hopes — with whatever reason, I have little apprehension of my own liability to the same evil. I have so much mixture of *silliness* in my intellectual frame that I think Providence has tempered me against this. My brother lived and acted and spoke with preternatural energy. My own manner is sluggish; my speech sometimes flippant, sometimes embarrassed and ragged; my actions (if I may say so) are of a passive kind. Edward had always great power of face. I have none. I laugh; I blush; I look ill-tempered; against my will and against my interest. But all this imperfection, as it appears to me, is a *caput mortuum*, is a ballast — as things go, is a defence.

EDUCATION

Cambridge, undated

I like to have a man's knowledge comprehend more than one class of topics, one row of shelves. I like a man who likes to see a fine barn as well as a good tragedy.

Cambridge, undated

The terms of intercourse in society are singularly unpropitious to the virtuous curiosity of young men with regard to the inner qualities of a beautiful woman. They may only see the outside of the house they want to buy.

Concord, New Hampshire, December 21, 1828

I have now been four days engaged to Ellen Louisa Tucker. Will my Father in Heaven regard us with kindness, and as he hath, as we trust, made us for each other, will he be pleased to strengthen and purify and prosper and eternize our affection!

1829-1832

[THE year 1829 opened happily. The letter to Aunt Mary of January 6, copied into the journal, expresses Emerson's unwonted sense of good fortune, as well as the ominous question 'Can this hold?' He accepted the call of the Second Church, and though Miss Tucker's health seemed frail, they were married in September. She was but eighteen. There was little time or interest for journalizing in this year.

By March, 1830, Ellen's health was declining and her husband took her South. Reverend Mr. Ware had gone to Europe, and Emerson was acting as sole pastor. His wife failed steadily, and she died in Boston on February 8, 1831. During the rest of this year Emerson fulfilled manfully his pastoral duties.

But by 1832 a certain restlessness is manifest in his journals. The entry for January 6 shows that he was already planning a book. Four days later he is rebelling against the 'official goodness' of a clergyman. By the first of June he had made known to his congregation his unwillingness to administer the Lord's Supper, believing as he did that Jesus 'did not intend to establish an institution for perpetual observance when he ate the Passover with his disciples.' (See his sermon on the 'Lord's Supper,' now printed in the *Miscellanies;* and also Edward W. Emerson's notes to that volume in the Centenary Edition.) While the congregation was making up its mind whether to retain him as pastor, under the conditions which he had laid down, Emerson went to the White Mountains to think the matter over in solitude. In September he returned, preached the sermon to which allusion has just been made, and resigned his pastorate, because, he said, 'It is my desire, in the office of a Christian minister, to do nothing which I cannot do with my whole heart.' The Second Church voted to accept his resignation. The entry in his journal for October 28, 1832, is his sole reference to this matter. On December 25 he sailed for Europe.]

Cambridge, January 6, 1829 [to Miss Emerson]

I lean always to that ancient superstition (if it is such, though drawn from a wise survey of human affairs) which taught men to beware of unmixed prosperity, for Nemesis keeps watch to overthrow the high. Well, now look at the altered aspect. William has begun to live by the law. Edward has recovered his reason and his health. Bulkeley was never more comfortable in his life. Charles is prospering in all ways. Waldo is comparatively well and comparatively successful — far more so than his friends, out of his family, anticipated. Now I add to all this felicity a particular felicity which makes my own glass very much larger and fuller. And I straightway say, Can this hold?

Cambridge, Sunday morning, January 17, 1829

My history has had its important days within a brief period. Whilst I enjoy the luxury of an unmeasured affection for an object so deserving of it all, and who requites it all, — I am called by an ancient and respectable

church to become its pastor. I recognize in these events,
accompanied as they are by so many additional occasions
of joy in the condition of my family, — I recognize with
acute sensibility, the hand of my heavenly Father. This
happiness awakens in me a certain awe: I know my im-
perfections: I know my ill-deserts; and the beauty of God
makes me feel my own sinfulness the more. I throw myself with humble gratitude upon his goodness, I feel my
total dependence. O God direct and guard and bless me,
and those and especially *her*, in whom I am blessed.

Boston, February 10, 1830

Is there not the sublime always in religion? I go down
to the vestry and I find a few plain men and women there,
come together not to eat or drink, or get money, or mirth,
but drawn by a great thought. Come thither to conceive
and form a connexion with an infinite Person. I thought
it was sublime, and not mean as others suppose.

Boston, March 3

Read with admiration and delight Mr. Webster's noble
speech in answer to Hayne. What consciousness of political rectitude, and what confidence in his intellectual
treasures must he have to enable him to take this master's
tone! Mr. Channing said he had great 'self-subsistence.'
The beauty and dignity of the spectacle he exhibits should
teach men the beauty and dignity of *principles*. This is
one that is not blown about by every wind of opinion, but
has mind great enough to see the majesty of moral nature
and to apply himself in all his length and breadth to it and
magnanimously trust thereto.

Boston, undated

The year is long enough for all that is to be done in it. The flowers blow; the fruit ripens; and every species of animals is satisfied and attains its perfection, but man does not; man has seen more than he has had time to do.

Brookline, July 24

Don't say that qualities are so radical in us that the fickle man can never persevere, let him try as he will, nor the selfish man ever distribute; for on the contrary, any quality of a man may be taken advantage of to lead him to any other that is desirable. I hate steady labour from morn till night, and therefore am not a learned man, but I have an omnivorous curiosity and facility of new undertaking. In voluntary exertions to gratify it, may I not become learned and acquire the habits of steady toil?

Brookline, August 18

The sun shines and warms and lights us and we have no curiosity to know why this is so; but we ask the reason of all evil, of pain, and hunger, and musquitoes and silly people.

Brookline, September 6

Mon amie à Concord.

Boston, November 5

When a man has got to a certain point in his career of truth he becomes conscious forevermore that he must take himself for better, for worse, as his portion; that what he can get out of his plot of ground by the sweat of his brow is his meat, and though the wide universe is full of good, not a particle can he add to himself but through his toil bestowed on this spot. It looks to him indeed a little spot, a poor barren possession, filled with thorns, and a lurking place for adders and apes and wolves. But cultivation will work wonders. It will enlarge to his eye as it is explored. That little nook will swell to a world of light and power and love.

Boston, February 8, 1831

Ellen Tucker Emerson died, 8th February, Tuesday morning, 9 o'clock. . . .

Boston, Chardon St., February 13, 1831

Five days are wasted since Ellen went to heaven to see, to know, to worship, to love, to intercede. . . . Reunite us, O thou Father of our spirits.

There is that which passes away and never returns. This miserable apathy, I know, may wear off. I almost fear when it will. Old duties will present themselves with no more repulsive face. I shall go again among my friends with a tranquil countenance. Again I shall be amused, I shall stoop again to little hopes and little fears and forget the graveyard. But will the dead be restored to me? Will the eye that was closed on Tuesday ever beam again in the fulness of love on me? Shall I ever again be able to connect the face of outward nature, the mists of the morn, the star of eve, the flowers, and all poetry, with the heart and life of an enchanting friend? No. There is one birth, and one baptism, and one first love, and the affections cannot keep their youth any more than men. . . .

Heu! quantominus est cum reliquis versari, quam tui meminisse!

Concord, March 4

The Religion that is afraid of science dishonours God and commits suicide.

Boston, April 3

Trust to that prompting within you. No man ever got above it. Men have transgressed and hated and blasphemed it, but no man ever sinned but he felt it towering above him and threatening him with ruin.

Boston, April 4

The days go by, griefs, and simpers, and sloth and disappointments. The dead do not return, and sometimes we are negligent of their image. Not of yours, Ellen. I know too well who is gone from me.

Boston, May 20

Blind men in Rome complained that the streets were dark. To the dull mind all nature is leaden. To the illuminated mind the whole world burns and sparkles with light.

Boston, June 15

After a fortnight's wandering to the Green Mountains and Lake Champlain, yet finding you, dear Ellen, nowhere and yet everywhere, I come again to my own place, and would willingly transfer some of the pictures that the eyes saw, in living language to my page; yea, translate the fair and magnificent symbols into their own sentiments. But this were to antedate knowledge. It grows into us, say rather, we *grow wise*, and not take wisdom; and only in God's own order, and by my concurrent effort, can I get the abstract sense of which mountains, sunshine, thunders, night, birds and flowers are the sublime alphabet.

Boston, June 20

I suppose it is not wise, not being natural, to belong to any religious party. In the Bible you are not directed to be a Unitarian, or a Calvinist or an Episcopalian. Now if a man is wise, he will not only not profess himself to be a Unitarian, but he will say to himself, I am not a member of that or of any party. I am God's child, a disciple of Christ, or, in the eye of God, a fellow disciple with Christ. Now let a man get into a stage-coach with this distinct understanding of himself, divorcing himself in his heart from every party, and let him meet with religious men of every different sect, and he will find scarce any proposition uttered by them to which he does not assent, and none to the sentiment of which he does not assent, though he may insist on varying the language. As fast as any man becomes great, that is, thinks, he becomes a new party. Socrates, Aristotle, Calvin, Luther, Abelard, what are these but names of parties? Which is to say, As fast as we use our own eyes, we quit these parties or Unthinking Corporations, and join ourselves to God in an unpartaken relation.

A sect or party is an elegant incognito devised to save a man from the vexation of thinking.

Since to govern my passions with absolute sway is the work I have to do, I cannot but think that the sect for the suppression of Intemperance, or a sect for the suppression of loose behaviour to women, would be a more reasonable and useful society than the Orthodox sect, which is a society for the suppression of Unitarianism, or the Unitarian, which is a society for the diffusion of useful knowledge.

Religion is the relation of the soul to God, and therefore the progress of Sectarianism marks the decline of religion. For, looking at God instantly reduces our disposition to dissent from our brother. A man may die by a fever as well as by consumption, and religion is as effectually destroyed by bigotry as by indifference.

Boston, Chardon St., June 29

Is not the law of compensation perfect? It holds as far as we can see. Different gifts to different individuals, but with a mortgage of responsibility on every one. 'The gods *sell* all things.' Well, old man, hast got no farther? Why, this was taught thee months and years ago. It was writ on the autumn leaves at Roxbury in keep-school days; it sounded in the blind man's ear at Cambridge. And all the joy and all the sorrow since have added nothing to thy wooden book. I can't help it. Heraclitus grown old complained that all resolved itself into identity. That thought was first his philosophy, and then his melancholy, — the life he lived and the death he died. And I have nothing charactered in my brain that outlives this word Compensation. Old Stubler, the Quaker in the Baltimore steamboat, said to me, that, if a man sacrificed

his impurity, purity should be the price with which it
would be paid; if a man gave up his hatred, he should
be rewarded with love — 'tis the same old melody
and it sounds through the vast of being.

Boston, July 6

President Monroe died on the fourth of July, — a
respectable man, I believe.

Boston, July 15

God in us worships God.

Boston, July 15

The things taught in colleges and schools are not an
education, but the means of education.

Boston, July 21 (?)

Dined with President Adams yesterday at Dr. Parkman's.

Boston, August 26

Yesterday I heard John Quincy Adams deliver an
eulogy upon President Monroe. But he held his notes so
close to his mouth that he could be ill heard. There was
nothing heroic in the subject, and not much in the feelings
of the orator, so it proved rather a spectacle than a
speech.

Boston, October 3

I wish the Christian principle, the *ultra* principle of non-
resistance and returning good for ill, might be tried

fairly. William Penn made one trial. The world was not
ripe, and yet it did well. An angel stands a poor chance
among wild beasts; a better chance among men: but among
angels best of all. And so I admit of this system that it
is, like the Free Trade, fit for one nation only on condition
that all adopt it. Still a man may try it in his own person, and even his sufferings by reason of it shall be its
triumphs. . . .

One thing more; it is said that it strips the good man
bare and leaves him to the whip and license of pirates and
butchers. But I suppose the exaltation of the general
mind by the influence of the principle will be a counteraction of the increased license. Not any influence acts
upon the highest man but a proportion of the same gets
down to the lowest man.

Boston, November

Have been at the Examination of Derry Academy, and
had some sad, some pleasant thoughts.

Is it not true that every man has before him in his
mind room in one direction to which there is no bound,
but in every other direction he runs against a wall in a
short time? One course of thought, affection, action is
for him — that is his *use*, as the new men say. Let me
embark in political economy, in repartee, in fiction, in
verse, in practical counsels (as here in the Derry case) and
I am soon run aground; but let my bark head its own
way toward the law of laws, toward the compensation or
action and reaction of the moral universe, and I sweep
serenely over God's depths in an infinite sea.

Boston, December 10

Charles has gone away to Porto Rico. God preserve
and restore him.

PAROCHIAL VISITS

Boston, December 19

When I talk with the sick they sometimes think I treat
death with unbecoming indifference and do not make the
case my own, or, if I do, err in my judgment. I do not
fear death. I believe those who fear it have borrowed the
terrors through which they see it from vulgar opinion, and
not from their own minds. My own mind is the direct
revelation which I have from God and far least liable to
mistake in telling his will of any revelation. Following
my own thoughts, especially as sometimes they have
moved me in the country (as in the Gulf Road in Vermont), I should lie down in the lap of earth as trustingly
as ever on my bed. But the terror to many persons is in
the vague notions of what shall follow death. The
judgment, an uncertain judgment to be passed upon
them, — whether they shall be saved? It ought to be
considered by them that there is no uncertainty about it.
Already they may know exactly what is their spiritual
condition. . . . He will not suffer his holy one to see
corruption. . . . What are your sources of satisfaction?
If they are meats and drinks, dress, gossip, revenge, hope
of wealth, they must perish with the body. If they are
contemplation, kind affections, admiration of what is
admirable, self-command, self-improvement, then they
survive death and will make you as happy then as
now.

Boston, December 25 [to Miss Emerson]

The rough and tumble old fellows, Bacons, Miltons, and Burkes, don't wire-draw. That's why I like Montaigne. No effeminate parlour workman is he, on an idea got at an evening lecture or a young man's debate, but roundly tells what he saw, or what he thought of when he was riding horse-back or entertaining a troop at his chateau. A gross, semisavage indecency debases his book, and ought doubtless to turn it out of doors; but the robustness of his sentiments, the generosity of his judgments, the downright truth without fear or favour, I do embrace with both arms. It is wild and savoury as sweet fern. Henry VIII. loved to see a *man*, and it is exhilarating, once in a while, to come across a genuine Saxon stump, a wild, virtuous man who knows books, but gives them their right place in his mind, lower than his reason. Books are apt to turn reason out of doors. You find men talking everywhere from their memories, instead of from their understanding. If I stole this thought from Montaigne, as is very likely, I don't care. I should have said the same myself.

Boston, December 28

The year hastens to its close. What is it to me? What I am, that is all that affects me. That I am 28, or 8, or 58 years old is as nothing. Should I mourn that the spring flowers are gone, that the summer fruit has ripened, that the harvest is reaped, that the snow has fallen?

Boston, January 6 [1832]

Shall I not write a book on topics such as follow? — Chapter 1. That the mind is its own place;

Chapter 2. That exact justice is done;

Chapter 3. That good motives are at the bottom of (many) bad actions; e. g. Business before friends;

Chapter 4. That the soul is immortal;

Chapter 5. On prayers;

Chapter 6. That the best is the true;

Chapter 7. That the mind discerns all things;

Chapter 8. That the mind seeks itself in all things.

Chapter 9. That truth is its own warrant.

Boston, January 10

It is the best part of the man, I sometimes think, that revolts most against his being a minister. His good revolts from official goodness. If he never spoke or acted but with the full consent of his understanding, if the whole man acted always, how powerful would be every act and every word. Well then, or ill then, how much power he sacrifices by conforming himself to say and do in other folks' time instead of in his own! The difficulty is that we do not make a world of our own, but fall into institutions already made, and have to accommodate ourselves to them to be useful at all, and this accommodation is, I say, a loss of so much integrity and, of course, of so much power.

Boston, January 20

Don't trust children with edge tools. Don't trust man, great God, with more power than he has, until he has learned to use that little better. What a hell should we make of the world if we could do what we would! Put a button on the foil till the young fencers have learned not to put each other's eyes out.

Boston, January 30

Every man hath his use, no doubt, and everyone makes ever the effort according to the energy of his character to suit his external condition to his inward constitution. If his external condition does not admit of such accommodation, he breaks the form of his life, and enters a new one which does. If it will admit of such accommodation, he gradually bends it to his mind. Thus Finney can preach, and so his prayers are short; Parkman can pray, and so his prayers are long; Lowell can visit, and so his church service is less. But what shall poor I do, who can neither visit nor pray nor preach to my mind?

Boston, Feb. 6

Take nothing for granted. That strikes you in hearing the discourse of a wise man, that he has brought to the crucible and the analysis all that other people receive without question, as chemists are directed to select what manufacturers throw away.

Boston, March 10

This year I have spent say $20 in wine and liquors which are drunk up, and the drinkers are the worse. It would have bought a beautiful print that would have pleased for a century; or have paid a debt. . . .

SHAKSPEARE

Boston, May 16

Shakspeare's creations indicate no sort of anxiety to be understood. There is the Cleopatra, an irregular, unfinished, glorious, sinful character, sink or swim, there she is, and not one in the thousand of his readers apprehends the noble dimensions of the heroine. Then Ariel, Hamlet, and all; all done in sport with the free, daring pencil of a master of the World. He leaves his children with God.

Boston, June 2

I have sometimes thought that, in order to be a good minister, it was necessary to leave the ministry. The profession is antiquated. In an altered age, we worship in the dead forms of our forefathers. Were not a Socratic paganism better than an effete, superannuated Christianity?

Conway, N. H., July 6

Here, among the mountains, the pinions of thought should be strong, and one should see the errors of men from a calmer height of love and wisdom. What is the message that is given me to communicate next Sunday? Religion in the mind is not credulity, and in the practice is not form. It is a life. It is the order and soundness of a man. It is not something else *to be got*, to be *added*, but is a new life of those faculties you have. It is to do right. It is to love, it is to serve, it is to think, it is to be humble.

Ethan Allen Crawford's, White Mountains, July 14

The good of going into the mountains is that life is reconsidered; it is far from the slavery of your own modes of living, and you have opportunity of viewing the town at such a distance as may afford you a just view, nor can you have any such mistaken apprehension as might be expected from the place you occupy and the round of customs you run at home.

White Mountains, July 15

The hour of decision. It seems not worth while for them who charge others with exalting forms above the moon to fear forms themselves with extravagant dislike. I am so placed that my *aliquid ingenii* may be brought into useful action. Let me not bury my talent in the earth in my indignation at this windmill. But though the thing may be useless and even pernicious, do not destroy what is good and useful in a high degree rather than comply with what is hurtful in a small degree. The Communicant celebrates on a foundation either of authority or of tradition an ordinance which has been the occasion to thousands, — I hope to thousands of thousands, — of contrition, of gratitude, of prayer, of faith, of love and of holy living. Far be it from any of my friends, — God forbid it be in my heart, — to interrupt any occasion thus blessed of God's influences upon the human mind. I will not, because we may not all think alike of the means, fight so strenuously against the means, as to miss of the end which we all value alike. I think Jesus did not mean to institute a perpetual celebration, but that a commemoration of him would be useful. Others think that Jesus did establish this one. We are agreed that one is useful, and we are agreed I hope in the way in which it must be made useful, viz., by each one's making it an original Commemoration.

I know very well that it is a bad sign in a man to be too conscientious, and stick at gnats. The most desperate

scoundrels have been the over-refiners. Without accommodation society is impracticable. But this ordinance is
esteemed the most sacred of religious institutions, and I
cannot go habitually to an institution which they esteem
holiest with indifference and dislike.

Boston, August 18

To be genuine. Goethe, they say, was wholly so. The
difficulty increases with the gifts of the individual. A
plough-boy can be, but a minister, an orator, an ingenious
thinker how hardly! George Fox was. 'What I am in
words,' he said, 'I am the same in life.' Swedenborg was.
'My writings will be found,' he said, 'another self.'
George Washington was; 'the irreproachable Washington.'

Boston, September 14

Don't tell me to get ready to die. I know not what
shall be. The only preparation I can make is by fulfilling
my present duties. This is the everlasting life.

Boston, October 1

I am cheered and instructed by this paper on Corn Law
Rhymes in the *Edinburgh* by my Germanick new-light
writer [Carlyle], whoever he be. He gives us confidence in
our principles. He assures the truth-lover everywhere of
sympathy. Blessed art that makes books, and so joins
me to that stranger by this perfect railroad.

Boston, October 19

My aunt [Mary Moody Emerson] had an eye that went
through and through you like a needle. 'She was en-

dowed,' she said, 'with the fatal gift of penetration.' She disgusted everybody because she knew them too well.

Boston, October 28

The vote on the question proposed to the proprietors of the Second Church this evening stood thus, Ayes 25; nays 34; blanks 2. On the acceptance of the pastor's letter, ayes 30; nays 20; blanks 4.

1833-1835

[THE first days of 1833 found Emerson on board the brig Jasper, 236 tons, bound for Malta. He passed Gibraltar on January 20, and landed at Malta on February 2. He visited Sicily, Naples, Rome, Florence, and Venice; then crossed the Alps, and after a brief stay in Switzerland, reached Paris on June 20. A month later he was in England. His visits to Landor in Italy, to Coleridge in London, to Wordsworth in the Lake Country, and to Carlyle at Ecclefechan were carefully recorded in his note-books, and later printed in *English Traits*. Most of these entries were therefore omitted from the *Journals* by the editors.

Emerson sailed from Liverpool on his return voyage September 4, landing in New York October 9. He joined his mother, for a time, at Newton Upper Falls, but during most of the winter, 1833–1834, he preached in New Bedford, Plymouth, and elsewhere, and delivered at least four lectures in Boston. He was in New York on October 18, 1834, when he received the news of the death of his brother Edward in Porto Rico. In November he moved to Concord with his mother and brother Charles, boarding with the venerable Dr. Ripley, his step-grandfather, in the Old Manse. The house had been built by Emerson's own grandfather, the Rev. William Emerson of Concord.

As the year 1835 opened, Emerson was busy with writing, lecturing, and occasional preaching. He had already met, while preaching in Plymouth, Miss Lydia Jackson, and by June they were betrothed. He bought in August the Concord house where he lived for the rest of his life. His marriage took place in Plymouth on September 14. In November and December he delivered in Boston a course of ten lectures on English literature.]

At Sea, January 2, 1833

Sailed from Boston for Malta, December 25, 1832, in Brig Jasper, Captain Ellis, 236 tons, laden with logwood, mahogany, tobacco, sugar, coffee, beeswax, cheese, etc. A long storm from the second morn of our departure consigned all the five passengers to the irremedial chagrins of the stateroom, to wit, nausea, darkness, unrest, uncleanness, harpy appetite and harpy feeding, the ugly 'sound of water in mine ears,' anticipations of going to the bottom, and the treasures of the memory. I remembered up nearly the whole of *Lycidas*, clause by clause, here a verse and there a word, as Isis in the fable the broken body of Osiris.

At Sea, January 3

I rose at sunrise, and under the lee of the spencer-sheet had a solitary, thoughtful hour. All right thought is devout.

The clouds were touched
And in their silent faces might be read
Unutterable love.

They shone with light that shines on Europe, Afric, and the Nile, and I opened my spirit's ear to their most an-

cient hymn. What, they said to me, goest thou so far to
seek — painted canvas, carved marble, renowned towns?
But fresh from us, new evermore, is the creative efflux
from whence these works spring. You now feel in gazing
at our fleecy arch of light the motions that express 'themselves in arts. You get no nearer to the principle in
Europe. . . .

This strong-winged sea-gull and striped sheer-water
that you have watched as they skimmed the waves under
our vault, they are works of art better worth your enthusiasm, masterpieces of Eternal power, strictly eternal
because now active, and ye need not go so far to seek what
ye would not seek at all if it were not within you. Yet
welcome and hail! So sang in my car the silver-grey
mists, and the winds and the sea said Amen.

At Sea, Saturday evening, January 5

I like the latitude of 37° better than my bitter native
42°. We have sauntered all this calm day at one or two
knots the hour, and nobody on board well pleased but I,
and why should I be pleased? I have nothing to record.
I have read little. I have done nothing. What then?
Need we be such barren scoundrels that the whole beauty
of heaven, the main, and man, cannot entertain us unless
we too must needs hold a candle and daub God's world
with a smutch of our own insignificance. Not I, for one.
I will be pleased, though I do not deserve it.

At Sea, January 15

I learn in the sunshine to get an altitude and the latitude, but am a dull scholar as ever in real figures. Seldom,

I suppose, was a more inapt learner of arithmetic, astronomy, geography, political economy, than I am, as I daily find to my cost. It were to brag much if I should there end the catalogue of my defects. My memory of history — put me to the pinch of a precise question — is as bad; my comprehension of a question in technical metaphysics very slow, and in all arts practick, in driving a bargain, or hiding emotion, or carrying myself in company as a man for an hour, I have no skill. What under the sun canst thou do then, pale face? Truly not much, but I can hope.

At Sea, January 16

The good Captain rejoices much in my ignorance. He confounded me the other day about the book in the Bible where God was not mentioned, and last night upon St. Paul's shipwreck. Yet I comforted myself at midnight with *Lycidas.* What marble beauty in that classic pastoral. I should like well to see an analysis of the pleasure it gives. That were criticism for the gods.

Past Gibraltar, January 25

If the sea teaches any lesson, it thunders this through the throat of all its winds, 'That there is no knowledge that is not valuable.' How I envied my fellow passenger who yesterday had knowledge and nerve enough to prescribe for the sailor's sore throat, and this morning to bleed him. In this little balloon of ours, so far from the human family and their sages and colleges and manufactories, every accomplishment, every natural or acquired talent, every piece of information is some time in request.

Malta, February

I am now pleased abundantly with St. John's church in Valetta. Welcome these new joys. Let my American eye be a child's again to these glorious picture-books. The chaunting friars, the carved ceilings, the madonnas and saints, they are living oracles, *quotidiana et perpetua.*

La Valetta, February 16

How beautiful to have the church always open, so that every tired wayfaring man may come in and be soothed by all that art can suggest of a better world when he is weary with this. I hope they will carve and paint and inscribe the walls of our churches in New England before this century, which will probably see many grand granite piles erected there, is closed.

Syracuse, February 23

Was it grand or mournful that I should hear mass in this Temple of Minerva this morn? Though in different forms, is it not venerable that the same walls should be devoted to divine worship for more than 2500 years? Is it not good witness to the ineradicableness of the religious principle? With the strange practice that in these regions everywhere confounds pagan and Christian antiquity, and half preserves both, they call this cathedral the church of 'Our Lady of the Pillar.'

Catania, March 1

I have been to the Opera, and thought three *taris*, the price of a ticket, rather too much for the whistle. It is doubtless a vice to turn one's eyes inward too much, but I am my own comedy and tragedy.

Naples, March 16

Last night, stayed at home at my black lodging in the Croce di Malta and read Goethe. This morn sallied out alone, and traversed, I believe for the seventh time, that superb mile of the Villa Reale; then to the tomb of Virgil.

Rome, March 29

I went to the Capitoline hill, then to its Museum and saw the Dying Gladiator, the Antinous, the Venus, — to the gallery, then to the Tarpeian Rock, then to the vast and splendid museum of the Vatican, a wilderness of marble. After traversing many a shining chamber and gallery I came to the Apollo and soon after to the Laocoön. 'Tis false to say that the casts give no idea of the originals. I found I knew these fine statues already by heart and had admired the casts long since much more than I ever can the originals.

Rome, Sunday, March 31

I have been to the Sistine Chapel to see the Pope bless the palms, and hear his choir chaunt the Passion. The Cardinals came in, one after another, each wearing a purple robe, an ermine cape, and a small red cap to cover the tonsure. A priest attended each one, to adjust the robes of their eminences. As each cardinal entered the chapel, the rest rose. One or two were fine persons. Then came the Pope in scarlet robes and bishop's mitre. After he was seated, the cardinals went in turn to the throne and kneeled and kissed his hand. After this ceremony the attendants divested the cardinals of their robes and put on them a gorgeous cope of cloth-of-gold. When this was arranged, a sort of ornamental baton made of the dried palm leaf was brought to his Holiness and blessed, and each of the cardinals went again to the throne and received one of these from the hands of the Pope. They were supplied from a large pile at the side of the papal chair. After the cardinals, came other dignitaries, bishops, deans, canons, — I know them not, but there was much etiquette, some kissing the hand only, and some the foot also of the Pope. Some received olive branches. Lastly several officers performed the same ceremony.

When this long procession of respect was over, and all the robed multitude had received their festal palms and olives, his Holiness was attended to a chair of state, and, being seated, was lifted up by his bearers, and, preceded by the long official array and by his chaunting choir, he rode out of the chapel.

It was hard to recognize in this ceremony the gentle Son of Man who sat upon an ass amidst the rejoicings of his fickle countrymen. Whether from age or from custom, I know not, but the Pope's eyes were shut or nearly shut as he rode. After a few minutes he reëntered the chapel in like state, and soon after retired and left the sacred college of cardinals to hear the Passion chaunted by themselves. The chapel is that whose walls Michel Angelo adorned with his Last Judgment. But to-day I have not seen the picture well.

All this pomp is conventional. It is imposing to those who know the customs of courts, and of what wealth and of what rank these particular forms are the symbols. But to the eye of an Indian I am afraid it would be ridiculous. There is no true majesty in all this millinery and imbecility. Why not devise ceremonies that shall be in as good and manly taste as their churches and pictures and music?

I counted twenty-one cardinals present. Music at St. Peter's in the afternoon, and better still at Chiesa Nuova in the evening. Those mutilated wretches sing so well it is painful to hear them.

Rome, Wednesday, April 3

The famous *Miserere* was sung this afternoon in the Sistine Chapel. The saying at Rome is, that it cannot be imitated, not only by any other choir, but in any other chapel in the world. The Emperor of Austria sent Mozart to Rome on purpose to have it sung at Vienna with like effect, but it failed.

Surely it is sweet music, and sounds more like the Eolian harp than anything else. The pathetic lessons of the day relate the treachery of Judas and apply select passages from the prophets and psalms to the circumstances of Jesus. Then whilst the choir chaunt the words '*Traditor autem dedit eis signum, dicens, Quem osculatus fuero, ipse est, tenete eum*,' all the candles in the chapel are extinguished but one. During the repetition of this verse the last candle is taken down and hidden under the altar. Then out of the silence and the darkness rises this most plaintive and melodious strain (the whole congregation kneeling), '*Miserere mei, Deus*,' etc. The sight and the sound are very touching.

Everything here is in good taste. The choir are concealed by the high fence which rises above their heads. We were in Michel Angelo's chapel which is full of noblest scriptural forms and faces.

Rome, April 4

To-night I heard the *Miserere* sung in St. Peter's and with less effect than yesterday. But what a temple! When night was settling down upon it and a long religious procession moved through a part of the church, I got an idea of its immensity such as I had not before. You walk about on its ample, marble pavement as you would on a common, so free are you of your neighbors; and throngs of people are lost upon it. And what beautiful lights and shades on its mighty gilded arches and vaults and far windows and brave columns, and its rich-clad priests that look as if they were the pictures come down from the walls and walking.

Thence we came out (I was walking with two painters, Cranch and Alexander) under the moon and saw the planet shine upon the finest fountain in the world, and upon all the stone saints on the piazza and the great church itself. This was a spectacle which only Rome can boast, — how faery beautiful! An Arabian Night's tale.

Rome, Sunday, April 14

Attended divine service at the English Chapel. To preach well you must speak the truth. It is vain to say what has been said every Sunday for a hundred years, if it is not true.

Florence, April 29

How like an archangel's tent is this great Cathedral of many-coloured marble set down in the midst of the city, and by its side its wondrous Campanile! I took a hasty glance at the gates of the Baptistery which Angelo said

ought to be the gates of Paradise, '*digne chiudere il Para-*
diso,' and then at his own David, and hasted to the
Tribune and to the Pitti Palace. I saw the statue that
enchants the world. And truly the Venus deserves to be
visited from far. It is not adequately represented by the
plaster casts, as the Apollo and the Laocoön are. I must
go again and see this statue. Then I went round this
cabinet and gallery and galleries till I was well-nigh
'dazzled and drunk with beauty.' I think no man has an
idea of the powers of painting until he has come hither.
Why should painters study at Rome? Here, here.

Florence, May 2

I revisited the Tribune this morning to see the Venus and
the Fornarina and the rest of that attractive company.
I reserve my admiration as much as I can; I make a continual effort not to be pleased except by that which ought
to please *me*, and I walked coolly round and round the
marble lady; but when I planted myself at the iron gate
which leads into the chamber of Dutch paintings, and
looked at the statue, I saw and felt that mankind have
had good reason for their preference of this excellent work,
and I gladly gave one testimony more to the surpassing
genius of the artist.

Florence, May 15

To-day I dined with Mr. Landor at his villa at San
Domenica di Fiesole. He lives in a beautiful spot in a fine
house full of pictures and with a family most engaging:
he has a wife and four children. He said good and pleasant things, and preferred Washington to all modern

great men. He is very decided, as I might have expected, in all his opinions, and very much a connoisseur,
in paintings.

Florence, May 18

When I walk up the piazza of Santa Croce I feel as if it
were not a Florentine, no, nor an European church, but
a church built by and for the human race. I feel equally
at home within its walls as the Grand Duke, so *hospitably*
sound to me the names of its mighty dead. Buonaroti and
Galileo lived for us all; as Don Ferranto says of Aristotle,
'*Non è nè antico nè moderno; è il filosofo senza più.*'

Florence, May 21

I like the sayers of No better than the sayers of Yes.

Ferrara, May 30

Arrived at Ferrara at 4 P. M. Visited Tasso's prison, a
real dungeon. There I saw Byron's name cut with his pen
knife in the wall. The guide said his father accompanied
him, and that Byron stayed an hour and a half in the
prison and there wrote.

Venice, June 2

I collect nothing that can be touched or tasted or
smelled, neither cameo, painting nor medallion; nothing
in my trunk but old clothes; but I value much the growing picture which the ages have painted and which I
reverently survey. It is wonderful how much we see in
five months, in how short a time we learn what it has
taken so many ages to teach.

Venice, June 3

I am speedily satisfied with Venice. It is a great oddity, a city for beavers, but, to my thought, a most disagreeable residence. You feel always in prison, and solitary. Two persons may live months in adjoining streets and never meet, for you go about in gondolas, and all the gondolas are precisely alike, and the persons within commonly concealed; then there are no news-rooms; except St. Mark's Piazza, no place of public resort. It is as if you were always at sea. And though, for a short time, it is very luxurious to lie on the eider-down cushions of your gondola and read or talk or smoke, drawing to, now the cloth-lined shutter, now the Venetian blind, now the glass window, as you please, yet there is always a slight smell of bilgewater about the thing, and houses in the water remind one of a freshet and of desolation, anything but comfort. I soon had enough of it. . . .

Milan, June 9

This cathedral is the only church in Italy that can pretend to compare with St. Peter's. It is a most impressive and glorious place, without and within. . . .

The walk upon the top of the church is delightful from the novelty and richness of the scene. Neighbored by this army of marble saints and martyrs, with scores of exquisitely sculptured pinnacles rising and flowering all around you, the noble city of Milan beneath, and all the Alps in the horizon, — it is one of the grandest views on earth.

Geneva, June 16

Yesterday, to oblige my companions, and protesting all the way upon the unworthiness of his memory, I went to Ferney to the château, the salon, the bedchamber, the gardens of Voltaire, the king of the scorners. His rooms were modest and pleasing, and hung with portraits of his friends. Franklin and Washington were there. The view of the lake and mountains commanded by the lawn behind the château is superior to that of Gibbon's garden at Lausanne. The old porter showed us some pictures belonging to his old master, and told a story that did full justice to his bad name. Yet it would be a sin against faith and philosophy to exclude Voltaire from toleration. He did his work as the buzzard and tarantula do theirs.

Paris, June 20

I arrived in Paris at noon on Thursday, 20 June. . . . We were presently lodged in the Hotel Montmorenci on the Boulevard Mont Martre. I have wandered round the city, but I am not well pleased. I have seen so much in five months that the magnificence of Paris will not take my eye to-day. The gardens of the Louvre looked pinched and the wind blew dust in my eyes, and before I got into the Champs Élysées I turned about and flatly refused to go farther. I was sorry to find that in leaving Italy I had left forever that air of antiquity and history which her towns possess, and in coming hither had come to a loud, modern New York of a place.

Paris, July 4

Dined to-day at Lointier's with General Lafayette and nearly one hundred Americans. I sought an opportunity of paying my respects to the hero, and inquiring after his health. His speech was as happy as usual.

Paris, July 11

A man who was no courtier, but loved men, went to Rome, — and there lived with boys. He came to France, and in Paris lives alone, and in Paris seldom speaks. If he do not see Carlyle in Edinburgh, he may go to America without saying anything in earnest, except to Cranch and to Landor.

The errors of traditional Christianity as it now exists, the popular faith of many millions, need to be removed to let men see the divine beauty of moral truth. I feel myself pledged, if health and opportunity be granted me, to demonstrate that all necessary truth is its own evidence; that no doctrine of God need appeal to a book; that Christianity is wrongly received by all such as take it for a system of doctrines, — its stress being upon moral truth; it is a rule of life, not a rule of faith.

And how men can toil and scratch so hard for things so dry, lifeless, unsightly, as these famous dogmas, when the divine beauty of the truths to which they are related lies behind them; how they can make such a fuss about the case, and never open it to see the jewel, is strange, pitiful.

Paris, July 13 [*Jardin des Plantes*]

The universe is a more amazing puzzle than ever, as you glance along this bewildering series of animated forms, — the hazy butterflies, the carved shells, the birds, beasts, fishes, insects, snakes, and the upheaving principle of life everywhere incipient, in the very rock aping organized

forms. Not a form so grotesque, so savage, nor so beautiful but is an expression of some property inherent in man
the observer, — an occult relation between the very scor-
pions and man. I feel the centipede in me, — cayman,
carp, eagle, and fox. I am moved by strange sympathies;
I say continually 'I will be a naturalist.'

Paris, July 15

At the *Théâtre Français*, where Talma played and
Madame Mars plays, I heard Delavigne's new piece,
Enfans d'Edouard, excellently performed; for although
Madame Mars speaks French beautifully and has the
manners of a princess, yet she scarcely excels the acting
of the less famous performers who support her. Each was
perfect in his part.

London, July 20

Went into St. Paul's, where service was saying. Poor
church.

London, July 28

Attended divine service at Westminster Abbey. The
Bishop of Gloucester preached. It is better than any
church I have seen except St. Peter's.

Carlisle in Cumberland, August 26

I am just arrived in merry Carlisle from Dumfries. A
white day in my years. I found the youth I sought in
Scotland, and good and wise and pleasant he seems to
me. Thomas Carlyle lives in the parish of Dunscore, 16
miles from Dumfries, amid wild and desolate heathery

hills, and without a single companion in this region out of
his own house. There he has his wife, a most accomplished
and agreeable woman. Truth and peace and faith dwell
with them and beautify them. I never saw more amiable-
ness than is in his countenance.

T. C. was born in Annandale. His reading multifarious,
Tristram Shandy, *Robinson Crusoe*, Robertson's *America.*
Rousseau's *Confessions* discovered to him that he was not
such an ass as he had imagined. Ten years ago he learned
German. London; heart of the world, wonderful only for
the mass of human beings. . . . Splendid bridge from the
new world to the old, built by Gibbon. . . .

T. C. had made up his mind to pay his taxes to William
and Adelaide Guelph with great cheerfulness as long as
William is able to compel the payment, and he shall cease
to do so the moment he ceases to compel them. Landor's
principle is mere rebellion, and he fears that is the American principle also. Himself worships the man that will
manifest any truth to him.

Mrs. Carlyle told of the disappointment when they had
determined to go to Weimar, and the letter arrived from
the bookseller to say the book did not sell, and they could
not go. The first thing Goethe sent was the chain she
wore round her neck, and how she capered when it came!
but since that time he had sent many things. Mrs. C.
said, when I mentioned the Burns piece, that it always
had happened to him upon those papers to hear of each
two or three years after. T. C. prefers London to any
other place to live in. John S. Mill the best mind he
knows, more purity, more force, has worked himself
clear of Benthamism.

Ambleside, August 28

This morning I went to Rydal Mount and called upon Mr. Wordsworth. . . .

The poet is always young, and this old man took the same attitudes that he probably had at seventeen, whilst he recollected the sonnet he would recite.

His egotism was not at all displeasing, obtrusive, as I had heard. To be sure it met no rock. I spoke as I felt, with great respect of his genius.

He spoke very kindly of Dr. Channing, who, he said, 'sat a long time in this very chair,' laying his hand upon an armchair.

He mentioned Burns's sons.

On my return to the inn, he walked near a mile with me, talking, and ever and anon stopping short to impress the word or the verse, and finally parted from me with great kindness and returned across the fields.

His hair is white, but there is nothing very striking about his appearance.

Liverpool, September 1

I thank the Great God who has led me through this European scene, this last schoolroom in which he has pleased to instruct me, from Malta's isle, through Sicily, through Italy, through Switzerland, through France, through England, through Scotland, in safety and pleasure, and has now brought me to the shore and the ship that steers westward. He has shown me the men I wished to see, — Landor, Coleridge, Carlyle, Wordsworth; he has thereby comforted and confirmed me in my convictions. Many things I owe to the sight of these men.

I shall judge more justly, less timidly, of wise men forevermore. To be sure not one of these is a mind of the very
first class, but what the intercourse with each of these
suggests is true of intercourse with better men, that they
never *fill the ear* — fill the mind — no, it is an *idealized*
portrait which always we draw of them. Upon an intelligent man, wholly a stranger to their names, they would
make in conversation no deep impression, none of a
world-filling fame, — they would be remembered as
sensible, well-read, earnest men, not more. Especially
are they all deficient, all these four, — in different
degrees, but all deficient, — in insight into religious truth.
They have no idea of that species of moral truth which I
call the first philosophy. . . .

The comfort of meeting men of genius such as these is
that they talk sincerely, they feel themselves to be so
rich that they are above the meanness of pretending to
knowledge which they have not, and they frankly tell
you what puzzles them. But Carlyle — Carlyle is so
amiable that I love him.

Wednesday, September 4

At 2 o'clock left Liverpool in the New York of N. Y.,
14 cabin passengers, 16 steerage. Ship 516 tons.

At Sea, September 6

I like my book about Nature, and wish I knew where
and how I ought to live. God will show me. I am glad to
be on my way home, yet not so glad as others, and my
way to the bottom I could find perchance with less regret,
for I think it would not hurt me, — that is, the ducking
or drowning.

At Sea, Sunday, September 8

Back again to myself. I believe that the error of re-
ligionists lies in this, that they do not know the extent or
the harmony or the depth of their moral nature; that they
are clinging to little, positive, verbal, formal versions of
the moral law, and very imperfect versions too, while the
infinite laws, the laws of the Law, the great circling truths
whose only adequate symbol is the material laws, the
astronomy, etc., are all unobserved, and sneered at when
spoken of, as frigid and insufficient. I call Calvinism such
an imperfect version of the moral law. Unitarianism is
another, and every form of Christian and of Pagan faith in
the hands of incapable teachers is such a version. On the
contrary, in the hands of a true Teacher, the falsehoods,
the pitifulnesses, the sectarianisms of each are dropped,
and the sublimity and the depth of the Original is pen-
etrated and exhibited to men. . . .

But the men of Europe will say, Expound; let us hear
what it is that is to convince the faithful and at the same
time the philosopher? Let us hear this new thing. It is
very old. It is the old revelation, that perfect beauty is
perfect goodness, it is the development of the wonderful
congruities of the moral law of human nature. Let me
enumerate a few of the remarkable properties of that
nature. A man contains all that is needful to his government within himself. He is made a law unto himself.
All real good or evil that can befall him must be from himself. . . . The purpose of life seems to be to acquaint a man
with himself. He is not to live to the future as described to
him, but to live to the real future by living to the real present. The highest revelation is that God is in every man.

At Sea, September 17

Yesterday I was asked what I mean by morals. I reply that I cannot define, and care not to define. It is man's business to observe, and the definition of moral nature must be the slow result of years, of lives, of states, perhaps of being. Yet in the morning watch on my berth I thought that morals is the science of the laws of human action as respects right and wrong. Then I shall be asked, And what is Right? Right is a conformity to the laws of nature as far as they are known to the human mind. . . .

Milton describes himself in his letter to Diodati as enamoured of moral perfection. He did not love it more than I. That which I cannot yet declare has been my angel from childhood until now. It has separated me from men. It has watered my pillow, it has driven sleep from my bed. It has tortured me for my guilt. It has inspired me with hope. It cannot be defeated by my defeats. It cannot be questioned, though all the martyrs apostatize. It is always the glory that shall be revealed; it is the 'open secret' of the universe; and it is only the feebleness and dust of the observer that makes it future, the whole *is* now potentially in the bottom of his heart. It is the soul of religion. Keeping my eye on this, I understand all heroism, the history of loyalty and of martyrdom and of bigotry, the heat of the Methodist, the nonconformity of the Dissenter, the patience of the Quaker.

Newton, October 20

God defend me from ever looking at a man as an animal. God defend me from the vice of my constitution, an excessive desire of sympathy.

Newton, October 21

I am sure of this, that by going much alone a man will get more of a noble courage in thought and word than from all the wisdom that is in books.

From Notebook, undated

The old jail in Cambridge was immediately back of Mrs. Kneeland's house. The inmates of the prison were very bad neighbors and used to take delight in pestering Mrs. Kneeland with foul names and profane language. Professor Hedge took great pains to get the nuisance removed, and at last the old jail was pulled down. Someone congratulated Mrs. K. upon the happy deliverance, but found her quite sad at the loss of her stimulus. 'She kind o' missed 'em,' she said.

From Notebook, undated

Jesus Christ was a minister of the pure Reason. The beatitudes of the Sermon on the Mount are all utterances of the mind contemning the phenomenal world. 'Blessed are the righteous poor, for theirs is the kingdom of heaven. Blessed are ye when men revile you,' etc. The Understanding can make nothing of it. 'Tis all nonsense. The Reason affirms its absolute verity.

Various terms are employed to indicate the counteraction of the Reason and the Understanding, with more or less precision, according to the cultivation of the speaker. A clear perception of it is the key to all theology, and a theory of human life. St. Paul marks the distinction by the terms natural man and spiritual man.

When Novalis says, 'It is the instinct of the under-

standing to counteract the Reason,' he only translates
into a scientific formula the sentence of St. Paul 'The
Carnal mind is enmity against God.'

January 1, 1834

This Book is my Savings Bank. I grow richer because I
have somewhere to deposit my earnings; and fractions are
worth more to me because corresponding fractions are waiting here that shall be made integers by their addition.

January 22

Luther and Napoleon are better treatises on the Will
than Edwards's.

Boston, February 19

A seaman in the coach told the story of an old sperm-
whale, which he called a white whale, which was known
for many years by the whalemen as Old Tom, and who
rushed upon the boats which attacked him, and crushed
the boats to small chips in his jaws, the men generally
escaping by jumping overboard and being picked up. A
vessel was fitted out at New Bedford, he said, to take him.
And he was finally taken somewhere off Payta Head by
the *Winslow* or the *Essex*.

April 11

Went yesterday to Cambridge and spent most of the
day at Mount Auburn; got my luncheon at Fresh Pond,
and went back again to the woods. After much wandering
and seeing many things, four snakes gliding up and down
a hollow for no purpose that I could see — not to eat, not

for love, but only gliding; then a whole bed of *Hepatica triloba*, cousins of the Anemone, all blue and beautiful, but constrained by niggard nature to wear their last year's faded jacket of leaves; then a black-capped titmouse, who came upon a tree, and when I would know his name, sang *chick-a-dee-dee;* then a far-off tree full of clamorous birds, I know not what, but you might hear them half a mile; I forsook the tombs, and found a sunny hollow where the east wind would not blow, and lay down against the side of a tree to most happy beholdings. At least I opened my eyes and let what would pass through them into the soul. I saw no more my relation, how near and petty, to Cambridge or Boston; I heeded no more what minute or hour our Massachusetts clocks might indicate — I saw only the noble earth on which I was born, with the great Star which warms and enlightens it. I saw the clouds that hang their significant drapery over us. It was Day — that was all Heaven said. The pines glittered with their innumerable green needles in the light, and seemed to challenge me to read their riddle. The drab oak-leaves of the last year turned their little somersets and lay still again. And the wind bustled high overhead in the forest top. This gay and grand architecture, from the vault to the moss and lichen on which I lay, — who shall explain to me the laws of its proportions and adornments?

Newton, April 12

All the mistakes I make arise from forsaking my own station and trying to see the object from another person's point of view.

Newton, April 13

We are always getting ready to live, but never living. We have many years of technical education; then many years of earning a livelihood, and we get sick, and take journeys for our health, and compass land and sea for improvement by travelling, but the work of self-improvement, — always under our nose, — nearer than the nearest, is seldom seldom engaged in. A few, few hours in the longest life.

Newton, May 1

In this still Newton we have seven Sabbaths in a week. The day is as calm as Eternity — quite a Chaldean time.

Newton, May 16

I remember when I was a boy going upon the beach and being charmed with the colors and forms of the shells. I picked up many and put them in my pocket. When I got home I could find nothing that I gathered — nothing but some dry, ugly mussel and snail shells. Thence I learned that composition was more important than the beauty of individual forms to effect. On the shore they lay wet and social by the sea and under the sky. [Compare his poem 'Each and All.']

Newton, May 21

I will trust my instincts. For always a reason halts after an instinct, and when I have deviated from the instinct, comes somebody with a profound theory teaching that I ought to have followed it: some Goethe, Swedenborg, or Carlyle. . . . I was the true philosopher in college, and Mr.

Farrar and Mr. Hedge and Dr. Ware the false, yet what
seemed then to me less probable?

Newton, June 10

Washington wanted a fit public. Aristides, Phocion,
Regulus, Hampden had worthy observers. But there is
yet a dearth of American genius.

Newton, June 18

Webster's speeches seem to be the utmost that the unpoetic West has accomplished or can. We all lean on
England; scarce a verse, a page, a newspaper, but is writ
in imitation of English forms; our very manners and
conversation are traditional, and sometimes the life seems
dying out of all literature, and this enormous paper
currency of Words is accepted instead. I suppose the
evil may be cured by this rank rabble party, the Jackson-
ism of the country, heedless of English and of all literature — a stone cut out of the ground without hands; —
they may root out the hollow dilettantism of our cultivation in the coarsest way, and the newborn may begin
again to frame their own world with greater advantage.

Newton, July 18

What is there of the divine in a load of bricks? What is
there of the divine in a barber's shop? . . . Much. All.

Newton, August 17

Is it not true that contemplation belongs to us, and
therefore outward worship, *because* our reason is at dis-
cord with our understanding? And that, whenever we

live rightly, thought will express itself in ordinary action
so fully as to make a special action, that is, a religious
form, impertinent? Is not Solomon's temple built because
Solomon is not a temple, but a brothel and a change-
house? Is not the meeting-house dedicated because men
are not? Is not the church opened and filled on Sunday
because the commandments are not kept by the wor-
shippers on Monday? But when he who worships there,
speaks the truth, follows the truth, is the truth's; when he
awakes by actual communion to the faith that God is in
him, will he need any temple, any prayer? The very fact
of worship declares that God is not at one with himself,
that there are two gods. Now does this sound like high
treason and go to lay flat all religion? It does threaten our
forms; but does not that very word 'form' already sound
hollow? It threatens our forms, but it does not touch in-
juriously Religion. Would there be danger if there were
real religion? If the doctrine that God is in man were faithfully taught and received, if I lived to speak the truth and
enact it, if I pursued every generous sentiment as one
enamoured, if the majesty of goodness were reverenced,
would not such a principle serve me by way of police at
least as well as a Connecticut Sunday? But the people, the
people. You hold up your pasteboard religion for the
people who are unfit for a true. So you say. But presently
there will arise a race of preachers who will take such hold
of the omnipotence of truth that they will blow the old
falsehood to shreds with the breath of their mouth.
There is no material show so splendid, no poem so
musical as the great law of Compensation in our moral
nature. When an ardent mind once gets a glimpse of that

perfect beauty, and sees how it envelopes him and de-
termines all his being, will he easily slide back to a
periodic shouting about 'blood atoning'? I apprehend
that the religious history of society is to show a pretty
rapid abandonment of forms of worship and the renova-
tion and exaltation of preaching into real anxious instruction.

September 15, *Afternoon*

No art can exceed the mellow beauty of one square rood
of ground in the woods this afternoon. The noise of the
locust, the bee, and the pine; the light, the insect forms, butterflies, cankerworms hanging, balloon-spiders swinging,
devils-needles cruising, chirping grasshoppers; the tints
and forms of the leaves and trees, — not a flower but its
form seems a type, not a capsule but is an elegant seedbox,
— then the myriad asters, polygalas, and golden-rods, and
through the bush the far pines, and overhead the eternal
sky. All the pleasing forms of art are imitations of these,
and yet before the beauty of a right action all this beauty
is cold and unaffecting.

October 14

Every involuntary repulsion that arises in your mind,
give heed unto. It is the surface of a central truth.

New York, October 18

Received the tidings of the death of my dear brother
Edward on the first day of this month at St. John, Porto
Rico. So falls one pile more of hope for this life. I see I
am bereaved of a part of myself.

October 29

We should hold to the usage until we are clear it is wrong.

Concord, November 15

Hail to the quiet fields of my fathers! Not wholly unattended by supernatural friendship and favor, let me come hither. Bless my purposes as they are simple and virtuous. . . .

Henceforth I design not to utter any speech, poem or book that is not entirely and peculiarly my work. I will say at public lectures, and the like, those things which I have meditated for their own sake, and not for the first time with a view to that occasion.

November 26

The shepherd or the beggar in his red cloak little knows what a charm he gives to the wide landscape that charms you on the mountain-top and whereof he makes the most agreeable feature, and I no more the part my individuality plays in the All. [Compare the poem 'Each and All.']

December 8

I rejoice in Time. I do not cross the common without a wild poetic delight, notwithstanding the prose of my demeanour. Thank God I live in the country.

December 18

I am writing my lecture of Michel Angelo, clothed with a coat which was made for me in Florence: I would I were clothed with the spirit of beauty which breathed life into Italian art.

December 19

The maker of a sentence, like the other artist, launches out into the infinite and builds a road into Chaos and old Night, and is followed by those who hear him with something of wild, creative delight.

December 22

It is very easy in the world to live by the opinion of the world. It is very easy in solitude to be self-centred. But the finished man is he who in the midst of the crowd keeps with perfect sweetness the independence of solitude.

Mr. Coleridge has thrown many new truths into circulation; Mr. Southey never one.

December 23

Do, dear, when you come to write Lyceum lectures, remember that you are not to say, What must be said in a Lyceum? but, What discoveries or stimulating thoughts have I to impart to a thousand persons? not what they will expect to hear, but what is fit for me to say.

December 27

I believe the Christian religion to be profoundly true; true to an extent that they who are styled its most orthodox defenders have never, or but in rarest glimpses, once or twice in a lifetime, reached.

I, who seek to be a realist, to deny and put off everything that I do not heartily accept, do yet catch myself continually in a practical unbelief of its deepest teachings.

It taught, it teaches the eternal opposition of the world to the truth, and introduced the absolute authority of the spiritual law. Milton apprehended its nature when he said, 'For who is there almost that measures wisdom by simplicity, strength by suffering, dignity by lowliness?' That do I in my sane moments, and feel the ineffable peace, yea and the influx of God, that attend humility and love, — and before the cock crows, I deny him thrice.

December 28

If I were called upon to charge a young minister, I would say Beware of Tradition: Tradition which embarrasses life and falsifies all teaching. The sermons that I hear are all dead of that ail.

December 29

Excite the soul, and it becomes suddenly virtuous. Touch the deep heart, and all these listless, stingy, beef-eating bystanders will see the dignity of a sentiment; will say, This is good, and all I have I will give for that. Excite the soul, and the weather and the town and your condition in the world all disappear; the world itself loses its solidity, nothing remains but the soul and the Divine Presence in which it lives.

Concord, January 6, 1835

No doubt we owe most valuable knowledge to our conversation, even with the frivolous; yet when I return, as just now, from more than usual opportunities of hearing and seeing, it seems to me that one good day here is worth more than three gadding days in town. Sunday I

went for the first time to the Swedenborg Chapel. The
sermon was in its style severely simple, and in method and
manner had much the style of a problem in geometry,
wholly uncoloured and unimpassioned. Yet was it, as I
told Sampson Reed, one that, with the exception of a
single passage, might have been preached without exciting
surprise in any church. At the opposite pole, say rather in
another Zone from this hard truist, was Taylor, in the
afternoon, wishing his sons a happy new year, praying
God for his servants of the brine, to favor commerce, to
bless the bleached sail, the white foam, and through commerce to Christianize the universe. 'May every deck,' he
said, 'be stamped by the hallowed feet of godly captains,
and the first watch and the second watch be watchful for
the Divine light.' He thanked God he had not been in
Heaven for the last twenty-five years, — then indeed had
he been a dwarf in grace, but now he had his redeemed
souls around him. And so he went on, — this poet of the
sailor and of Ann Street, — fusing all the rude hearts of
his auditory with the heat of his own love, and making the
abstractions of philosophers accessible and effectual to
them also. He is a fine study to the metaphysician or the
life philosopher. He is profuse of himself; he never remembers the looking-glass. They are foolish who fear that notice will spoil him. They never made him, and such as they
cannot unmake him; he is a real man of strong nature, and
noblest, richest lines on his countenance. He is a work of
the same hand that made Demosthenes and Shakspear
and Burns, and is guided by instincts diviner than rules.
His whole discourse is a string of audacious felicities
harmonized by a spirit of joyful love. Everybody is

cheered and exalted by him. He is a living man and explains at once what Whitefield and Fox and Father Moody were to their audiences, by the total infusion of his own soul into his assembly, and consequent absolute dominion over them. How puny, how cowardly, other preachers look by the side of this preaching! He shows us what a man can do. As I sat last Sunday in my country pew, I thought this Sunday I would see two living chapels, the Swedenborg and the Seamen's, and I was not deceived.

January 7

Bitter cold days, yet I read of that inward fervor which ran as fire from heart to heart through England in George Fox's time. How precisely parallel are the biographies of religious enthusiasts — Swedenborg, Guyon, Fox, Luther, and perhaps Boehmen. Each owes all to the discovery that God must be sought within, not without. That is the discovery of Jesus.

January 8

The Teacher that I look for and await shall enunciate with more precision and universality, with piercing poetic insight those beautiful yet severe compensations that give to moral nature an aspect of mathematical science. He will not occupy himself in laboriously reanimating a historical religion, but in bringing men to God by showing them that he is, not was, and speaks, not spoke. [Compare the 'Divinity School Address.']

February 2

Let Christianity speak ever for the poor and the low. Though the voice of society should demand a defence of slavery, from all its organs, that service can never be expected from me. My opinion is of no worth, but I have not a syllable of all the language I have learned, to utter for the planter. If by opposing slavery I go to undermine institutions, I confess I do not wish to live in a nation where slavery exists.

February 16

If Milton, if Burns, if Bryant, is in the world, we have more tolerance, and more love for the changing sky, the mist, the rain, the bleak, overcast day, the indescribable sunrise and the immortal stars. If we believed no poet survived on the planet, nature would be tedious.

March 23

There is no greater lie than a voluptuous book like Boccaccio. For it represents the pleasures of appetite, which only at rare intervals, a few times in a life-time, are intense, and to whose acme continence is essential, as frequent, habitual, and belonging to the incontinent. . . .

March 26

I went by him in the night. Who can tell the moment when the pine outgrew the whortleberry that shaded its first sprout. It went by in the night.

April 10

I fretted the other night at the hotel at the stranger who broke into my chamber after midnight, claiming to share

it. But after his lamp had smoked the chamber full and I
had turned round to the wall in despair, the man blew out
his lamp, knelt down at his bedside, and made in low
whisper a long earnest prayer. Then was the relation
entirely changed between us. I fretted no more, but
respected and liked him.

June 20

The good of publishing one's thoughts is that of hooking
to you like-minded men, and of giving to men whom you
value, such as Wordsworth or Landor, one hour of
stimulated thought. Yet, how few! Who in Concord
cares for the first philosophy in a book? The woman
whose child is to be suckled? The man at Nine-acre-
Corner who is to cart sixty loads of gravel on his meadow?
the stageman? the gunsmith? Oh, no! Who then?

August 6

I think I may undertake, one of these days, to write a
chapter on Literary Ethics, or the Duty and Discipline of
a Scholar.

August 8

Yesterday I delighted myself with Michel de Montaigne. With all my heart I embrace the grand old
sloven. He pricks and stings the sense of virtue in me —
the wild Gentile stock, I mean, for he has no Grace. But
his panegyric of Cato, and of Socrates in his essay of
Cruelty (volume ii) do wind up again for us the spent
springs and make virtue possible without the discipline
of Christianity, or rather do shame her of her eye-

service and put her upon her honor. I read the Essays in Defence of Seneca and Plutarch; on Books; on Drunkenness; and on Cruelty. And at some fortunate line which I cannot now recall, the spirit of some Plutarch hero or sage touched mine with such thrill as the war-trump makes in Talbot's ear and blood.

August 15

I bought my house and two acres six rods of land of John T. Coolidge for 3,500 dollars.

August 31

Use of Harvard College to clear the head of much nonsense that gathers in the inferior colleges.

September 14

I was married to Lydia Jackson.

October 13

Do you see what we preserve of history? a few anecdotes of a moral quality of some momentary act or word, — the word of Canute on the seashore, the speech of the Druid to Edwin, the anecdote of Alfred's learning to read for Judith's gift, the box on the ear by the herdman's wife, the tub of Diogenes, the gold of Crœsus, and Solon, and Cyrus, the emerald of Polycrates; these things, reckoned insignificant at the age of their occurrence, have floated, whilst laws and expeditions and books and kingdoms have sunk and are forgotten. So potent is this simple element of humanity or moral common sense.

My will never gave the images in my mind the rank

they now take there. The four college years and the three years' course of Divinity have not yielded me so many grand facts as some idle books under the bench at the Latin School. We form no guess, at the time of receiving a thought, of its comparative value.

November 6

Charles says the nap is worn off the world.

December 12

I wrote H. Ware, Jr., that his 4th topic, the circumstances which show a tendency toward war's abolition, seemed to me the nearest to mine; for I strongly feel the inhumanity or unmanlike character of war, and should gladly study the outward signs and exponents of that progress which has brought us to this feeling.

1836–1838

[EARLY in 1836 it is apparent that Emerson is occupied with writing his first book, *Nature*. He also furnished a preface for the Boston edition of Carlyle's *Sartor Resartus*. By April his brother Charles, who had spent the winter with Waldo and was engaged to be married to Elizabeth Hoar, was stricken fatally with consumption. Emerson took him to New York, where he died on May 9.

As for a year past, Emerson felt a keen interest in A. Bronson Alcott, who was teaching school in Boston. There are many references to him henceforth in the journal. By August *Nature* was nearly ready, and it was published early in September. On October 31 his son Waldo was born. Emerson was now preaching regularly in the tiny village of East Lexington, and lecturing, each winter, to good-sized audiences in Boston. The financial panic of 1837 is often referred to in the journal. By July Emerson was at work upon one of the most famous of all his utterances, the Phi Beta Kappa oration on 'The American Scholar,' delivered in Cambridge on August 31. He says nothing of his triumph, however, in his journal except to record in October the sale of the entire edition of 500 copies in just one month after publication. He was now arranging for the republication in Boston of Carlyle's *French Revolution*.

In the winter of 1837–1838 he delivered a course of lectures in Boston on 'Human Culture.' An epoch-

making event in his career was the address to the graduat-
ing class of the Harvard Divinity School on July 15, 1838.
There are echoes of it in the journal, and in Emerson's
correspondence with Carlyle. A few days later he drove
to Hanover, N.H., to deliver his Dartmouth address on
'Literary Ethics.']

January 22, 1836

Upham [Charles W.] thinks it fatal to the happiness of
a young man to set out with ultra-conservative notions
in this country. He must settle it in his mind that the
human race have got possession, and, though they will
make many blunders and do some great wrongs, yet on
the whole will consult the interest of the whole.

February 8

Women have less accurate measure of time than men.
There is a clock in Adam: none in Eve.

February 28

Cold, bright Sunday morn, white with deep snow.
Charles thinks if a superior being should look into
families, he would find natural relations existing, and man
a worthy being, but if he followed them into shops, sen-
ates, churches, and societies, they would appear wholly
artificial and worthless. Society seems noxious. I believe
that against these baleful influences Nature is the antidote. The man comes out of the wrangle of the shop and
office, and sees the sky and the woods, and is a man again.
He not only quits the cabal, but he finds himself. But how
few men see the sky and the woods!

February, undated

God manifest in the flesh of every man is a perfect rule of social life. Justify yourself to an infinite Being in the ostler and dandy and stranger, and you shall never repent.

March 5

I have no curiosity respecting historical Christianity; respecting persons and miracles: I take the phenomenon as I find it, and let it have its effect on me, careless whether it is a poem or a chronicle.

March 21

I thought yesterday morning of the sweetness of that fragrant piety which is almost departed out of the world, which makes the genius of À-Kempis, Scougal, Herbert, Jeremy Taylor. It is a beautiful mean, equi-distant from the hard, sour, iron Puritan on one side, and the empty negation of the Unitarian on the other. It is the spirit of David and of Paul. . . .

April 1

Beautiful morn, follower of a beautiful moon. Yet lies the snow on the ground. Birds sing, mosses creep, grass grows on the edge of the snow-bank. Read yesterday Goethe's Iphigenia. A pleasing, moving, even heroic work, yet with the great deduction of being an imitation of the antique.

May 16

Charles died at New York, Monday afternoon, 9 May. His prayer that he might not be sick was granted him. He was never confined to a bed. He rode out on Monday afternoon with Mother, promised himself to begin his journey with me on my arrival, the next day; on reaching home, he stepped out of the carriage alone, walked up the steps and into the house without assistance, sat down on the stairs, fainted and never recovered. Beautiful without any parallel in my experience of young men, was his life, happiest his death. Miserable is my own prospect from whom my friend is taken. Clean and sweet was his life, untempted almost, and his action on others all-healing, uplifting and fragrant. I read now his pages, I remember all his words and motions without any pang, so healthy and human a life it was, and not like Edward's, a tragedy of poverty and sickness tearing genius.

His virtues were like the victories of Timoleon, and Homer's verses, they were so easy and natural. I cannot understand why his manuscript journal should have so bitter a strain of penitence and deprecation. I mourn that in losing him I have lost his all, for he was born an orator, not a writer. His written pages do him no justice, and as he felt the immense disparity between his power of conversation and his blotted paper, it was easy for him to speak with scorn of written composition. . . .

His senses were those of a Greek. I owe to them a thousand observations. To live with him was like living with a great painter. I used to say that I had no leave to see things till he pointed them out, and afterwards I never ceased to see them.

May 19

I find myself slowly, after this helpless mourning. I remember states of mind that perhaps I had long lost

before this grief, the native mountains whose tops re-
appear after we have traversed many a mile of weary
region from home.

June 7

Many letters from friends who loved or honored Charles.
I know not why it is, but a letter is scarcely welcome to
me. I expect to be lacerated by it, and if I come safe to the
end of it, I feel like one escaped.

June 10

I gladly pay the rent of my house because I therewith
get the horizon and the woods which I pay no rent for.
For daybreak and evening and night, I pay no tax. I
think it is a glorious bargain which I drive with the town.

June 16

Yesterday I went to Mr. Alcott's school and heard a
conversation upon the Gospel of St. John. I thought the
experiment of engaging young children upon questions of
taste and truth successful. A few striking things were said
by them. I felt strongly as I watched the gradual dawn of
a thought upon the minds of all, that to truth is no age or
season. It appears, or it does not appear, and when the
child perceives it, he is no more a child; age, sex, are
nothing: we are all alike before the great whole. Little
Josiah Quincy, now six years, six months old, is a child
having something wonderful and divine in him. He is a
youthful prophet.

June 22

Mr. Alcott has been here with his Olympian dreams. He is a world-builder. Evermore he toils to solve the problem, whence is the world? The point at which he prefers to begin is the mystery of the Birth of a child. I tell him it is idle for him to affect to feel an interest in the compositions of any one else. Particulars — particular thoughts, sentences, facts even — cannot interest him, except as for a moment they take their place as a ray from his orb. The Whole, — Nature proceeding from himself, is what he studies. But he loses, like other sovereigns, great pleasures by reason of his grandeur. I go to Shakspear, Goethe, Swift, even to Tennyson, submit myself to them, become merely an organ of hearing, and yield to the law of their being. I am paid for thus being nothing by an entire new mind, and thus, a Proteus, I enjoy the universe through the powers and organs of a hundred different men. But Alcott cannot delight in Shakspear, cannot get near him. And so with all things. What is characteristic also, he cannot recall one word or part of his own conversation or of any one's, let the expression be never so happy. He made here some majestic utterances, but so inspired me that even I forgot the words often.

July 21

Make your own Bible. Select and collect all the words and sentences that in all your reading have been to you like the blast of triumph out of Shakspear, Seneca, Moses, John and Paul.

August 27

To-day came to me the first proof-sheet of *Nature* to be corrected, like a new coat, full of vexations; with the first sentences of the chapters perched like mottoes aloft in small type! The peace of the author cannot be wounded by such trifles, if he sees that the sentences are still good. A good sentence can never be put out of countenance by any blunder of compositors.

September 13

I went to the College Jubilee on the 8th instant. A noble and well-thought-of anniversary. The pathos of the occasion was extreme, and not much noted by the speakers. Cambridge at any time is full of ghosts; but on that day the anointed eye saw the crowd of spirits that mingled with the procession in the vacant spaces, year by year, as the classes proceeded; and then the far longer train of ghosts that followed the company, of the men that wore before us the college honors and the laurels of the State — the long, winding train reaching back into eternity. But among the living was more melancholy reflection, namely, the identity of all the persons with that which they were in youth, in college halls. I found my old friends the same; the same jokes pleased, the same straws tickled; the manhood and offices they brought hither to-day seemed masks; underneath we were still boys.

September 20

What interest has Greenough to make a good statue? Who cares whether it is good? a few prosperous gentlemen and ladies; but the universal Yankee nation roaring in the

Capitol to approve or condemn would make his eye and hand and heart go to a new tune.

September 24

There is no truth in the proverb, that if you get up your name, you may safely play the rogue. Thence the balancing proverb, that in every wit is a grain of fool. You are known. . . .

Look into the stage-coach and see the faces! Stand in State Street and see the heads and the gait and gesture of the men; they are doomed ghosts going under Judgment all day long.

September 28

Why is there no genius in the Fine Arts in this country?

In sculpture Greenough is picturesque; in painting, Allston; in Poetry, Bryant; in Eloquence, Channing; in Architecture, ——; in Fiction, Irving, Cooper; in all, feminine, no character.

1st reason: Influence of Europe, mainly of England. . . .

2nd reason. They are not called out by the necessity of the people. Poetry, music, sculpture, painting were all enlisted in the service of Patriotism and Religion. The statue was to be worshipped, the picture also. The poem was a confession of faith. A vital faith built the cathedrals of Europe. But who cares to see a poem of Bryant's, or a statue of Greenough, or a picture of Allston? The people never see them. The mind of the race has taken another direction, — Property.

October 6

Transcendentalism means, says our accomplished Mrs. B., with a wave of her hand, *a little beyond.*

October 23

The literary man in this country has no critic.

October 29

There is one advantage which every man finds in setting himself a literary task, — as these my lectures, — that it gives him the high pleasure of reading, which does not in other circumstances attain all its zest. . . . When the mind is braced by the weighty expectation of a prepared work, the page of whatever book we read becomes luminous with manifold allusion. Every sentence is doubly significant, and the sense of our author is as broad as the world. There is creative reading as well as creative writing.

October 31

Last night, at 11 o'clock, a son [Waldo] was born to me. Blessed child! a lovely wonder to me, and which makes the universe look friendly to me.

November 5

This day I have been scrambling in the woods, and with help of Peter Howe I have got six hemlock trees to plant in my yard, which may grow whilst my boy is sleeping.

November 8

I dislike to hear the patronizing tone in which the self-sufficient young men of the day talk of ministers 'adapt-

ing their preaching to the great mass.' Was the sermon
good? 'O yes, good for you and me, but not understood
by the great mass.' Don't you deceive yourself, say I, the
great mass understand what's what, as well as the little
mass.

November 12

How many attractions for us have our passing fellows
in the streets, both male and female, which our ethics
forbid us to express, which yet infuse so much pleasure
into life. A lovely child, a handsome youth, a beautiful
girl, a heroic man, a maternal woman, a venerable old
man, charm us, though strangers, and we cannot say so,
or look at them but for a moment.

November 28

Come, let us not be an appanage to Alexander, Charles
V, or any of history's heroes. Dead men all! But for me
the earth is new to-day, and the sun is raining light.

December 10

Rhetoric. — I cannot hear a sermon without being
struck by the fact that amid drowsy series of sentences
what a sensation a historical fact, a biographical name, a
sharply objective illustration makes! Why will not the
preacher heed the admonition of the momentary silence
of his congregation and (often what is shown him) that
this particular sentence is all they carry away?

January 8, 1837

Can you not show the man of genius that always genius is situated in the world as it is with him?

Lidian Emerson.
Waldo Emerson.
R. Waldo Emerson.[1]

I have come no farther in my query than this, when mine Asia came in and wrote her name, her son's and her husband's to warm my cold page.

February 6

In these Lectures which from week to week I read, each on a topic which is a main interest of man, and may be made an object of exclusive interest, I seem to vie with the brag of Puck; — 'I can put a girdle round about the world in forty minutes.' I take fifty.

March 4

I have finished, on Thursday evening last, my course of twelve Lectures on the Philosophy of History. I read the first on the 8 December, 1836. The audience attending them might average 350 persons. I acknowledge the Divine Providence which has given me perfect health and smoothed the way unto the end.

March 14

Edward Taylor came last night and gave us in the old church a Lecture on Temperance. A wonderful man; I had almost said, a perfect orator. The utter want and loss of all method, the ridicule of all method, the bright chaos come again of his bewildering oratory, certainly bereaves it of power, — but what splendor! what sweetness! what richness! what depth! what cheer! How he conciliates,

[1] These names are in Mrs. Emerson's handwriting.

how he humanizes! how he exhilarates and ennobles!
Beautiful philanthropist! Godly poet! the Shakspear of
the sailor and the poor.

March 29

Carlyle again. I think he has seen, as no other in our
time, how inexhaustible a mine is the language of Conversation. He does not use the *written* dialect of the time,
in which scholars, pamphleteers and the clergy write, nor
the Parliamentary dialect, in which the lawyer, the statesman, and the better newspapers write, but draws strength
and mother-wit out of a poetic use of the spoken vocabulary, so that his paragraphs are all a sort of splendid
conversation.

April 8

Ah! my darling boy, so lately received out of Heaven,
leave me not now! Please God, this sweet symbol of love
and wisdom may be spared to rejoice, teach and ac-
company me.

April 22

Cold April; hard times; men breaking who ought not to
break; banks bullied into the bolstering of desperate
speculators; all the newspapers a chorus of owls.

April 22

I say to Lidian that in composition the *What* is of no
importance compared with the *How*. The most tedious of
all discourses are on the subject of the Supreme Being.

April 29

I will add it to my distinctive marks of man and woman — the man loves hard wood, the woman loves pitch-pine.

May 6

Sad is this continual postponement of life. I refuse sympathy and intimacy with people, as if in view of some better sympathy and intimacy to come. But whence and when? I am already thirty-four years old. Already my friends and fellow workers are dying from me. Scarcely can I say that I see any new men or women approaching me; I am too old to regard fashion; too old to expect patronage of any greater or more powerful. Let me suck the sweetness of those affections and consuetudes that grow near me — that the Divine Providence offers me. These old shoes are easy to the feet. But no, not for mine, if they have an ill savor. I was made a hermit, and am content with my lot. I pluck golden fruit from rare meetings with wise men. I can well abide alone in the intervals, and the fruit of my own tree shall have a better flavor.

May 7

In my childhood, Aunt Mary herself wrote the prayers which first my brother William, and, when he went to college, I read aloud morning and evening at the family devotions, and they still sound in my ear with their prophetic and apocalyptic ejaculations. . . .

This day my boy was baptized in the old church by Dr. Ripley. They dressed him in the self-same robe in which,

twenty-seven years ago, my brother Charles was baptized.

May 9

Yesterday in the woods I followed the fine humble bee
with rhymes and fancies fine. [Compare the poem 'The
Humble-Bee.']

May 19

Yesterday Alcott left me after three days spent here.
I had 'lain down a man and waked up a bruise,' by reason
of a bad cold, and was lumpish, tardy and cold. Yet could
I see plainly that I conversed with the most extraordinary
man and the highest genius of the time. He is a Man. . . .

He is, to be sure, monotonous; you may say, one gets
tired of the uniformity, — he will not be amused, he
never cares for the pleasant side of things, but always
truth and their origin he seeketh after.

May 22

Among provocatives, the next best thing to good
preaching is bad preaching. I have even more thoughts
during or enduring it than at other times.

May 25

'My dear sir, clear your mind of cant,' said Dr. Johnson. Wordsworth, whom I read last night, is garrulous
and weak often, but quite free from cant. I think I could
easily make a small selection from his volumes which
should contain all their poetry. It would take Fidelity,
Tintern Abbey, Cumberland Beggar, Ode to Duty, Sep-

tember, The Force of Prayer, Lycoris, Lines on the
Death of Fox, Dion, Happy Warrior, Laodamia, the
Ode.

May 31

We have had two peerless summer days after all our
cold winds and rains. I have weeded corn and straw-
berries, intent on being fat, and have foreborne study.
The Maryland yellow-throat pipes to me all day long,
seeming to say Extacy! Extacy! and the Bob-o'-Lincoln
flies and sings. I read during the heat of the day *Beppo*
and *Manfred*. What famine of meaning! *Manfred* is
ridiculous for its purposeless raving, not all the genuine
love of nature, nor all the skill of utterance can save it.
It is all one circular proposition.

July 21

Crabbe knew men, but to read one of his poems seems
to me all one with taking a dose of medicine.

July 26

Yesterday I went to the Athenæum and looked through
journals and books — for wit, for excitement, to wake in
me the muse. In vain, and in vain. And am I yet to
learn that the God dwells within? That books are but
crutches, the resorts of the feeble and lame, which, if used
by the strong, weaken the muscular power, and become
necessary aids. I return home. Nature still solicits me.
Overhead the sanctities of the stars shine forevermore,
and to me also, pouring satire on the pompous business of
the day which they close, and making the generations of

men show slight and evanescent. A man is but a bug, the earth but a boat, a cockle, drifting under their old light.

July 29

If the All-wise would give me light, I should write for the Cambridge men a theory of the Scholar's office. It is not all books which it behooves him to know, least of all to be a book-worshipper, but he must be able to read in all books that which alone gives value to books — in all to read one, the one incorruptible text of truth. That alone of their style is intelligible, acceptable to him.

Books are for the scholar's idle times. . . .

Pope and Johnson and Addison write as if they had never seen the face of the country, but had only read of trees and rivers in books.

August 2

An enchanting night of south wind and clouds; mercury at 73°; all the trees are wind-harps; blessed be light and darkness; ebb and flow, cold and heat; these restless pulsations of nature which by and by will throb no more.

August 4

After raffling all day in Plutarch's morals, or shall I say angling there, for such fish as I might find, I sallied out this fine afternoon through the woods to Walden water.

August 9

Carlyle: how the sight of his handwriting warms my heart at the little post-window; how noble it seems to me that his words should run out of Nithsdale or London over land and sea to Weimar, to Rome, to America, to Watertown, to Concord, to Louisville; that they should cheer and delight and invigorate me. . . .

How noble that, alone and unpraised, he should still write for he knew not whom, and find at last his readers in the valley of the Mississippi, and they should brood on the pictures he had painted, and untwist the many-colored meanings which he had spun and woven into so rich a web of sentences; and domesticate in so many and remote heads the humor, the learning and the philosophy which, year by year, in summer and in frost, this lonely man had lived in the moors of Scotland. This man upholds and propels civilization. For every wooden post he knocks away he replaces one of stone.

August 9

The Southerner asks concerning any man, 'How does he fight?' The Northerner asks, 'What can he do?'

August 18

The hope to arouse young men at Cambridge to a worthier view of their literary duties prompts me to offer the theory of the Scholar's function. He has an office to perform in Society. What is it? To arouse the intellect; to keep it erect and sound; to keep admiration in the hearts of the people; to keep the eye open upon its spiritual aims. How shall he render this service? By being a soul among those things with which he deals.

August 18

They say the insane like a master; so always does the human heart hunger after a leader, a master through truth.

August 20

Lidian remembers the religious terrors of her childhood, when Young tinged her day and night thoughts, and the doubts of Cowper were her own; when every lightning seemed the beginning of conflagration, and every noise in the street the crack of doom. I have some parallel recollections at the Latin School when I lived in Beacon Street. Afterwards, what remained for one to learn was cleansed by books and poetry and philosophy, and came in purer forms of literature at College. These spiritual crises no doubt are periods of as certain occurrence in some form of agitation to every mind as dentition or puberty. Lidian was at that time alarmed by the lines on the gravestones.

August 21

I believe I shall some time cease to be an individual, that the eternal tendency of the soul is to become Universal, to animate the last extremities of organization.

September 19

On the 29th August, I received a letter from the Salem Lyceum, signed I. F. Worcester, requesting me to lecture before the institution next winter, and adding, 'The subject is, of course, discretionary with yourself, provided no allusions are made to religious controversy, or other exciting topics upon which the public mind is honestly divided!' I replied, on the same day, to Mr. W. by quoting these words, and adding, 'I am really sorry that any person in Salem should think me capable of accepting an invitation so incumbered.'

September 28

I hope New England will come to boast itself in being a nation of Servants, and leave to the planters the misery of being a nation of served.

October 8

The young Southerner comes here a spoiled child, with graceful manners, excellent self-command, very good to be spoiled more, but good for nothing else, — a mere parader. He has conversed so much with rifles, horses and dogs that he has become himself a rifle, a horse and a dog, and in civil, educated company, where anything human is going forward, he is dumb and unhappy, like an Indian in a church. Treat them with great deference, as we often do, and they accept it all as their due without misgiving. Give them an inch, and they take a mile. They are mere bladders of conceit. Each snipper-snapper of them all undertakes to speak for the entire Southern States. 'At the South, the reputation of Cambridge,' etc., etc., which being interpreted, is, In my negro village of Tuscaloosa, or Cheraw, or St. Mark's, I supposed so and so. 'We, at the South,' forsooth. They are more civilized than the Seminoles, however, in my opinion; a little more. Their question respecting any man is like a Seminole's, — How can he fight? In this country, we ask, What can he do? His pugnacity is all they prize in man, dog, or turkey. The proper way of treating them is not deference, but to say as Mr. Ripley does, 'Fiddle faddle,' in answer to each solemn remark about 'The South.' 'It must be confessed,' said the young man, 'that in Alabama, we are dead to everything, as respects politics.' 'Very true,' replied Mr. Ripley, 'leaving out the last clause.'

October 16

The babe stands alone to-day for the first time.

October 16

I looked over the few books in the young clergyman's study yesterday till I shivered with cold: Priestley; Noyes; Rosenmuller; Joseph Allen, and other Sunday School books; Schleusner; Norton; and the *Saturday Night* of Taylor; the dirty comfort of the farmer could easily seem preferable to the elegant poverty oi the young clergyman.

October 16

A lovely afternoon and I went to Walden Water, and read Goethe on the bank.

October 18

One of the last secrets we learn as scholars is to confide in our own impressions of a book. If Æschylus is that man he is taken for, he has not yet done his office when he has educated the learned of Europe for a thousand years. He is now to approve himself a master of delight to me. If he cannot do that, all his fame shall avail him nothing. I were a fool not to sacrifice a thousand Æschyluses to my intellectual integrity.

October 20

When I commended the adroit New York broker to Alcott, he replied that he saw he had more austerity than I, and that he gave his hand with some reluctance to mere merchant or banker. What is so comic, I pray, as the mutual condescension with which Alcott and Colonel Perkins would give the hand to each other?

October 20

The same complaint I have heard is made against the Boston Medical College as against the Cambridge Divinity School, that those who there receive their education, want faith, and so are not as successful as practitioners from the country schools who believe in the power of medicine.

October 21

I said when I awoke, After some more sleepings and wakings I shall lie on this mattress sick; then, dead; and through my gay entry they will carry these bones. Where shall I be then? I lifted my head and beheld the spotless orange light of the morning beaming up from the dark hills into the wide Universe.

October 23

It is very hard to be simple enough to be good.

October 24

I find, in town, the Phi Beta Kappa Oration, of which 500 copies were printed, all sold, in just one month.

October 28

When the conversation soars to principles Unitarianism is boyish.

November 3

Last night I wrote to Carlyle to inform him of the new edition of his history. [*The French Revolution.*]

November 6

'Miracles have ceased.' Have they indeed? When? They had not ceased this afternoon when I walked into the wood and got into bright, miraculous sunshine, in shelter from the roaring wind. Who sees a pine-cone, or the turpentine exuding from the tree, or a leaf, the unit of vegetation, fall from its bough, as if it said, 'the year is finished,' or hears in the quiet, piny glen the chickadee chirping his cheerful note, or walks along the lofty promontory-like ridges which, like natural causeways, traverse the morass, or gazes upward at the rushing clouds, or downward at a moss or a stone and says to himself, 'Miracles have ceased'? Tell me, good friend, when this hillock on which your foot stands swelled from the level of the sphere by volcanic force; pick up that pebble at your foot; look at its gray sides, its sharp crystal, and tell me what fiery inundation of the world melted the minerals like wax, and, as if the globe were one glowing crucible, gave this stone its shape. There is the truth-speaking pebble itself, to affirm to endless ages the thing was so. Tell me where is the manufactory of this air, so thin, so blue, so restless, which eddies around you, in which your life floats, of which your lungs are but an organ, and which you coin into musical words. I am agitated with curiosity to know the secret of nature. Why cannot geology, why cannot botany speak and tell me what has been, what is, as I run along the forest promontory, and ask when it rose like a blister on heated steel? Then I looked up and saw the sun shining in the vast sky, and heard the wind bellow above and the water glistened in the vale. These were the forces that wrought then and work now. Yes, there they grandly speak to all plainly, in proportion as we are quick to apprehend.

November 8

Right-minded men have recently been called to decide for Abolition.

November 24

The self-subsistent shakes like a reed before a sneering paragraph in the newspaper, or even at a difference of opinion, concerning something to be done, expressed in a private letter from just such another shaking bullrush as himself. He sits expecting a dinner-guest with a suspense which paralyses his inventive or his acquiring faculties. He finds the solitude of two or three entire days, when mother, wife and child are gone, tedious and dispiriting. Let him not wrong the truth and his own experience by too stiffly standing on the cold and proud doctrine of self-sufficiency.

November 24

It seems to me that the circumstances of man are historically somewhat better here and now than ever, — that more freedom exists for Culture. It will not now run against an axe at the first step. In other places it is not so. The brave Lovejoy has given his breast to the bullet for his part, and has died when it was better not to live. He is absolved. There are always men enough ready to die for the silliest punctilio; to die like dogs, who fall down under each other's teeth, but I sternly rejoice that one was bound to die for humanity and the rights of free speech and opinion.

November 25

I do not like to see a sword at a man's side. If it threaten man, it threatens me. A company of soldiers is an offensive spectacle.

December 3

Lidian says, it is wicked to go to church Sundays.

December 8

Waldo walks alone.

January 26, 1838

All this mild winter, Hygeia and the Muse befriend with the elements the poor, driven scribe. Eight lectures have been read on eight fine evenings, and to-day the mercury stands at 52° (3 o'clock P. M.) in the shade. To-day I send the oration to press again. ['The American Scholar.']

February 3

Five days ago came Carlyle's letter, and has kept me warm ever since with its affection and praise. It seems his friend John Sterling loves Waldo Emerson also, by reason of reading the book *Nature*. I am quite bewitched, maugre all my unamiableness, with so dainty a relation as a friendship for a scholar and poet I have never seen, and he Carlyle's friend. I read his papers immediately in *Blackwood*, and see a thinker, if not a poet. Thought he has, and right in every line, but music he cares not for. I had certainly supposed that a lover of Carlyle and of me must needs love rhythm and music of style.

February 9

In Boston, Wednesday night, I read at the Masonic Temple the tenth and last lecture of my Course on Human Culture.

Lecture I, Introductory. II, The Hands. III, The Head. IV, The Eye and The Ear. V, The Heart. VI, The Heart, Continued. VII, Prudence. VIII, Heroism. IX, Holiness. X, General Views.

The pecuniary advantage of the Course has been considerable.

```
Season tickets sold 319 for $620.
Single tickets sold 373 for  186.
                            ─────
                            $800.
Deduct error somewhere        13
                            ─────
                            $793.
Deduct expenses              225
                            ─────
                            $568. net profit.
```

The attendance on this course (adding to the above list 85 tickets distributed by me to friends) will be about 439 persons, on the average, of an evening — and, as it was much larger at the close than at the beginning, I think five hundred persons at the closing lectures.

A very gratifying interest on the part of the audience was evinced in the views offered, which were drawn chiefly out of the materials already collected in this Journal. The ten lectures were read on ten pleasant winter evenings, on consecutive Wednesdays. Thanks to the Teacher, of me and of all, the Upholder, the Health-giver; thanks and lowliest wondering acknowledgment.

February 17

My good Henry Thoreau made this else solitary afternoon sunny with his simplicity and clear perception.
How comic is simplicity in this double-dealing, quacking
world. Everything that boy says makes merry with
society, though nothing can be graver than his meaning.
I told him he should write out the history of his college
life, as Carlyle has his tutoring. We agreed that the seeing the stars through a telescope would be worth all the
astronomical lectures.

February 17

How much self-reliance it implies to write a true description of anything, for example, Wordsworth's picture
of skating; that leaning back on your heels and stopping
in mid-career. So simple a fact no common man would
have trusted himself to detach as a thought.

March 4

Last night a remembering and remembering talk with
Lidian. I went back to the first smile of Ellen on the door-
stone at Concord. [N. H.] I went back to all that delicious
relation to feel, as ever how many shades, how much reproach. Strange is it that I can go back to no part of
youth, no past relation, without shrinking and shrinking.
Not Ellen, not Edward, not Charles. Infinite compunctions embitter each of those dear names, and all who sur-
rounded them. Ah! could I have felt in the presence of
the first, as now I feel, my own power and hope, and so
have offered her in every word and look the heart of a
man humble and wise, but resolved to be true and perfect

with God, and not, as I fear it seemed, the uneasy, un-
centred joy of one who received in her a good — a lovely
good — out of all proportion to his deserts, I might haply
have made her days longer and certainly sweeter, and at
least have recalled her seraph smile without a pang. I
console myself with the thought that if Ellen, if Edward,
if Charles, could have read my entire heart, they should
have seen nothing but rectitude of purpose and generosity
conquering the superficial coldness and prudence. But I
ask now, Why was not I made like all these beatified
mates of mine, *superficially* generous and noble, as well as
internally so? They never needed to shrink at any remembrance; — and I at so many sad passages that look
to me now as if I had been blind and mad. Well, O God,
I will try and learn from this sad memory to be brave and
circumspect and true henceforth and weave now a web
that will not shrink. This is the thorn in the flesh.

March 5

What shall I answer to these friendly youths who ask
of me an account of Theism, and think the views I have
expressed of the impersonality of God desolating and
ghastly? I say, that I cannot find, when I explore my own
consciousness, any truth in saying that God is a person,
but the reverse. I feel that there is some profanation in
saying, He is personal. To represent him as an individual
is to shut him out of my consciousness.

March 5

Take Cousin's Philosophy — (a kissed finger cannot
write) [Mrs. Emerson had evidently brought little Waldo

into the study.] — Well, this book (if the pretention they make be good) ought to be wisdom's wisdom, and we can hug the volume to our heart and make a bonfire of all the libraries.

March 5

I have read with astonishment and unabated curiosity and pleasure Carlyle's *Revolution* again, half through the second volume. I cannot help feeling that he squanders his genius. Why should an imagination such as never rejoiced before the face of God, since Shakespeare, be content to play? Why should he trifle and joke? ... that there is, therefore, some inequality between his power of painting, which is matchless, and his power of explaining, which satisfies not.

March 5

I regret one thing omitted in my late course of Lectures: that I did not state with distinctness and conspicuously the great error of modern society in respect to religion, and say, You can never come to any peace or power until you put your whole reliance in the moral constitution of man, and not at all in a historical Christianity.

The Belief in Christianity that now prevails is the Unbelief of men. They will have Christ for a Lord and not for a Brother. Christ preaches the greatness of man, but we hear only the greatness of Christ.

March 18

I have read the second volume of poems by Tennyson, with like delight to that I found in the first and with like

criticism. Drenched he is in Shakspear, born, baptized
and bred in Shakspear, yet has his own humor, and
original rhythm, music and images.

March 18

There is no better subject for effective writing than the
Clergy. I ought to sit and think, and then write a discourse to the American Clergy, showing them the ugli-
ness and unprofitableness of theology and churches at
this day, and the glory and sweetness of the moral nature
out of whose pale they are almost wholly shut.

March 18

Astronomy is sedative to the human mind. In skeptical
hours when things go whirling and we doubt if all is not an
extemporary dream: the calm, remote and secular character of astronomical facts composes us to a sublime peace.

March 21

Last night, George Minot says he heard, in his bed, the
screaming and squalling of the wild geese flying over, between nine and ten o'clock. The newspaper notices the
same thing. I, riding from Framingham at the same hour,
heard nothing. The collar of my wrapper did shut out
nature.

April 1

Cool or cold, windy, clear day. The Divinity School
youths wish to talk with me concerning Theism. I went
rather heavy-hearted, for I always find that my views
chill or shock people at the first opening. But the conversation went well and I came away cheered. I told them

that the preacher should be a poet smit with love of the harmonies of moral nature; — and yet look at the Unitarian Association and see if its aspect is poetic. They all smiled No. A minister nowadays is plainest prose, the prose of prose. He is a warming-pan, a night-chair at sickbeds and rheumatic souls; and the fire of the minstrel's eye and the vivacity of his word is exchanged for intense, grumbling enunciation of the Cambridge sort, and for Scripture phraseology.

April 1

Preaching, especially false preaching, is for able men a sickly employment. Study of books is also sickly; and the garden and the family, wife, mother, son, and brother are a balsam. There is health in table-talk and nursery play. We must wear old shoes and have aunts and cousins.

April 19

I have been to New York and seen Bryant and Dewey, and at home seen young Jones Very, and two youthful philosophers who came here from Cambridge, — Edward Washburn and Renouf, — and who told me fine hopeful things of their mates in the senior class. And now young Eustis has been here and tells me of more aspiring and heroical young men, and I begin to conceive hopes of the Republic.

April 20

I said to Bryant and to these young people, that the high poetry of the world from the beginning has been ethical, and it is the tendency of the ripe modern mind to produce it. Wordsworth's 'merit is that he saw the truly great across the perverting influences of society and of English literature; and though he lacks executive power, yet his poetry is of the right kind.

April 24

Lidian says that when she gives any new direction in the kitchen she feels like a boy who throws a stone and runs.

April 26

Yesterday afternoon I went to the Cliff with Henry Thoreau. Warm, pleasant, misty weather, which the great mountain amphitheatre seemed to drink in with gladness. A crow's voice filled all the miles of air with sound. A bird's voice, even a piping frog, enlivens a solitude and makes world enough for us. At night I went out into the dark and saw a glimmering star and heard a frog, and Nature seemed to say, Well do not these suffice? Here is a new scene, a new experience. Ponder it, Emerson, and not like the foolish world, hanker after thunders and multitudes and vast landscapes, the sea or Niagara.

April 26

Lidian came into the study this afternoon and found the towerlet that Wallie had built, half an hour before, of two spools, a card, an awl-case and a flower-box top, each perpendicularly balanced on the other, and could scarce believe that her boy had built the pyramid, and then fell

into such a fit of affection that she lay down by the structure and kissed it down and declared she could possibly
stay no longer with papa, but must go off to the nursery
to see with eyes the lovely creature; and so departed.

May 6

Dark though the hour be, and dull the wit, no flood of
thoughts, no lovely pictures in memory or in hope, only
heavy, weary duty, moving on cart-wheels along the old
ruts of life, — I will still trust. Was not Luther's Bible,
Shakspear's Hamlet, Paul's letter, a deed as notable and
far-reaching as Marengo or the dike of Arcola. Yet these
were written by dint of flagging spirits. Sobs of the heart,
and dull, waste, unprofitable hours, taught the master
how to write to apprehensive thousands the tragedy of
these same.

May 11

Last night the moon rose behind four distinct pine-tree
tops in the distant woods and the night at ten was so
bright that I walked abroad. But the sublime light of
night is unsatisfying, provoking; it astonishes but explains not. Its charm floats, dances, disappears, comes
and goes, but palls in five minutes after you have left the
house. Come out of your warm, angular house, resound-
ing with few voices, into the chill, grand, instantaneous
night, with such a Presence as a full moon in the clouds,
and you are struck with poetic wonder. In the instant
you leave far behind all human relations, wife, mother
and child, and live only with the savages — water, air,
light, carbon, lime, and granite. I think of Kuhleborn.

I become a moist, cold element. 'Nature grows over me.' Frogs pipe; waters far off tinkle; dry leaves hiss; grass bends and rustles, and I have died out of the human world and come to feel a strange, cold, aqueous, terra-queous, aerial, ethereal sympathy and existence. I sow the sun and moon for seeds.

May 13

Last night walking under the pleasant, cloud-strown, dim-starred sky, I sought for topics for the young men at Dartmouth, and could only think one thing, namely, that the cure for bigotry and for all partiality is the recurrence to the experience, that we have been in our proper person Robinson Crusoe and Saint John, Dr. Pedant and Sardanapalus.

May 14

A Bird-while. In a natural chronometer, a Bird-while may be admitted as one of the metres, since the space most of the wild birds will allow you to make your observations on them when they alight near you in the woods, is a pretty equal and familiar measure.

May 24

I was at Medford the other day at a meeting of Hedge's Club. I was unlucky in going after several nights of vigils, and heard as though I heard not, and among gifted men I had not one thought or aspiration. But Alcott acquitted himself well, and made a due impression. So the meeting was good. I nevertheless read to-day with wicked pleasure the saying ascribed to Kant, that 'de-

testable was the society of mere literary men.' It must be
tasted sparingly to keep its gusto. If you do not quit the
high chair, lie quite down and roll on the ground a good
deal, you become nervous and heavy-hearted. The
poverty of topics, the very names of Carlyle, Channing,
Cambridge, and the Reviews become presently insup-
portable. The dog that was fed on sugar died. So all this
summer I shall talk of Chenangoes and my new garden
spout; have you heard of my pig? I have planted forty-
four pine-trees; what will my tax be this year? — and
never a word more of Goethe or Tennyson.

May 26

In the wood, God was manifest, as he was not in the
sermon. In the cathedralled larches the ground-pine
crept him, the thrush sung him, the robin complained
him, the cat-bird mewed him, the anemone vibrated him,
the wild apple bloomed him; the ants built their little
Timbuctoo wide abroad; the wild grape budded; the rye
was in the blade; high overhead, high over cloud, the
faint, sharp-horned moon sailed steadily west through
fleets of little clouds; the sheaves of the birch brightened
into green below. The pines kneaded their aromatics in
the sun. All prepared itself for the warm thunder-days of
July.

June 6

When I told Alcott that I would not criticise his compositions; that it would be as absurd to require them to
conform to my way of writing and aiming, as it would
be to reject Wordsworth because he was wholly unlike

Campbell; that here was a new mind, and it was welcome
to a new style; — he replied, well pleased, 'That is
criticism.'

June 8

A good deal of character in our abused age. The rights
of woman, the antislavery-, temperance-, peace-, health-,
and money-movements; female speakers, mobs and martyrs, the paradoxes, the antagonism of old and new, the
anomalous church, the daring mysticism and the plain
prose, the uneasy relation of domestics, the struggling
toward better household arrangements, — all indicate
life at the heart, not yet justly organized at the surface.

June 8

A man must have aunts and cousins, must buy carrots
and turnips, must have barn and woodshed, must go to
market and to the blacksmith's shop, must saunter and
sleep and be inferior and silly.

June 10. *Noon*

Mercury 90° in the shade. Rivers of heat, yea, a cir-
cumambient sea. Welcome as truly as finer and coarser
influences to this mystic, solitary 'purple island' that I
am! I celebrate the holy hour at church amid these fine
creative deluges of light and heat which evoke so many
gentle traits, — gentle and bold, — in man and woman.
Man in summer is Man intensated.

June 10

Everett has put more stories, sentences, verses, names
in amber for me than any other person.

'*A Wise Limitation.*' Very refreshing it is to me to see Minot: he is a man of no extravagant expectations; of no hypocrisy; of no pretension. He would not have his corn eaten by worms, — he picks them out and kills them; he would have his corn grow, — he weeds and hoes every hill; he would keep his cow well, — and he feeds and waters her. Means to ends and George Minot forever! They say he sleeps in his field. They say he hurts his corn by too much hoeing it.

Elizabeth Peabody brought me yesterday Hawthorne's *Footprints on the Seashore* to read. I complained that there was no inside to it. Alcott and he together would make a man.

The unbelief of the age is attested by the loud condemnation of trifles. Look at our silly religious papers. Let a minister wear a cane, or a white hat, go to a theatre, or avoid a Sunday School, let a school-book with a Calvinistic sentence or a Sunday School book without one be heard of, and instantly all the old grannies squeak and gibber and do what they call 'sounding an alarm,' from Bangor to Mobile. Alike nice and squeamish is its ear. You must on no account say 'stink' or 'Damn.'

Quite as much as Lord Byron I hate scenes. I think I have not the common degree of sympathy with dark, turbid, mournful, passionate natures.

June 21

Animal magnetism peeps. If an adept should attempt to put me to sleep by the concentration of his will without my leave, I should feel unusual rights over that person's person and life. Keep away from keyholes.

June 24

The softness and peace, the benignant humanity that hovers over our assembly when it sits down in the morning service in church, the cold gentleness of the women, the quietude of the men, are like that beautiful invention of the Dew, whereby the old hard-peaked earth and its old selfsame productions are made new every morning, just dazzling with the latest touch of the Artist's hand.

June 28

The moon and Jupiter side by side last night stemmed the sea of clouds and plied their voyage in convoy through the sublime Deep as I walked the old and dusty road. The snow and the enchantment of the moonlight make all landscapes alike, and the road that is so tedious and homely that I never take it by day, — by night is Italy or Palmyra. In these divine pleasures permitted to me of walks in the June night under moon and stars, I can put my life as a fact before me and stand aloof from its honor and shame.

July 1

I think Tennyson got his inspiration in gardens, and that in this country, where there are no gardens, his musky verses could not be written. The Villa d'Este is a memorable poem in my life.

Saw beautiful pictures yesterday. Miss Fuller brought
with her a portfolio of Sam Ward's, containing a chalk
sketch of one of Raphael's Sibyls, of Cardinal Bembo, and
the angel in Heliodorus's profanation; and Thorwaldsen's
Entry of Alexander, etc., etc. I have said sometimes that
it depends little on the object, much on the mood, in art.
I have enjoyed more from mediocre pictures, casually
seen when the mind was in equilibrium, and have reaped
a true benefit of the art of painting, — the stimulus of
color, the idealizing of common life into this gentle, elegant, unoffending fairy-land of a picture, than from many
masterpieces seen with much expectation and tutoring,
and so not with equipoise of mind. The mastery of a great
picture comes slowly over the mind. If I see a fine
picture with other people, I am driven almost into in-
evitable affectations. The scanty vocabulary of praise
is quickly exhausted, and we lose our common sense,
and, much worse, our reason, in our *superlative degrees*.
But these pictures I looked at with leisure and with
profit.

Dr. Ripley prays for rain with great explicitness on
Sunday, and on Monday the showers fell. When I spoke
of the speed with which his prayers were answered, the
good man looked modest.

The address to the Divinity School is published, and
they are printing the Dartmouth Oration. The correction
of these two pieces for the press has cost me no small

labor, now nearly ended. There goes a great deal of work into a correct literary paper, though of few pages.

August 31

Yesterday at Φ B K anniversary. Steady, steady. I am convinced that if a man will be a true scholar, he shall have perfect freedom. The young people and the mature hint at odium, and aversion of faces to be presently encountered in society. I say, No: I fear it not. . . . Society has no bribe for me, neither in politics, nor church, nor college, nor city. My resources are far from exhausted. If they will not hear me lecture, I shall have leisure for my book which wants me.

August 31

We came home, Elizabeth Hoar and I, at night from Waltham. The moon and stars and night wind made coolness and tranquillity grateful after the crowd and the festival. Elizabeth, in Lincoln woods, said that the woods always looked as if they waited whilst you passed by — waited for you to be gone.

September 5

How rare is the skill of writing? I detected a certain unusual unity of purpose in the paragraph levelled at me in the Daily Advertiser, and I now learn it is the old tyrant of the Cambridge Parnassus himself, Mr. [Andrews] Norton, who wrote it.

September 12

Alcott wants a historical record of conversations holden by you and me and him. I say, how joyful rather is some

Montaigne's book which is full of fun, poetry, business, divinity, philosophy, anecdote, smut, which dealing of bone and marrow, of cornbarn and flour barrel, of wife, and friend, and valet, of things nearest and next, never names names, or gives you the glooms of a recent date or relation, but hangs there in the heaven of letters, unrelated, untimed, a joy and a sign, an autumnal star.

September 16. *Sunday eve.*

I went at sundown to the top of Dr. Ripley's hill and renewed my vows to the Genius of that place. Somewhat of awe, somewhat grand and solemn mingles with the beauty that shines afar around. In the West, where the sun was sinking behind clouds, one pit of splendour lay as in a desert of space, — a deposit of *still light*, not radiant. Then I beheld the river, like God's love, journeying out of the grey past on into the green future.

September 21

Tennyson is a beautiful half of a poet.

September 29

Censure and Praise. — I hate to be defended in a newspaper. As long as all that is said is said *against* me, I feel a certain sublime assurance of success, but as soon as honied words of praise are spoken for me, I feel as one that lies unprotected before his enemies.

October 5

Books. — It seems meritorious to read: but from everything but history or the works of the old commanding writers I come back with a conviction that the slightest *wood-thought*, the least significant native emotion of my own, is more to me.

October 12

It seems not unfit that the scholar should deal plainly with society and tell them that he saw well enough before he spoke the consequence of his speaking; that up there in his silent study, by his dim lamp, he fore-heard this Babel of outcries. The nature of man he knew, the insanity that comes of inaction and tradition, and knew well that when their dream and routine were disturbed, like bats and owls and nocturnal beasts they would howl and shriek and fly at the torch-bearer. But he saw plainly that under this their distressing disguise of bird-form and beast form, the divine features of man were hidden, and he felt that he would dare to be so much their friend as to do them this violence to drag them to the day and to the healthy air and water of God, that the unclean spirits that had possessed them might be exorcised and depart. The taunts and cries of hatred and anger, the very epithets you bestow on me, are so familiar long ago in my reading that they sound to me ridiculously old and stale. The same thing has happened so many times over (that is, with the appearance of every original observer) that, if people were not very ignorant of literary history, they would be struck with the exact coincidence. I, whilst I see this, that you must have been shocked and must cry out at what I have said, I see too that we cannot easily be reconciled, for I have a great deal more to say that will shock you out of all patience.

October 19

Steady, steady! When this fog of good and evil affections falls, it is hard to see and walk straight.

October 19

It is plain from all the noise that there is atheism somewhere; the only question is now, Which is the atheist?

October 21

Edward Palmer asked me if I liked two services in a Sabbath. I told him, Not very well. If the sermon was good I wished to think of it; if it was bad, one was enough.

October 26

Jones Very came hither, two days since, and gave occasion to many thoughts on his peculiar state of mind and his relation to society. His position accuses society as much as society names it false and morbid; and much of his discourse concerning society, the church, and the college was perfectly just.

October 26

Let me study and work contentedly and faithfully; I do not remember my critics. I forget them, — I depart from them by every step I take. If I think then of them, it is a bad sign.

October 29

Sincerity is the highest compliment you can pay. Jones Very charmed us all by telling us he hated us all.

October 30

There are some men above grief and some men below it.

November 14

What is the hardest task in the world? To think. . . .

1839-1841

[As 1839 opened, Emerson was busy with his annual course of lectures in Boston, taking the subject of 'Human Life.' His first daughter, Ellen, was born on February 24. In that spring he began slowly to prepare the first volume of his *Essays*. In August he drove with a friend to visit the White Mountains again, but upon the whole this was a year of enfeebled health.

In January, 1840, Emerson was once more engaged with his Boston lectures, the subject being 'The Present Age.' The journal for February 19 records his disappointment with what he felt to be their cold and decorous quality. *The Dial*, to which he rendered such valiant service during the two years of Margaret Fuller's editorship, issued its first number in July. The volume of *Essays* came gradually into shape. In the autumn the Brook Farm project began to enlist the enthusiasm of many of Emerson's friends, but in spite of his interest in the experiment, he kept personally aloof.

He celebrated the beginning of the new year, 1841, by sending his first volume of *Essays* to the press. In April Henry Thoreau, then twenty-four, became a member of the Emerson household for two years. In November Emerson's second daughter, Edith, was born.]

February 25, 1839

Yesterday morning, 24 February at 8 o'clock, a daughter was born to me, a soft, quiet, swarthy little creature,

apparently perfect and healthy. My sacred child!
Blessings on thy head, little winter bud! And comest
thou to try thy luck in this world, and know if the things
of God are things for thee? Well assured, and very soft
and still, the little maiden expresses great contentment
with all she finds, and her delicate but fixed determination
to stay where she is, and grow. So be it, my fair child!
Lidian, who magnanimously makes my gods her gods,
calls the babe Ellen. I can hardly ask more for thee, my
babe, than that name implies. Be that vision, and remain with us, and after us.

March 19

'*It is in bad taste*,' is the most formidable word an
Englishman can pronounce.

April 21

In Landor's noble book, *Pericles and Aspasia*, is honor
and elegance enough to polish a nation for an age. All
the elements of the gentleman are there, except holiness.
Religion in a high degree he does not know.

May 23

A College. — My College should have Allston, Greenough, Bryant, Irving, Webster, Alcott, summoned for
its domestic professors. And if I must send abroad (and,
if we send for dancers and singers and actors, why not at
the same prices for scholars?), Carlyle, Hallam, Campbell, should come and read lectures on History, Poetry,
Letters. I would bid my men come for the love of God
and man, promising them an open field and a bound-

less opportunity, and they should make their own terms. Then I would open my lecture rooms to the wide nation; and they should pay, each man, a fee that should give my professor a remuneration fit and noble. Then I should see the lecture-room, the college, filled with life and hope. Students would come from afar; for who would not ride a hundred miles to hear some one of these men giving his selectest thoughts to those who received them with joy? I should see living learning; the Muse once more in the eye and cheek of the youth.

May 26

Allston's pictures are Elysian; fair, serene, but unreal. I extend the remark to all the American geniuses. Irving, Bryant, Greenough, Everett, Channing, even Webster in his recorded Eloquence, all lack nerve and dagger.

May 30

'T is pity we should leave with the children all the romance, all that is daintiest in life, and reserve for ourselves as we grow old only the prose. Goethe fell in love in his old age, and I would never lose the capacity of delicate and noble sentiments.

June 6

My life is a May game, I will live as I like. I defy your strait-laced, weary, social ways and modes. Blue is the sky, green the fields and groves, fresh the springs, glad the rivers, and hospitable the splendor of sun and star. I will play my game out.

June 6

Love is thaumaturgic. It converts a chair, a box, a scrap of paper, or a line carelessly drawn on it, a lock of hair, a faded weed, into amulets worth the world's fee. If we see out of what straws and nothings he builds his Elysium, we shall read nothing miraculous in the New Testament.

June 12

I know no means of calming the fret and perturbation into which too much sitting, too much talking, brings me, so perfect as labor. I have no animal spirits; therefore, when surprised by company and kept in a chair for many hours, my heart sinks, my brow is clouded and I think I will run for Acton woods, and live with the squirrels henceforward. But my garden is nearer, and my good hoe, as it bites the ground, revenges my wrongs, and I have less lust to bite my enemies. I confess I work at first with a little venom, lay to a little unnecessary strength. But by smoothing the rough hillocks, I smooth my temper; by extracting the long roots of the piper-grass, I draw out my own splinters; and in a short time I can hear the bobolink's song and see the blessed deluge of light and colour that rolls around me.

June 22

It is one of the signs of our time, the ill health of all people. All the young people are nearsighted in the towns.

July 9

I like my boy, with his endless, sweet soliloquies and iterations, and his utter inability to conceive why I should not leave all my nonsense business and writing, and come to tie up his toy horse, as if there was or could be any end to nature beyond his horse.

July 20

Night in this enchanting season is not night, but a miscellany of lights. The journeying twilight, the half-moon, the kindling Venus, the beaming Jove, — Saturn and Mars something less bright, and, fainter still, 'the common people of the sky,' as Crashaw said: then, below, the meadows and thickets flashing with the fireflies, and all around the farms the steadier lamps of men compose the softest, warmest illumination.

August 1

Last night came to me a beautiful poem from Henry Thoreau, 'Sympathy.' The purest strain, and the loftiest, I think, that has yet pealed from this unpoetic American forest. I hear his verses with as much triumph as I point to my Guido when they praise half-poets and half-painters.

August 16

With those devouring eyes, with that portraying hand, Carlyle has seen Webster.

September 14

How sad a spectacle, so frequent nowadays, to see a young man after ten years of college education come out, ready for his voyage of life, — and to see that the entire ship is made of rotten timber, of rotten, honeycombed, traditional timber without so much as an inch of new plank in the hull.

September 18

All conversation among literary men is muddy. I derive from literary meetings no satisfaction. Yet it is pity that meetings for conversation should end as quickly as they ordinarily do. They end as soon as the blood is up, and we are about to say daring and extraordinary things. They adjourn for a fortnight, and when we are reassembled we have forgot all we had to say.

September 18

It is no easy matter to write a dialogue. Cooper, Sterling, Dickens, and Hawthorne cannot.

September 20

'*These Men.*' — In Massachusetts a number of young and adult persons are at this moment the subject of a revolution. They are not organized into any conspiracy: they do not vote, or print, or meet together. They do not know each other's faces or names. They are united only in a common love of truth and love of its work. They are of all conditions and natures. They are, some of them, mean in attire, and some mean in station, and some mean in body, having inherited from their parents faces and forms scrawled with the traits of every vice. Not in churches, or in courts, or in large assemblies; not in solemn holidays, where men were met in festal dress, have these pledged themselves to new life, but in lonely and obscure places, in servitude, in solitude, in solitary compunctions and shames and fears, in disappointments, in diseases, trudging beside the team in the dusty road, or drudging, a hireling in other men's cornfields, schoolmasters who teach a few children rudiments for a pittance, ministers of small parishes of the obscurer sects, lone women in dependent condition, matrons and young maidens, rich and poor, beautiful and hard-favoured, without conceit or proclamation of any kind, have silently given in their several adherence to a new hope.

September 24

I have read *Oliver Twist* in obedience to the opinions of so many intelligent people as have praised it. The author has an acute eye for costume; he sees the expression of dress, of form, of gait, of personal deformities; of furniture, of the outside and inside of houses; but his eye rests always on surfaces; he has no insight into character.

September 28

Also I hate Early Poems.

September 29

When I was thirteen years old, my Uncle Samuel Ripley one day asked me, 'How is it, Ralph, that all the boys dislike you and quarrel with you, whilst the grown people are fond of you?' Now am I thirty-six and the fact is reversed, — the old people suspect and dislike me, and the young love me.

October 11

Horace Walpole, whose letters I read so attentively in
the past summer, is a type of the dominant Englishman at
this day. He has taste, common sense, love of facts, im-
patience of humbug, love of history, love of splendor, love
of justice, and the sentiment of honour among gentlemen,
but no life whatever of the higher faculties, no faith, no
hope, no aspiration, no question even touching the secret
of nature.

October 18

Lectures. — In these golden days it behooves me once
more to make my annual inventory of the world. For
the five last years I have read each winter a new course of
lectures in Boston, and each was my creed and confession
of faith. Each told all I thought of the past, the present
and the future. Once more I must renew my work, and I
think only once in the same form, though I see that he who
thinks he does something for the last time ought not to do
it at all. Yet my objection is not to the thing, but with
the form: and the concatenation of errors called *society*
to which I still consent, until my plumes be grown, makes
even a duty of this concession also. So I submit to sell
tickets again.

October 19

Who can blame men for seeking excitement? They are
polar, and would you have them sleep in a dull eternity
of equilibrium? Religion, love, ambition, money, war,
brandy, — some fierce antagonism must break the round
of perfect circulation or no spark, no joy, no event can be.

As good not be. In the country, the lover of nature dreaming through the wood would never awake to thought if the scream of an eagle, the cries of a crow or a curlew near his head, did not break the continuity. Nay, if the truth must out, the finest lyrics of the poet come of this coarse parentage; the imps of matter beget such child on the Soul, fair daughter of God.

October 27

In our modern reforms there's a little too much commentary on the movement by the mover.

October 28

The world can never be learned by learning all its details.

October 31

No article so rare in New England as Tone.

November 14

Systems. — I need hardly say to anyone acquainted with my thoughts that I have no System. When I was quite young, I fancied that by keeping a manuscript Journal by me, over whose pages I wrote a list of the great topics of human study, as, *Religion, Poetry, Politics, Love,* etc., in the course of a few years I should be able to complete a sort of encyclopædia containing the net value of all the definitions at which the world had yet arrived. But at the end of a couple of years, my Cabinet Cyclopædia, though much enlarged, was no nearer to a completeness than on its first day. Nay, somehow the whole plan of it needed alteration, nor did the following months promise any speedier term to it than the foregoing. At last I discovered that my curve was a parabola whose arcs would never meet, and came to acquiesce in the perception that, although no diligence can rebuild the universe in a model by the best accumulation of disposition of details, yet does the world reproduce itself in miniature in every event that transpires, so that all the laws of nature may be read in the smallest fact. So that the truth-speaker may dismiss all solicitude as to the proportion and congruency of the aggregate of his thoughts, so long as he is a faithful reporter of particular impressions.

November 20

Ah, Nature! the very look of the woods is heroical and stimulating. This afternoon in a very thick grove where Henry Thoreau showed me the bush of mountain laurel, the first I have seen in Concord, the stems of pine and hemlock and oak almost gleamed like steel upon the excited eye.

December 22

Some books leave us free and some books make us free.

February 19, 1840

I closed last Wednesday, 12th instant, my course of lectures in Boston, on 'The Present Age,' which were read on ten consecutive Wednesday evenings (except Christmas evening).

> I. Introductory. (4 December.)
> II. Literature.
> III. Literature.

IV. Politics.
V. Private Life.
VI. Reforms.
VII. Religion.
VIII. Ethics.
IX. Education.
X. Tendencies.

I judge from the account rendered me by the sellers of tickets, added to an account of my own distribution of tickets to my friends, that the average audience at a lecture consisted of about 400 persons. 256 course tickets were sold and 305 evening tickets or passes. I distributed about 110 to 120 course tickets.

These lectures give me little pleasure. I have not done what I hoped when I said, I will try it once more. I have not once transcended the coldest self-possession. I said I will agitate others, being agitated myself, I dared to hope for extasy and eloquence. . . . Alas! alas! I have not the recollection of one strong moment. A cold mechanical preparation for a delivery as decorous, — fine things, pretty things, wise things, — but no arrows, no axes, no nectar, no growling, no transpiercing, no loving, no en chantment.

And why?

I seem to lack constitutional vigor to attempt each topic as I ought. I ought to seek to lay myself out utterly, — large, enormous, prodigal, upon the subject of the week. But a hateful experience has taught me that I can only expend, say, twenty-one hours on each lecture, if I would also be ready and able for the next. Of course,

I spend myself prudently; I economize; I cheapen; whereof nothing grand ever grew. Could I spend sixty hours on each, or, what is better, had I such energy that I could rally the lights and mights of sixty hours into twenty, I should hate myself less, I should help my friend.

Providence, March 28

Send Very's Poems to Carlyle and Wordsworth.

April 7

At Providence I was made very sensible of the desire of all open minds for religious teaching. The young men and several good women freely expressed to me their wish for more light, their sympathy in whatever promised a better life. They inquired about the new Journal of next July. I was compelled to tell them that the aims of that paper were rather literary than psychological or religious. But the inquiry and the tone of these inquirers showed plainly what one may easily see in Boston and Cambridge and the villages also — that what men want is a Religion.

April 7

In all my lectures, I have taught one doctrine, namely, the infinitude of the private man. This the people accept readily enough, and even with loud commendation, as long as I call the lecture Art, or Politics, or Literature, or the Household; but the moment I call it Religion, they are shocked, though it be only the application of the same truth which they receive everywhere else, to a new class of facts.

April 9

We walked this afternoon to Edmund Hosmer's and Walden Pond. The South wind blew and filled with bland and warm light the dry sunny woods. The last year's leaves flew like birds through the air. As I sat on the bank of the Drop, or God's Pond, and saw the amplitude of the little water, what space, what verge, the little scudding fleets of ripples found to scatter and spread from side to side and take so much time to cross the pond, and saw how the water seemed made for the wind, and the wind for the water, dear playfellows for each other, — I said to my companion, I declare this world is so beautiful that I can hardly believe it exists. At Walden Pond the waves were larger and the whole lake in pretty uproar. Jones Very said, 'See how each wave rises from the midst with an original force, at the same time that it partakes the general movement!'

He said that he went to Cambridge, and found his brother reading Livy. 'I asked him if the Romans were masters of the world? My brother said they had been: I told him they were still. Then I went into the room of a senior who lived opposite, and found him writing a theme. I asked him what was his subject? And he said, Cicero's Vanity. I asked him if the Romans were masters of the world? He replied they had been: I told him they were still. This was in the garret of Mr. Ware's house. Then I went down into Mr. Ware's study, and found him reading Bishop Butler, and I asked him if the Romans were masters of the world? He said they had been: I told him they were still.'

May, undated

Wordsworth has done as much as any living man to restore sanity to cultivated society

May 17

Latent heat performs a great office in nature. Not less does *latent joy* in life. You may have your stock of well-being condensed into extasies, trances of good fortune and delight, preceded and followed by blank or painful weeks and months; or, you may have your joy spread over all the days in a bland, vague, uniform sense of power and hope.

May 28

Old Age. — Sad spectacle that a man should live and be fed that he may fill a paragraph every year in the newspapers for his wonderful age, as we record the weight and girth of the Big Ox, or Mammoth Girl. We do not count a man's years until he has nothing else to count.

June 4

Waldo says, 'The flowers talk when the wind blows over them.' My little boy grows thin in the hot summer, and runs all to eyes and eyelashes.

June 11

I finish this morning transcribing my old essay on Love, but I see well its inadequateness. I, cold because I am hot, — cold at the surface only as a sort of guard and compensation for the fluid tenderness of the core, — have much more experience than I have written there, more than I will, more than I can write. In silence we must wrap much of our life, because it is too fine for speech, because also we cannot explain it to others, and because somewhat we cannot yet understand.

June 24

Montaigne. — The language of the street is always strong. What can describe the folly and emptiness of scolding like the word *jawing?* I feel too the force of the double negative, though clean contrary to our grammar rules. And I confess to some pleasure from the stinging rhetoric of a rattling oath in the mouth of truckmen and teamsters. How laconic and brisk it is by the side of a page of the *North American Review.* Cut these words and they would bleed; they are vascular and alive; they walk and run. Moreover they who speak them have this elegancy, that they do not trip in their speech. It is a shower of bullets, whilst Cambridge men and Yale men correct themselves and begin again at every half sentence.

I know nobody among my contemporaries except Carlyle who writes with any sinew and vivacity comparable to Plutarch and Montaigne. Yet always this profane swearing and bar-room wit has salt and fire in it. I cannot now read Webster's speeches. Fuller and Browne and Milton are quick, but the list is soon ended. Goethe seems to be well alive, no pedant. Luther too.

June 24

Now for near five years I have been indulged by the gracious Heaven in my long holiday in this goodly house

of mine, entertaining and entertained by so many worthy
and gifted friends, and all this time poor Nancy Barron,
the mad-woman, has been screaming herself hoarse at the
Poor-house across the brook and I still hear her whenever
I open my window.

July 6

Whenever I read Plutarch or look at a Greek vase I am
inclined to accept the common opinion of the learned that
the Greeks had cleaner wits than any other people in the
Universe. But there is anything but Time in my idea of
the antique. A clear and natural expression by word or
deed is that which we mean when we love and praise the
antique. In society I do not find it; in modern books
seldom; but the moment I get into the pastures I find
antiquity again. Once in the fields with the lowing cattle,
the birds, the trees, the waters and satisfying outlines of
the landscape, and I cannot tell whether this is Tempe,
Thessaly and Enna, or Concord and Acton.

September 8

I went into the woods. I found myself not wholly
present there. If I looked at a pine-tree or an aster, *that*
did not seem to be Nature. Nature was still elsewhere:
this, or this was but outskirt and far-off reflection and
echo of the triumph that had passed by and was now at
its glancing splendor and heyday, — perchance in the
neighboring fields, or, if I stood in the field, then in the adjacent woods. Always the present object gave me this
sense of the stillness that follows a pageant that has just
gone by.

September 12

Sarah Clarke, who left us yesterday, is a true and high-minded person, but has her full proportion of our native frost. She remarked of the *Dial*, that the spirit of many of the pieces was lonely.

September 16

A sleeping child gives me the impression of a traveller in a very far country.

October 7

I have been writing with some pains essays on various matters as a sort of apology to my country for my apparent idleness. But the poor work has looked poorer daily, as I strove to end it. My genius seemed to quit me in such a mechanical work, a seeming wise — a cold exhibition of dead thoughts. When I write a letter to anyone whom I love, I have no lack of words or thoughts. I am wiser than myself and read my paper with the pleasure of one who receives a letter, but what I write to fill up the gaps of a chapter is hard and cold, is grammar and logic; there is no magic in it; I do not wish to see it again.

October 17

Yesterday George and Sophia Ripley, Margaret Fuller and Alcott discussed here the Social Plans. [Brook Farm.] I wished to be convinced, to be thawed, to be made nobly mad by the kindlings before my eye of a new dawn of human piety. But this scheme was arithmetic and comfort: this was a hint borrowed from the Tremont House and United States Hotel; a rage in our poverty

and politics to live rich and gentlemanlike, an anchor to
leeward against a change of weather; a prudent forecast
on the probable issue of the great questions of Pauperism
and Poverty. And not once could I be inflamed, but sat
aloof and thoughtless; my voice faltered and fell. It was
not the cave of persecution which is the palace of spiritual
power, but only a room in the Astor House hired for the
Transcendentalists. I do not wish to remove from my
present prison to a prison a little larger. I wish to break
all prisons. I have not yet conquered my own house. It
irks and repents me. Shall I raise the siege of this hen-
coop, and march baffled away to a pretended siege of
Babylon? It seems to me that so to do were to dodge the
problem I am set to solve, and to hide my impotency in
the thick of a crowd. I can see too, afar, — that I should
not find myself more than now, — no, not so much, in
that select, but not by me selected, fraternity. Moreover, to join this body would be to traverse all my long
trumpeted theory, and the instinct which spoke from it,
that one man is a counterpoise to a city, — that a man is
stronger than a city, that his solitude is more prevalent
and beneficent than the concert of crowds.

October 24

What a pity that we cannot curse and swear in good
society! Cannot the stinging dialect of the sailors be do-
mesticated? It is the best rhetoric, and for a hundred
occasions those forbidden words are the only good ones.
My page about 'Consistency' would be better written
thus: Damn Consistency!

November 5

It is not irregular hours or irregular diet that make the romantic life. A sylvan strength, a united man, whose character leads the circumstances, and is not led by them, — this makes romance, and no condition.

November 21

A. [Alcott] is a tedious archangel.

January 1, 1841

I begin the year by sending my little book of Essays to the press.

January 21

When I look at the sweeping slect amid the pine woods, my sentences look very contemptible, and I think I will never write more: but the words prompted by an irresistible charity, the words whose path from the heart to the lips I cannot follow, — are fairer than the snow. It is pitiful to be an artist. . . .

January 31

All my thoughts are foresters. I have scarce a daydream on which the breath of the pines has not blown, and their shadows waved. Shall I not then call my little book Forest Essays?

January 31

These novels will give way, by and by, to diaries or autobiographies; — captivating books, if only a man knew how to choose among what he calls his experiences that which is really his experience, and how to record truth truly!

February 4

If I judge from my own experience I should unsay all my fine things, I fear, concerning the manual labor of literary men. They ought to be released from every species of public or private responsibility. To them the grasshopper is a burden. I guard my moods as anxiously as a miser his money; for company, business, my own household chares, untune and disqualify me for writing. I think then the writer ought not to be married; ought not to have a family. I think the Roman Church with its celibate clergy and its monastic cells was right. If he must marry, perhaps he should be regarded happiest who has a shrew for a wife, a sharp-tongued notable dame who can and will assume the total economy of the house, and, having some sense that her philosopher is best in his study, suffers him not to intermeddle with her thrift.

April 19

I am tempted lately to wish, for the benefit of our literary society, that we had the friendly institution of the *Café.* How much better than Munroe's bookshop would be a coffee-room wherein one was sure at one o'clock to find what scholars were abroad taking their walk after the morning studies were ended.

April 24

I frequently find the best part of my ride in the Concord Coach from my house to Winthrop Place to be in

Prince Street, Charter Street, Ann Street, and the like places at the North End of Boston. The dishabille of both men and women, their unrestrained attitudes and manners, make pictures greatly more interesting than the clean-shaved and silk-robed procession in Washington and Tremont streets. I often see that the attitudes of both men and women engaged in hard work are more picturesque than any which art and study could contrive, for the Heart is in these first. I say *picturesque;* because when I pass these groups, I instantly know whence all the fine pictures I have seen had their origin: I feel the painter in me: these are the traits which make us feel the force and eloquence of *form* and the sting of color. But the painter is only *in* me; it does not come to the fingers' ends. But whilst I see a true painting, I feel how it was made; I feel that genius organizes, or it is lost.

May 4

Aunt Mary, whose letters I read all yesterday afternoon, is Genius always new, subtle, frolicsome, musical, unpredictable. All your learning of all literatures and states of society, Platonistic, Calvinistic, English or Chinese, would never enable you to anticipate one thought or expression. She is embarrassed by no Moses or Paul, no Angelo or Shakspeare, after whose type she is to fashion her speech: her wit is the wild horse of the desart, who snuffs the sirocco and scours the palm-grove without having learned his paces in the Stadium or at Tattersall's. . . . In reading these letters of M. M. E. I acknowledge (with surprise that I could ever forget it) the debt of myself and my brothers to that old religion which, in those years, still dwelt like a Sabbath peace in the country population of New England, which taught privation, self-denial, and sorrow. A man was born, not for prosperity, but to suffer for the benefit of others, like the noble rock-maple tree which all around the villages bleeds for the service of man. Not praise, not men's acceptance of our doing, but the Spirit's holy errand through us, absorbed the thought. How dignified is this! how all that is called talents and worth in Paris and in Washington dwindles before it! . . . I value Andover, Yale, and Princeton as altars of this same old fire, though I fear they have done burning cedar and sandalwood there also, and have learned to use chips and pine.

June 6

I am sometimes discontented with my house because it lies on a dusty road, and with its sills and cellar almost in the water of the meadow. But when I creep out of it into the Night or the Morning and see what majestic and what tender beauties daily wrap me in their bosom, how near to me is every transcendent secret of Nature's love and religion, I see how indifferent it is where I eat and sleep. This very street of hucksters and taverns the moon will transform to a Palmyra, for she is the apologist of all apologists, and will kiss the elm trees alone and hides every meanness in a silver-edged darkness.

June 7

Critics. — The borer on our peach trees bores that she may deposit an egg: but the borer into theories and institutions and books bores that he may bore.

July, undated

But woe to him who is always successful, who still speaks the best word, and does the handiest thing, for that man has no heavenly moment.

July. undated

Lidian says that the only sin which people never forgive in each other is a difference of opinion.

Nantasket, July, undated

Do not waste yourself in rejection; do not bark against the bad, but chant the beauty of the good.

Nantasket, July, undated

Let us answer a book of ink with a book of flesh and blood.

August 22

I remember, when a child, in the pew on Sundays amusing myself with saying over common words as 'black,' 'white,' 'board,' etc., twenty or thirty times, until the word lost all meaning and fixedness, and I began to doubt which was the right name for the thing, when I saw that neither had any natural relation, but all were arbitrary. It was a child's first lesson in Idealism.

August 31

Alas, that I must hint to you that poverty is not an unmixed good; that labor may easily exceed. The sons of the rich have finer forms and in some respects a better organization than the sons of the laborer. The Irish

population in our towns is the most laborious, but neither
the most moral nor the most intelligent: the experience of
the colleagues of Brook Farm was unanimous, 'We have
no thoughts.'

August, undated

At Cambridge, the last Wednesday, I met twenty
members of my college class and spent the day with them.
Governor Kent of Maine presided, Upham, Quincy,
Lowell, Gardner, Loring, Gorham, Motte, Wood, Blood,
Cheney, Withington, Bulfinch, Reed, Burton, Stetson,
Lane, Angier, Hilliard, Farnsworth, Dexter, Emerson.
It was strange how fast the company returned to their old
relation, and the whole mass of college nonsense came
back in a flood. They all associated perfectly, were an
unit for the day — men who now never meet. Each resumed his old place. The change in them was really very
little in twenty years, although every man present was
married, and all but one fathers. I too resumed my old
place and found myself as of old a spectator rather than
a fellow. I drank a great deal of wine (for me) with the
wish to raise my spirits to the pitch of good fellowship,
but wine produced on me its old effect, and I grew graver
with every glass. Indignation and eloquence will excite
me, but wine does not.

August, undated

The trumpet-like lowing of a cow — what does that
speak to in me? Not to my understanding. No. Yet
somewhat in me hears and loves it well.

August, undated

Lotus-eaters. I suppose there is no more abandoned epicure or opium-eater than I. I taste every hour of these autumn days. Every light from the sky, every shadow on the earth, ministers to my pleasure. I love this gas. I grudge to move or to labor or to change my book or to will, lest I should disturb the sweet dream.

September, undated

Life. Osman. We are all of us very near to sublimity. As one step freed Wordsworth's Recluse on the mountains from the blinding mist and brought him to the view of 'Glory beyond all glory ever seen,' so near are all to a vision of which Homer and Shakspeare are only hints and types, and yet cannot we take that one step. [By 'Osman' Emerson often means himself considered as a poet. Sometimes he uses the word as a symbol for the ideal man.]

September 21

Dr. Ripley died this morning. The fall of this oak of ninety years makes some sensation in the forest, old and doomed as it was. He has identified himself with the forms at least of the old church of the New England Puritans, his nature was eminently loyal, not in the least adventurous or democratical; and his whole being leaned backward on the departed, so that he seemed one of the rear-guard of this great camp and army which have filled the world with fame, and with him passes out of sight almost the last banner and guidon flag of a mighty epoch. For these Puritans, however in our last days they have declined into ritualists, solemnized the heyday of their strength by the planting and the liberating of America.

Great, grim, earnest men, I belong by natural affinity to other thoughts and schools than yours, but my affection hovers respectfully about your retiring footprints, your unpainted churches, strict platforms, and sad offices; the iron-gray deacon and the wearisome prayer rich with the diction of ages.

September, undated

Sarah Alden Ripley is a bright foreigner: she signalizes herself among the figures of this masquerade. I do not hope when I see her to gain anything, any thought: she is choked, too, by the multitude of all her riches, Greek and German, Biot and Bichat, chemistry and philosophy. All this is bright obstruction. But capable she is of high and calm intelligence, and of putting all the facts, all life aloof, as we sometimes have done. But when she does not, and only has a tumultuous time, it is time well wasted. I think her worth throwing time away upon.

September, undated

I told Henry Thoreau that his freedom is in the form, but he does not disclose new matter. I am very familiar with all his thoughts, — they are my own quite originally drest. But if the question be, what new ideas has he thrown into circulation, he has not yet told what that is which he was created to say.

September, undated

Poetry. But now of poetry I would say, that when I go out into the fields in a still sultry day, in a still sultry

humor, I do perceive that the finest rhythms and cadences
of poetry are yet unfound, and that in that purer state
which glimmers before us, rhythms of a faery and dreamlike music shall enchant us, compared with which the
finest measures of English poetry are psalm-tunes. I
think now that the very finest and sweetest closes and
falls are not in our metres, but in the measures of eloquence, which have greater variety and richness than
verse. . . .

October 8

The view taken of Transcendentalism in State Street is
that it threatens to invalidate contracts.

October 9

I would have my book read as I have read my favorite
books, not with explosion and astonishment, a marvel
and a rocket, but a friendly and agreeable influence stealing like the scent of a flower, or the sight of a new landscape on a traveller. I neither wish to be hated and defied
by such as I startle, nor to be kissed and hugged by the
young whose thoughts I stimulate.

October 9

The sum of life ought to be valuable when the fractions
and particles are so sweet.

October 12

I would that I could, I know afar off that I cannot, give
the lights and shades, the hopes and outlooks that come
to me in these strange, cold-warm, attractive-repelling

conversations with Margaret, whom I always admire, most revere when I nearest see, and sometimes love, — yet whom I freeze, and who freezes me to silence, when we seem to promise to come nearest.

October, undated

I saw in Boston Fanny Elssler in the ballet of *Nathalie*. She must show, I suppose, the whole compass of her instrument, and add to her softest graces of motion or 'the wisdom of her feet,' the feats of the rope-dancer and tumbler: and perhaps on the whole the beauty of the exhibition is enhanced by this that is strong and strange, as when she stands erect on the extremities of her toes or on one toe, or 'performs the impossible' in attitude. But the chief beauty is in the extreme grace of her movement, the variety and nature of her attitude, the winning fun and spirit of all her little coquetries, the beautiful erectness of her body, and the freedom and determination which she can so easily assume, and, what struck me much, the air of perfect sympathy with the house, and that mixture of deference and conscious superiority which puts her in perfect spirits and equality to her part. When she courtesies, her sweet and slow and prolonged salaam which descends and still descends whilst the curtain falls, until she seems to have invented new depths of grace and condescension, — she earns well the profusion of bouquets of flowers which are hurled on to the stage.

As to the morals, as it is called, of this exhibition, that lies wholly with the spectator. The basis of this exhibition, like that of every human talent, is moral, is the sport and triumph of health or the virtue of organiza-

tion. Her charm for the house is that she dances for them
or they dance in her, not being (fault of some defect in
their forms and educations) able to dance themselves.
We must be expressed. Hence all the cheer and exhilaration which the spectacle imparts and the intimate property which each beholder feels in the dancer, and the joy
with which he hears good anecdotes of her spirit and her
benevolence. They know that such surpassing grace must
rest on some occult foundations of inward harmony.

But over and above her genius for dancing are the in-
cidental vices of this individual, her own false taste or her
meretricious arts to please the groundlings and which
must displease the judicious. The immorality the immoral will see; the very immoral will see that only; the
pure will not heed it, — for it is not obtrusive, — perhaps
will not see it at all. I should not think of danger to young
women stepping with their father or brother out of happy
and guarded parlors into this theatre to return in a few
hours to the same; but I can easily suppose that it is not
the safest resort for college boys who have left metaphysics, conic sections, or Tacitus to see these tripping
satin slippers, and they may not forget this graceful,
silvery swimmer when they have retreated again to their
baccalaureate cells.

It is a great satisfaction to see the best in each kind,
and as a good student of the world, I desire to let pass
nothing that is excellent in its own kind unseen, unheard.

October, undated

I saw Webster on the street, — but he was changed
since I saw him last, — black as a thunder-cloud, and

careworn; the anxiety that withers this generation among
the young and thinking class had crept up also into the
great lawyer's chair, and too plainly, too plainly he was
one of us. I did not wonder that he depressed his eyes
when he saw me, and would not meet my face. The
cankerworms have crawled to the topmost bough of the
wild elm and swing down from that. No wonder the elm
is a little uneasy.

October 24

I told Garrison that I thought he must be a very young
man, or his time hang very heavy on his hands, who can
afford to think much and talk much about the foibles of
his neighbors, or '*denounce*,' and play 'the son of thunder'
as he called it.

October, undated

It seems to me sometimes that we get our education
ended a little too quick in this country. As soon as we
have learned to read and write and cipher, we are dismissed from school and we set up for ourselves. We are
writers and leaders of opinion and we write away without
check of any kind, play whatsoever mad prank, indulge
whatever spleen, or oddity, or obstinacy, comes into our
dear head, and even feed our complacency thereon, and
thus fine wits come to nothing, as good horses spoil themselves by running away and straining themselves. I cannot help seeing that Doctor Channing would have been a
much greater writer had he found a strict tribunal of
writers, a graduated intellectual empire established in the
land, and knew that bad logic would not pass, and that

the most severe exaction was to be made on all who enter these lists. Now, if a man can write a paragraph for a newspaper, next year he writes what he calls a history, and reckons himself a classic incontinently, nor will his contemporaries in critical Journal or Review question his claims. It is very easy to reach the degree of culture that prevails around us; very hard to pass it, and Doctor Channing, had he found Wordsworth, Southey, Coleridge, and Lamb around him, would as easily have been severe with himself and risen a degree higher as he has stood where he is. I mean, of course, a genuine intellectual tribunal, not a literary junto of Edinburgh wits, or dull conventions of Quarterly or Gentleman's Reviews.

October 28

We are very near to greatness: one step and we are safe: can we not take the leap?

October 30

The Age. Shelley is wholly unaffecting to me. I was born a little too soon: but his power is so manifest over a large class of the best persons, that he is not to be overlooked.

October 30

Soldier. Can one nowadays see a soldier without a slight feeling — the slightest possible — of the ridiculous?

November 13

As to the *Miracle*, too, of Poetry. There is truly but one miracle, the perpetual fact of Being and Becoming, the ceaseless saliency, the transit from the Vast to the

particular, which miracle, one and the same, has for its
most universal name the word *God*. Take one or two or
three steps where you will, from any fact in Nature or
Art, and you come out full on this fact; as you may
penetrate the forest in any direction and go straight on,
you will come to the sea.

November 22

Edith. There came into the house a young maiden, but
she seemed to be more than a thousand years old. She
came into the house naked and helpless, but she had for
her defence more than the strength of millions. She
brought into the day the manners of the Night.

December, undated

When Jones Very was in Concord, he said to me, 'I
always felt when I heard you speak or read your writings
that you saw the truth better than others, yet I felt that
your spirit was not quite right. It was as if a vein of
colder air blew across me.'

December, undated

All writing is by the grace of God. People do not deserve to have good writing, they are so pleased with bad.
In these sentences that you show me, I can find no beauty,
for I see death in every clause and every word. There is a
fossil or a mummy character which pervades this book.
The best sepulchres, the vastest catacombs, Thebes and
Cairo, Pyramids, are sepulchres to me. I like gardens and
nurseries. Give me initiative, spermatic, prophesying,
man-making words.

1842–1844

[PERHAPS the sharpest sorrow of Emerson's life came in the death of his five-year-old son Waldo, on January 27, 1842. The journal makes pathetic record of the father's grief. He lectured in New York in March, and shortly afterward succeeded Margaret Fuller in the thankless task of editing *The Dial*. This was the year of Alcott's visit to England and his return with Wright and Lane, who were soon to be associated with him in the ill-starred community experiment at Fruitlands. There are many references to Alcott and his friends in the journal, — for the most part keenly critical. Emerson's walking trip with Hawthorne in September was one of the pleasantest episodes of the year.

As 1843 opened, Emerson was making a long lecturing trip to New York, Philadelphia, Baltimore, and Washington. His references to Webster in the journal grow more hostile, though he admired the Bunker Hill oration on June 17, and heard him argue a notable case in Concord in August.

There were few events in Emerson's life during 1844, and the journal records are scantier than usual. *The Dial* perished in this year, and the Second Series of *Essays* was published. Emerson's youngest child, Edward Waldo, was born on July 10.]

January 28, 1842

Yesterday night, at fifteen minutes after eight, my little Waldo ended his life.

January 30

The morning of Friday, I woke at three o'clock, and every cock in every barnyard was shrilling with the most unnecessary noise. The sun went up the morning sky with all his light, but the landscape was dishonored by this loss. For this boy, in whose remembrance I have both slept and awaked so oft, decorated for me the morning star, the evening cloud. . . . A boy of early wisdom, of a grave and even majestic deportment, of a perfect gentleness.

Every tramper that ever tramped is abroad, but the little feet are still.

He gave up his little innocent breath like a bird.

Sorrow makes us all children again, — destroys all differences of intellect. The wisest knows nothing.

March 18

Home from New York, where I read six lectures on the Times, viz., Introductory; The Poet; The Conservative; The Transcendentalist; Manners; Prospects. They were read in the 'Society Library,' were attended by three or four hundred persons, and after all expenses were paid yielded me about two hundred dollars.

In New York I became acquainted with Henry James, John James, William Greene, Mrs. Rebecca Black, Thomas Truesdale, Horace Greeley, Albert Brisbane, J. L. H. McCracken, Mr. Field, Maxwell, Mason, Nathan, Delf, Eames, besides Bryant and Miss Sedgwick, whom I knew before.

Letters from beloved persons found me there. My lectures had about the same reception there as elsewhere: very fine and poetical, but a little puzzling. One thought it 'as good as a kaleidoscope.' Another, a good Staten Islander, would go hear, 'for he had heard I was a rattler.'

March 20

The *Dial* is to be sustained or ended, and I must settle the question, it seems, of its life or death. I wish it to live, but do not wish to be its life. Neither do I like to put it in the hands of the Humanity and Reform Men, because they trample on letters and poetry; nor in the hands of the Scholars, for they are dead and dry.

March 20

I comprehend nothing of this fact [Waldo's death] but its bitterness. Explanation I have none, consolation none that rises out of the fact itself; only diversion; only oblivion of this, and pursuit of new objects.

March 23

Here prepares now the good Alcott to go to England, after so long and strict acquaintance as I have had with him for seven years   I saw him for the first time in Boston in 1835.

What shall we say of him to the wise Englishman? [Carlyle]

He is a man of ideas, a man of faith. Expect contempt for all usages which are simply such. His social nature and his taste for beauty and magnificence will betray him into tolerance and indulgence, even, to men and to magnificence, but a statute or a practice he is condemned to measure by its essential wisdom or folly.

He delights in speculation, in nothing so much, and is

very well endowed and weaponed for that work with a
copious, accurate and elegant vocabulary; I may say
poetic; so that I know no man who speaks such good
English as he, and is so inventive withal. He speaks
truth truly; or the expression is adequate. Yet he knows
only this one language. He hardly needs an antagonist,
— he needs only an intelligent ear. Where he is greeted
by loving and intelligent persons, his discourse soars to a
wonderful height, so regular, so lucid, so playful, so new
and disdainful of all boundaries of tradition and experience, that the hearers seem no longer to have bodies or
material gravity, but almost they can mount into the air
at pleasure, or leap at one bound out of this poor solar
system. I say this of his speech exclusively, for when he
attempts to write, he loses, in my judgment, all his power,
and I derive more pain than pleasure from the perusal.
The *Post* expresses the feeling of most readers in its rude
joke, when it said of his *Orphic Sayings* that they 're-
sembled a train of fifteen railroad cars with one passenger.'
He has moreover the greatest possession both of mind and
of temper in his discourse, so that the mastery and
moderation and foresight, and yet felicity, with which he
unfolds his thought, are not to be surpassed. This is of
importance to such a broacher of novelties as he is, and to
one baited, as he is very apt to be, by the sticklers for old
books or old institutions. He takes such delight in the
exercise of this faculty that he will willingly talk the whole
of a day, and most part of the night, and then again to-
morrow, for days successively, and if I, who am impatient
of much speaking, draw him out to walk in the woods or
fields, he will stop at the first fence and very soon propose

either to sit down or to return. He seems to think society
exists for this function, and that all literature is good or
bad as it approaches colloquy, which is its perfection.
Poems and histories may be good, but only as adumbra-
tions of this; and the only true manner of writing the
literature of a nation would be to convene the best heads
in the community, set them talking, and then introduce
stenographers to record what they say. He so swiftly and
naturally plants himself on the moral sentiment in any
conversation that no man will ever get any advantage of
him, unless he be a saint, as Jones Very was. Every one
else Alcott will put in the wrong.

It must be conceded that it is speculation which he
loves, and not action. Therefore he dissatisfies everybody
and disgusts many. When the conversation is ended, all
is over. He lives to-morrow, as he lived to-day, for further
discourse, not to begin, as he seemed pledged to do, a new
celestial life. . . . He has no vocation to labor, and, although he strenuously preached it for a time, and made
some efforts to practise it, he soon found he had no genius
for it, and that it was a cruel waste of his time. It depressed his spirits even to tears. . . . He is quite ready at
any moment to abandon his present residence and employment, his country, nay, his wife and children, on very
short notice, to put any new dream into practice which
has bubbled up in the effervescence of discourse. If it is so
with his way of living, much more so is it with his opinions. He never remembers. He never affirms anything
to-day because he has affirmed it before. You are rather
astonished, having left him in the morning with one set of
opinions, to find him in the evening totally escaped from

all recollection of them, as confident of a new line of conduct and heedless of his old advocacy. . . .

Alcott sees the law of man truer and farther than any one ever did. Unhappily, his conversation never loses sight of his own personality. He never quotes; he never refers; his only illustration is his own biography. His topic yesterday is Alcott on the 17th October; to-day, Alcott on the 18th October; to-morrow, on the 19th. So will it be always. The poet, rapt into future times or into deeps of nature admired for themselves, lost in their law, cheers us with a lively charm; but this noble genius discredits genius to me. I do not want any more such persons to exist.

April 5

Truth; Realism. Are you not scared by seeing that the Gypsies are more attractive to us than the Apostles? For though we love goodness and not stealing, yet also we love freedom and not preaching.

April 5

Swedenborg never indicates any emotion, — a cold, passionless man.

April 6

The history of Christ is the best Document of the power of Character which we have. A youth who owed nothing to fortune and who was 'hanged at Tyburn,' — by the pure quality of his nature has shed this epic splendor around the facts of his death which has transfigured every particular into a grand universal symbol for the eyes of all mankind ever since.

He did well. This great Defeat is hitherto the highest fact we have. But he that shall come shall do better. The mind requires a far higher exhibition of character, one which shall make itself good to the senses as well as to the soul; a success to the senses as well as to the soul. This was a great Defeat; we demand Victory. More character will convert judge and jury, soldier and king; will rule human and animal and mineral nature; will command irresistibly and blend with the course of Universal Nature.

April 6

I am *Defeated* all the time; yet to Victory I am born.

April 6

A saint, an angel, a chorus of saints, a myriad of Christs, are alike worthless and forgotten by the soul, as the leaves that fall, or the fruit that was gathered in the garden of Eden in the golden age. A new day, a new harvest, new duties, new men, new fields of thought, new powers call you, and an eye fastened on the past unsuns nature, bereaves me of hope, and ruins me with a squalid indigence which nothing but death can adequately symbolize.

April, undated

If I go into the churches in these days, I usually find the preacher in proportion to his intelligence to be cunning, so that the whole institution sounds hollow. X, the ablest of all the Unitarian clergy, spread popular traps all over the lecture which I heard in the Odeon. But in the days of the Pilgrims and the Puritans, the preachers were the

victims of the same faith with which they whipped and
persecuted other men, and their sermons are strong,
imaginative, fervid, and every word a cube of stone.

April, undated

The gates of thought, — how slow and late they discover themselves! Yet when they appear, we see that
they were always there, always open.

April 14

If I should write an honest diary, what should I say?
Alas, that life has halfness, shallowness. I have almost
completed thirty-nine years, and I have not yet adjusted
my relation to my fellows on the planet, or to my own
work. Always too young or too old, I do not justify myself; how can I satisfy others?

May 15

'Abou ben Adhem' seems to promise its own immortality beyond all the contemporary poems.

June 16

I read the *Timæus* in these days, but am never sufficiently in a sacred and holiday health for the task. The
man must be equal to the book. A man does not know how
fine a morning he wants until he goes to read Plato and
Proclus.

June, undated

Elizabeth Hoar says that Shelley is like shining sand; it
always looks attractive and valuable, but, try never so

many times, you cannot get anything good. And yet the
mica-glitter will still remain after all.

June, undated

Charles King Newcomb took us all captive. . . . Let it
be his praise that when I carried his manuscript story to
the woods, and read it in the armchair of the upturned
root of a pine tree, I felt for the first time since Waldo's
death some efficient faith again in the repairs of the Universe, some independency of natural relations whilst
spiritual affinities can be so perfect and compensating.

June, undated

I hear with pleasure that a young girl in the midst of
rich, decorous Unitarian friends in Boston is well-nigh
persuaded to join the Roman Catholic Church. Her
friends, who are also my friends, lamented to me the
growth of this inclination. But I told them that I think
she is to be greatly congratulated on the event. She has
lived in great poverty of events. In form and years a
woman, she is still a child, having had no experiences, and
although of a fine, liberal, susceptible, expanding nature,
has never yet found any worthy object of attention; has
not been in love, not been called out by any taste, except
lately by music, and sadly wants adequate objects. In this
church, perhaps, she shall find what she needs, in a power
to call out the slumbering religious sentiment. It is unfortunate that the guide who has led her into this path is a
young girl of a lively, forcible, but quite external character,
who teaches her the historical argument for the Catholic
faith. I told A. that I hoped she would not be misled by

attaching any importance to that. If the offices of the church attracted her, if its beautiful forms and humane spirit draw her, if St. Augustine and St. Bernard, Jesus and Madonna, cathedral music and masses, then go, for thy dear heart's sake, but do not go out of this icehouse of Unitarianism, all external, into an icehouse again of external. At all events, I charged her to pay no regard to dissenters, but to suck that orange thoroughly.

June, undated

In Boston I saw the new second volume of Tennyson's *Poems*. It has many merits, but the question might remain whether it has *the* merit. One would say it was the poetry of an exquisite; that it was prettiness carried out to the infinite, but with no one great heroic stroke; a too vigorous exclusion of all mere natural influences.

July 12

Carlyle represents very well the literary man, makes good the place of and function of Erasmus and Johnson, of Dryden and Swift, to our generation. He is thoroughly a gentleman and deserves well of the whole fraternity of scholars, for sustaining the dignity of his profession of Author in England. Yet I always feel his limitation, and praise him as one who plays his part well according to his light, as I praise the Clays and Websters. For Carlyle is worldly, and speaks not out of the celestial region of Milton and Angels.

August 3

Some play at chess, some at cards, some at the Stock Exchange. I prefer to play at Cause and Effect.

August, undated

The only poetic fact in the life of thousands and thousands is their death. No wonder they specify all the circumstances of the death of another person.

August 20

Last night a walk to the river with Margaret, and saw the moon broken in the water, interrogating, interrogating.

September 1

I have so little vital force that I could not stand the dissipation of a flowing and friendly life; I should die of consumption in three months. But now I husband all my strength in this bachelor life I lead; no doubt shall be a well-preserved old gentleman.

September, undated

Nathaniel Hawthorne's reputation as a writer is a very pleasing fact, because his writing is not good for anything, and this is a tribute to the man.

September, undated

I question when I read Tennyson's *Ulysses*, whether there is taste in England to do justice to the poet.

September, undated

How slowly, how slowly we learn that witchcraft and ghostcraft, palmistry and magic, and all the other so-called superstitions, which, with so much police, boastful skepticism, and scientific committees, we had finally

dismissed to the moon as nonsense, are really no nonsense
at all, but subtle and valid influences, always starting up,
mowing, muttering in our path, and shading our day.

September, undated

It pains me never that I cannot give you an accurate
answer to the question, What is God? What is the
operation we call Providence? and the like. There lies the
answer: there it exists, present, omnipresent to you, to
me. . . .

September, undated

All persons are puzzles until at last we find in some word
or act the key to the man, to the woman; straightway all
their past words and actions lie in light before us.

September, undated

Milnes brought Carlyle to the railway, and showed
him the departing train. Carlyle looked at it and then
said, 'These are our poems, Milnes.' Milnes ought to
have answered, 'Aye, and our histories, Carlyle.'

September, undated

Edward Everett. There was an influence on the young
people from Everett's genius which was almost comparable to that of Pericles in Athens. That man had an
inspiration that did not go beyond his head, but which
made him the genius of elegance. He had a radiant beauty
of person, of a classic style, a heavy, large eye, marble
lids, which gave the impression of mass which the slight-
ness of his form needed, sculptured lips, a voice of such

rich tones, such precise and perfect utterance that, although slightly nasal, it was the most mellow and beautiful and correct of all the instruments of the time. The word that he spoke, in the manner in which he spoke it, became current and classical in New England.

Especially beautiful were his poetic quotations. He quoted Milton; more rarely Byron; and sometimes a verse from Watts, and with such sweet and perfect modulation that he seemed to give as much beauty as he borrowed, and whatever he had quoted will seldom be remembered by any who heard him without inseparable association with his voice and genius. This eminently beautiful person was followed like an Apollo from church to church, wherever the fame that he would preach led, by all the most cultivated and intelligent youths with grateful admiration. His appearance in any pulpit lighted up all countenances with delight. The smallest anecdote of behavior or conversation was eagerly caught and repeated, and every young scholar could repeat brilliant sentences from his sermons with mimicry, good or bad, of his voice. . . . The church was dismissed, but the bright image of that eloquent form followed the boy home to his bedchamber, and not a sentence was written in a theme, not a declamation attempted in the College Chapel, but showed the omnipresence of his genius to youthful heads. He thus raised the standard of taste in writing and speaking in New England.

Meantime all this was a pure triumph of Rhetoric. This man had neither intellectual nor moral principles to teach. He had no thoughts. It was early asked, when Massachusetts was full of his fame, what truths he had thrown into circulation, and how he had enriched the general mind, and agreed that only in graces of manner, only in a new perception of Grecian beauty, had he opened our eyes. It was early observed that he had no warm personal friends. Yet his genius made every youth his defender and boys filled their mouths with arguments to prove that the orator had a heart. . . .

September, undated

September 27 was a fine day, and Hawthorne and I set forth on a walk. . . .

Our walk had no incidents. It needed none, for we were in excellent spirits, had much conversation, for we were both old collectors who had never had opportunity before to show each other our cabinets, so that we could have filled with matter much longer days.

September, undated

If in this last book of Wordsworth there be dulness, it is yet the dulness of a great and cultivated mind.

September, undated

Perhaps, as we live longer, we begin to compare more narrowly the chances of life with the things to be seen in it, and count the Niagaras we have not visited. For me, not only Niagara, but the Prairie, and the Ohio and the Mississippi rivers are still only names.

October, undated

Le Peau d'Ane. You *can* do two things at a time; and when you have got your pockets full of chestnuts, and say

I have lost my half-hour, behold you have got something besides, for the tops of the Silver Mountains of the White Island loomed up whilst you stood under the tree, and glittered for an instant; therefore there is no *peau de chagrin*. [The title of Balzac's novel.]

October, undated

Life. Everything good, we say, is on the highway. A *virtuoso* hunts up with great pains a landscape of Guercino, a crayon sketch of Salvator, but the Transfiguration, The Last Judgment, The Communion, are on the walls of the Vatican where every footman may see them without price. You have got for five hundred pounds an autograph receipt of Shakspeare; but for nothing a schoolboy can read *Hamlet*, and, if he has eyes, can detect secrets yet unpublished and of highest concernment therein. I think I will never read any but the commonest of all books: the Bible, Shakspeare, Milton, Dante, Homer.

October, undated

The sannup and the squaw do not get drunk at the same time. They take turns in keeping sober, and husband and wife should never be low-spirited at the same time, but each should be able to cheer the other.

October, undated

I told Hawthorne yesterday that I think every young man at some time inclines to make the experiment of a dare-God and dare-devil originality like that of Rabelais. He would jump on the top of the nearest fence and crow. He makes the experiment, but it proves like the flight of

pig-lead into the air, which cannot cope with the poorest
hen. Irresistible custom brings him plump down, and he
finds himself, instead of odes, writing gazettes and leases.
Yet there is imitation and model, or suggestion, to the
very archangels, if we knew their history, and if we knew
Rabelais's reading we should see the rill of the Rabelais
river. Yet his hold of his place in Parnassus is as firm as
Homer's. A jester, but his is the jest of the world, and
not of Touchstone or Clown or Harlequin. His wit is
universal, not accidental, and the anecdotes of the time,
which made the first butt of the satire and which are lost,
are of no importance, as the wit transcends any particular
mark, and pierces to permanent relations and interests.
His joke will fit any town or community of men.

The style at once decides the high quality of the man.
It flows like the river Amazon, so rich, so plentiful, so
transparent, and with such long reaches, that longanimity
or longsightedness which belongs to the Platos. No sand
without lime, no short, chippy, indigent epigrammatist or
proverbialist with docked sentences, but an exhaustless
affluence.

October, undated

This feeling I have respecting Homer and Greek, that
in this great, empty continent of ours, stretching enormous almost from pole to pole, with thousands of long
rivers and thousands of ranges of mountains, the rare
scholar, who, under a farmhouse roof, reads Homer and
the Tragedies, adorns the land. He begins to fill it with
wit, to counterbalance the enormous disproportion of the
unquickened earth. He who first reads Homer in America

is its Cadmus and Numa, and a subtle but unlimited
benefactor.

October, undated

Thou shalt read Homer, Æschylus, Sophocles, Eurip-
ides, Aristophanes, Plato, Proclus, Plotinus, Jamblichus,
Porphyry, Aristotle, Virgil, Plutarch, Apuleius, Chaucer,
Dante, Rabelais, Montaigne, Cervantes, Shakspeare,
Jonson, Ford, Chapman, Beaumont and Fletcher, Bacon,
Marvell, More, Milton, Molière, Swedenborg, Goethe.

October, undated

You shall have joy, or you shall have power, said
God; you shall not have both.

October, undated

Every man writes after a trick, and you need not read
many sentences to learn his whole trick. Richter is a
perpetual exaggeration and I get nervous.

October 26

Boston is not quite a mean place, since in walking
yesterday in the street I met George Bancroft, Horatio
Greenough, Sampson Reed, Sam Ward, Theodore Parker,
George Bradford, and had a little talk with each of them.

October 26

Alcott is a singular person, a natural Levite, a priest
forever after the order of Melchizedek, whom all good
persons would readily combine, one would say, to maintain as a priest by voluntary contribution to live in his

own cottage, literary, spiritual, and choosing his own
methods of teaching and action. But for a founder of a
family or institution, I would as soon exert myself to
collect money for a madman.

October, undated

Henry Thoreau made, last night, the fine remark that,
as long as a man stands in his own way, everything seems
to be in his way, governments, society, and even the sun
and moon and stars, as astrology may testify.

November 11

Do not gloze and prate and mystify. Here is our dear,
grand Alcott says, You shall dig in my field for a day and
I will give you a dollar when it is done, and it shall not be
a business transaction! It makes me sick. Whilst money
is the measure *really* adopted by us all as the most convenient measure of all material values, let us not affectedly
disuse the name, and mystify ourselves and others; let
us not 'say no, and take it.'

November 11

Do not be too timid and squeamish about your actions.
All life is an experiment. The more experiments you
make the better. What if they are a little coarse, and
you may get your coat soiled or torn? What if you do fail,
and get fairly rolled in the dirt once or twice? Up again
you shall never be so afraid of a tumble.

November 11

Last night Henry Thoreau read me verses which
pleased, if not by beauty of particular lines, yet by the

honest truth, and by the length of flight and strength of
wing; for most of our poets are only writers of lines or of
epigrams. These of Henry's at least have rude strength,
and we do not come to the bottom of the mine. Their
fault is, that the gold does not yet flow pure, but is drossy
and crude.

November 11

Time is the little grey man who takes out of his breast-
pocket first a pocketbook, then a Dollond telescope, then
a Turkey carpet, then four saddled and bridled nags and a
sumptuous canvas tent. We are accustomed to chemistry
and it does not surprise us. But chemistry is but a name
for changes and developments as wonderful as those of
this Breast-Pocket.

I was a little chubby boy trundling a hoop in Chauncy
Place, and spouting poetry from Scott and Campbell at
the Latin School. But Time, the little grey man, has taken
out of his vest-pocket a great, awkward house (in a
corner of which I sit down and write of him), some acres
of land, several full-grown and several very young persons, and seated them close beside me; then he has taken
that chubbiness and that hoop quite away (to be sure he
has left the declamation and the poetry), and here left a
long, lean person threatening to be a little grey man, like
himself.

November 11

Religion has failed! Yes, the religion of another man
has failed to save me. But it has saved him. We speak of
the Past with pity and reprobation, but through the

enormities, evils, and temptations of the past, saints and
heroes slipped into heaven. There is no spot in Europe
but has been a battle-field; there is no religion, no church,
no sect, no year of history, but has served men to rise by,
to scale the walls of heaven, and enter into the banquets
of angels. Our fathers are saved. The same, precisely the
same conflicts have always stood as now, with slight
shiftings of scene and costume.

November 19

I begged Alcott to paint out his project, and he proceeded to say that there should be found a farm of a
hundred acres in excellent condition, with good buildings,
a good orchard, and grounds which admitted of being laid
out with great beauty; and this should be purchased and
given to them, in the first place. I replied, You ask too
much. This is not solving the problem; there are hundreds
of innocent young persons, whom, if you will thus stablish
and endow and protect, will find it no hard matter to keep
their innocency. And to see their tranquil household,
after all this has been done for them, will in no wise
instruct or strengthen me. But he will instruct and
strengthen me, who, there where he is, unaided, in the
midst of poverty, toil, and traffic, extricates himself
from the corruptions of the same and builds on his land
a house of peace and benefit, good customs, and free
thoughts. But, replied Alcott, how is this to be done?
How can I do it who have a wife and family to maintain?
I answered that he was not the person to do it, or he
would not ask the question.

November 25

Yesterday I read Dickens's *American Notes*. It answers its end very well, which plainly was to make a readable book, nothing more. Truth is not his object for a single instant, but merely to make good points in a lively sequence, and he proceeds very well. As an account of America it is not to be considered for a moment: it is too short, and too narrow, too superficial, and too ignorant, too slight, and too fabulous, and the man totally unequal to the work. . . . As a picture of American manners nothing can be falser.

November 26

Bancroft and Bryant are historical democrats who are interested in dead or organized, but not in organizing, liberty. Bancroft would not know George Fox, whom he had so well eulogized, if he should meet him in the street. It is like Lyell's science, who did not know by sight, when George B. Emerson showed him them, the shells he has described in his Geology.

November 26

Conservatism stands on this, that a man cannot jump out of his skin; and well for him that he cannot, for his skin is the world; and the stars of heaven do hold him there: in the folly of men glitters the wisdom of God.

November 26

This old Bible, if you pitch it out of the window with a fork, it comes bounce back again.

December, undated

'Full many a glorious morning have I seen.' That is a bold saying. Few men have seen many mornings. This day when I woke I felt the peace of the morning, and knew that I seldom behold it.

December 10

The harvest will be better preserved and go farther, laid up in private bins, in each farmer's corn-barn, and each woman's basket, than if it were kept in national granaries. In like manner, an amount of money will go farther if expended by each man and woman for their own wants, and in the feeling that this is their all, than if expended by a great Steward, or National Commissioners of the Treasury. Take away from me the feeling that I must depend on myself, give me the least hint that I have good friends and backers there in reserve who will gladly help me, and instantly I relax my diligence.

December 10

Elizabeth Hoar affirms that religion bestows a refinement which she misses in the best-bred people not religious, and she considers it essential therefore to the flower of gentleness.

Come dal fuoco il caldo, esser diviso
Non può 'l bel dall' eterno.
MICHEL ANGELO.

December 10

I have no thoughts to-day; What then? What difference does it make? It is only that there does not chance to-day

to be an antagonism to evolve them, the electricity is the
more accumulated; a week hence you shall meet somebody
or something that shall draw from you a shower of sparks.

Baltimore, Barnum's Hotel, January 7, 1843

Here to-day from Philadelphia. The railroad, which
was but a toy coach the other day, is now a dowdy, lumber-
ing country wagon. . . . The Americans take to the little
contrivance as if it were the cradle in which they were
born.

New York, February 7

Dreamlike travelling on the railroad. The towns
through which I pass between Philadelphia and New York
make no distinct impression. They are like pictures on a
wall. The more, that you can read all the way in a car a
French novel.

New York, February 7

Webster. Webster is very dear to the Yankees because
he is a person of very commanding understanding with
every talent for its adequate expression. . . . His external
advantages are very rare and admirable; his noble and
majestic frame, his breadth and projection of brows, his
coal-black hair, his great cinderous eyes, his perfect self-
possession, and the rich and well-modulated thunder of
his voice (to which I used to listen, sometimes, abstract-
ing myself from his sense merely for the luxury of such
noble explosions of sound) distinguish him above all other
men. . . .

The faults that shade his character are not such as to

hurt his popularity. He is very expensive, and always in debt; but this rather commends him, as he is known to be generous. . . . It is sometimes complained of him that he is a man of pleasure, and all his chosen friends are easy epicures and debauchees. But this is after Talleyrand's taste, who said of his foolish wife that he found nonsense very refreshing: so Webster, after he has been pumping his brains in the courts and the Senate, is, no doubt, heartily glad to get among cronies and gossips where he can stretch himself at his ease and drink his mulled wine. They also quote as his *three rules* of living: (1) Never to pay any debt that can by any possibility be avoided; (2) Never to do anything to-day that can be put off till to-morrow; (3) Never to do anything himself which he can get anybody else to do for him.

All is forgiven to a man of such surpassing intellect, and such prodigious powers of business which have so long been exerted. There is no malice in the man, but broad good humor and much enjoyment of the hour; so that Stetson said of him, 'It is true that he sometimes commits crimes, but without any guilt.' . . .

He has misused the opportunity of making himself the darling of the American world in all coming time by abstaining from putting himself at the head of the Anti-slavery interest by standing for New England and for man against the bullying and barbarism of the South.

New York, February 7

Earth Spirit, living, a black river like that swarthy stream which rushes through the human body is thy nature, demoniacal, warm, fruitful, sad, nocturnal.

New York, February 8

Mr. Adams chose wisely and according to his constitution, when, on leaving the Presidency, he went into Congress. He is no literary old gentleman, but a bruiser, and loves the *mêlée*. When they talk about his age and venerableness and nearness to the grave, he knows better, he is like one of those old cardinals, who, as quick as he is chosen Pope, throws away his crutches and his crookedness, and is as straight as a boy.

March, undated

The philosophers at Fruitlands have such an image of virtue before their eyes, that the poetry of man and nature they never see; the poetry that is in man's life, the poorest pastoral clownish life; the light that shines on a man's hat, in a child's spoon, the sparkle on every wave and on every mote of dust, they see not.

March, undated

Montaigne. In Roxbury, in 1825, I read Cotton's translation of Montaigne. It seemed to me as if I had written the book myself in some former life, so sincerely it spoke my thought and experience. No book before or since was ever so much to me as that.

March, undated

It is not in the power of God to make a communication of his will to a Calvinist. For to every inward revelation he holds up his silly book, and quotes chapter and verse against the Book-Maker and Man-Maker, against that which quotes not, but is and cometh. There is a light older than intellect, by which the intellect lives and works, always new, and which degrades every past and particular shining of itself. This light, Calvinism denies, in its idolatry of a certain past shining.

April 10

Daniel Webster is a great man with a small ambition. Nature has built him and holds him forth as a sample of the heroic mould to this puny generation. He was virtual President of the United States from the hour of the Speech on Foot's Resolutions in the United States Senate in 1830, being regarded as the Expounder of the Constitution and the Defender of Law. But this did not suffice; he wished to be an officer, also; wished to add a title to his name, and be a President. That ruined him.

April, undated

I wrote to Thomas Carlyle of his new book, *Past and Present.* . . .

April, undated

I went to Washington and spent four days. The two poles of an enormous political battery, galvanic coil on coil, self-increased by series on series of plates from Mexico to Canada and from the sea westward to the Rocky Mountains, here terminate and play and make the air electric and violent. Yet one feels how little, more than how much, Man is represented there.

May 7

Yesterday, English visitors, and I waited all day when they should go.

If we could establish the rule that each man was a guest in his own house, and when we had shown our visitors the passages of the house, the way to fire, to bread, and water, and thus made them as much at home as the inhabitant, did then leave them to the accidents of intercourse, and went about our ordinary business, a guest would no longer be formidable.

May 10

Brook Farm will show a few noble victims, who act and suffer with temper and proportion, but the larger part will be slight adventurers and will shirk work.

May 18

My garden is an honest place. Every tree and every vine are incapable of concealment, and tell after two or three months exactly what sort of treatment they have had. The sower may mistake and sow his peas crookedly: the peas make no mistake, but come up and show his line.

May 20

All the physicians I have ever seen call themselves believers, but are materialists; they believe only in the existence of matter, and not in matter as an appearance, but as substance, and do not contemplate a cause. Their idea of spirit is a chemical agent.

May 20

I enjoy all the hours of life. Few persons have such susceptibility to pleasure; as a countryman will say, 'I

was at sea a month and never missed a meal,' so I eat my
dinner and sow my turnips, yet do I never, I think,
fear death.   It seems to me so often a relief, a render-
ing-up of responsibility, a quittance of so many vexa-
tious trifles.

May 20

It is greatest to believe and to hope well of the world,
because he who does so, quits the world of experience, and
makes the world he lives in.

May 25

The sky is the daily bread of the eyes. What sculpture
in these hard clouds; what expression of immense amplitude in this dotted and rippled rack, here firm and conti-
nental, there vanishing into plumes and auroral gleams.
No crowding; boundless, cheerful, and strong.

June 10

Hawthorne and I talked of the number of superior
young men we have seen. H. said, that he had seen several
from whom he had expected much, but they had not distinguished themselves; and he had inferred that he must
not expect a popular success from such; he had in nowise
lost his confidence in their power.

June 18

Yesterday at Bunker Hill, a prodigious concourse of
people, but a village green could not be more peaceful,
orderly, sober, and even affectionate. Webster gave us
his plain statement like good bread, yet the oration was

feeble compared with his other efforts, and even seemed poor and Polonius-like with its indigent conservations. When there is no antagonism, as in these holiday speeches, and no religion, things sound not heroically. It is a poor oration that finds Washington for its highest mark. The audience give one much to observe, they are so light-headed and light-timbered, every man thinking more of his inconveniences than of the objects of the occasion, and the hurrahs are so slight and easily procured. Webster is very good America himself.

June 22

Life. Fools and clowns and sots make the fringes of every one's tapestry of life, and give a certain reality to the picture. What could we do in Concord without Bigelow's and Wesson's bar-rooms and their dependencies? What without such fixtures as Uncle Sol, and old Moore who sleeps in Doctor Hurd's barn, and the red charity-house over the brook? Tragedy and comedy always go hand in hand.

July 8

The sun and the evening sky do not look calmer than Alcott and his family at Fruitlands. . . .

I will not prejudge them successful. They look well in July. We will see them in December.

July 16

Montaigne has the *de quoi* which the French cherubs had not, when the courteous Archbishop implored them to sit down. His reading was Plutarch.

August 17

Webster at Concord. Mr. Webster loses nothing by comparison with brilliant men in the legal profession: he is as much before them as before the ordinary lawyer. At least I thought he appeared among these best laywers of the Suffolk Bar, like a schoolmaster among his boys. His wonderful organization, the perfection of his elocution, and all that thereto belongs, — voice, accent, intonation, attitude, manner, — are such as one cannot hope to see again in a century; then he is so thoroughly simple and wise in his rhetoric. Understanding language and the use of the positive degree, all his words tell, and his rhetoric is perfect, so homely, so fit, so strong. Then he manages his matter so well, he hugs his fact so close, and will not let it go, and never indulges in a weak flourish, though he knows perfectly well how to make such exordiums and episodes and perorations as may give perspective to his harangue, without in the least embarrassing his plan or confounding his transitions. . . . And one feels every moment that he goes for the actual world, and never one moment for the ideal. . . .

I looked at him sometimes with the same feeling with which I see one of these strong Paddies on the railroad. Perhaps it was this, perhaps it was a mark of having outlived some of my once finest pleasures, that I found no appetite to return to the Court in the afternoon and hear the conclusion of his argument. The green fields on my way home were too fresh and fair, and forbade me to go again. . . .

Rockwood Hoar said, nothing amused him more than to see Mr. Webster adjourn the Court every day, which

he did by rising, and taking his hat and looking the
Judge coolly in the face; who then bade the Crier adjourn
the Court.

August, undated

Choate and Webster. Rufus Choate is a favorite with the
bar, and a nervous, fluent speaker, with a little too much
fire for the occasion, yet with a certain temperance in his
fury and a perfect self-command; but he uses the superlative degree, and speaks of affairs altogether too rhetori-
cally.

August, undated

Webster behaves admirably well in Society. These
village parties must be dishwater to him, yet he shows
himself just good-natured, just nonchalant *enough*, and
has his own way without offending any one or losing
any ground. He told us that he never read by candle-
light.

August, undated

Webster quite fills our little town, and I doubt if I shall
get settled down to writing until he is well gone from the
county. . . .

Elizabeth Hoar says that she talked with him, as one
likes to go behind the Niagara Falls, so she tried to
look into those famed caverns of eyes, and see how
deep they were, and the whole man was magnificent.
Mr. Choate told her that he should not sleep for a week
when a cause like this was pending, but that when they
met in Boston on Saturday afternoon to talk over the

matter, the rest of them were wide awake, but Mr. Webster went fast asleep amidst the consultation.

It seems to me the Quixotism of Criticism to quarrel with Webster because he has not this or that fine evangelical property. He is no saint, but the wild olive wood, ungrafted yet by grace, but according to his lights a very true and admirable man. His expensiveness seems to be necessary to him. Were he too prudent a Yankee it would be a sad deduction from his magnificence. I only wish he would never truckle; I do not care how much he spends.

August 25

There is nothing in history to parallel the influence of Jesus Christ. The Chinese books say of Wan Wang, one of their kings, 'From the west, from the east, from the south, and from the north there was not one thought not brought in subjection to him.' This can be more truly said of Jesus than of any mortal.

August 25

Henry Thoreau sends me a paper with the old fault of unlimited contradiction. The trick of his rhetoric is soon learned: it consists in substituting for the obvious word and thought its diametrical antagonist. He praises wild mountains and winter forests for their domestic air; snow and ice for their warmth; villagers and wood-choppers for their urbanity, and the wilderness for resembling Rome and Paris. With the constant inclination to dispraise cities and civilization, he yet can find no way to know woods and woodmen except by paralleling them with towns and townsmen. Channing declared the piece is excellent: but it makes me nervous and wretched to read it, with all its merits.

September 3

The capital defect of my nature for society (as it is of so many others) is the want of animal spirits. They seem to me a thing incredible, as if God should raise the dead.

September undated

A visit to the railroad yesterday, in Lincoln, showed me the laborers — how grand they are; all their postures, their air, and their very dress. They are men, manlike employed, and the art of the sculptor is to take these forms and set on them a cultivated face and head. But cultivation never, except in war, makes such forms and carriage as these.

September, undated

Life. A great lack of vital energy; excellent beginners, infirm executors. I should think there were factories above us which stop the water. . . .

September, 26

This morning Charles Lane left us after a two days' visit. He was dressed in linen altogether, with the exception of his shoes, which were lined with linen, and he wore no stockings. He was full of methods of an improved life.

September, undated

Hard clouds, and hard expressions, and hard manners, I love.

September, undated

The only straight line in Nature that I remember is the spider swinging down from a twig.

September, undated

Tennyson is a master of metre, but it is as an artist who has learned admirable mechanical secrets. He has no wood-notes. Great are the dangers of education.

October, undated

Autobiography. My great-grandfather was Rev. Joseph Emerson of Malden, son of Edward Emerson, Esq., of Newbury(port). I used often to hear that when William, son of Joseph, was yet a boy walking before his father to church, on a Sunday, his father checked him: 'William, you walk as if the earth was not good enough for you.' 'I did not know it, Sir,' he replied, with the utmost humility. This is one of the household anecdotes in which I have found a relationship. 'Tis curious, but the same remark was made to me, by Mrs. Lucy Brown, when I walked one day under her windows here in Concord.

October, undated

People came, it seems, to my lectures with expectation that I was to realize the Republic I described, and ceased to come when they found this reality no nearer. They mistook me. I am and always was a painter. I paint still with might and main, and choose the best subjects I can. Many have I seen come and go with false hopes and fears, and dubiously affected by my pictures. But I paint on.

October, undated

Alcott came, the magnificent dreamer, brooding, as ever, on the renewal or reëdification of the social fabric after ideal law, heedless that he had been uniformly rejected by every class to whom he has addressed himself, and just as sanguine and vast as ever. . . . Very pathetic it is to see this wandering Emperor from year to year making his round of visits from house to house of such as do not exclude him, seeking a companion, tired of pupils.

December 31

We rail at trade, but the historian of the world will see that it was the principle of liberty; that it settled America, and destroyed feudalism, and made peace and keeps peace; that it will abolish slavery.

January, 1844, *undated*

Finish each day before you begin the next, and interpose a solid wall of sleep between two. This you cannot do without temperance.

January 30

I wrote to Mr. F. that I had no experiences nor progress to reconcile me to the calamity whose anniversary returned the second time last Saturday. [Waldo's death.] The senses have a right to their method as well as the mind; there should be harmony in facts as well as in truths. Yet these ugly breaks happen there, which the continuity of theory does not contemplate. The amends are of a different kind from the mischief.

February, undated

When I address a large assembly, as last Wednesday, I am always apprised what an opportunity is there: not for reading to them, as I do, lively miscellanies, but for painting in fire my thought, and being agitated to agitate.

February, undated

Skeptic. Pure intellect is the pure devil when you have got off all the masks of Mephistopheles. It is a painful symbol to me that the index or forefinger is always the most soiled of all the fingers.

March 12

On Sunday evening, 10th instant, at the close of the fifteenth year since my ordination as minister in the Second Church, I made an address to the people on the occasion of closing the old house, now a hundred and twenty-three years old, and the oldest church in Boston. Yesterday they began to pull it down.

March, undated

I have always found our American day short. The constitution of a Teutonic scholar with his twelve, thirteen, or fourteen hours a day, is fabulous to me. I become nervous and peaked with a few days editing the *Dial*, and watching the stage-coach to send proofs to printers. If I try to get many hours in a day, I shall not have any.

March, undated

But in America I grieve to miss the strong black blood of the English race: ours is a pale, diluted stream. What

a company of brilliant young persons I have seen with so
much expectation! the sort is very good, but none is good
enough of his sort. Every one an imperfect specimen;
respectable, not valid. Irving thin, and Channing thin,
and Bryant and Dana; Prescott and Bancroft. There is
Webster, but he cannot do what he would; he cannot do
Webster.

March, undated

I wish to have rural strength and religion for my children, and I wish city facility and polish. I find with
chagrin that I cannot have both.

May 8

Our people are slow to learn the wisdom of sending
character instead of talent to Congress. Again and again
they have sent a man of great acuteness, a fine scholar, a
fine forensic orator, and some master of the brawls has
crunched him up in his hand like a bit of paper. At last
they sent a man with a back, and he defied the whole
Southern delegation when they attempted to smother
him, and has conquered them. Mr. Adams is a man of
great powers, but chiefly he is a sincere man and not a
man of the moment and of a single measure. And besides
the success or failure of the measure, there remains to him
the respect of all men for his earnestness.

June 15

Be an opener of doors for such as come after thee, and
do not try to make the universe a blind alley.

October, undated

Wendell Phillips. I wish that Webster and Everett and also the young political aspirants of Massachusetts should hear Wendell Phillips speak, were it only for the capital lesson in eloquence they might learn of him. This, namely, that the first and the second and the third part of the art is, to keep your feet always firm on a fact.

1845–1848

[THE journal for 1845 has many allusions to the Texan question and the allied topic of Slavery. Emerson lectured frequently in this year on Napoleon, a discourse afterward printed in his *Representative Men*, and by the summer he had prepared other lectures in this series.

For January and February, 1846, there are no entries in the journal. Emerson was giving the course on Representative Men in Boston, Providence, and Lowell. He was also arranging for the publication of an American edition of Carlyle's *Cromwell*. The declaration of war with Mexico was made on May 13. Emerson's volume of *Poems* came out at Christmas time, but was dated 1847.

There were few events for Emerson in 1847 until he sailed for Liverpool on October 14. He lectured in Liverpool, Manchester, and London, and in many other cities of England and Scotland, and was entertained most hospitably by Englishmen of all parties and social stations. His experiences, set down in great detail in the journal, later furnished the material for *English Traits*. Early in May, 1848, Emerson went to Paris, in spite of the turmoil incident to the recent revolution. He visited many political clubs and saw some rioting. In June he was back in London, lecturing, and going constantly into fashionable society, then at the height of its season. He sailed home from Liverpool on July 15. Thoreau had lived in Emerson's house during his absence.]

March, [1845] *undated*

Napoleon was entitled to his crowns; he won his victories in his head before he won them on the field. He was not lucky only.

March, *undated*

Alas! our Penetration increases as we grow older, and we are no longer deceived by great words when unrealized and unembodied. Say rather, we detect littleness in expressions and thoughts that once we should have taken and cited as proofs of strength.

March, *undated*

Good manners require a great deal of time, as does a wise treatment of children. Orientals have time, the desert, and stars; the Occidentals have not.

March, *undated*

The State is our neighbors; our neighbors are the State. It is a folly to treat the State as if it were some individual, arbitrarily willing thus and so. It is the same company of poor devils we know so well, of William and Edward and John and Henry, doing as they are obliged to do, and trying hard to do conveniently what must and will be done. They do not impose a tax. God and the nature of things imposes the tax, requires that the land shall bear its burden, of road and of social order, and defence; and I confess I lose all respect for this tedious denouncing of the State by idlers who rot in indolence, selfishness, and envy in the chimney corner.

March, undated

After this generation one would say mysticism should go out of fashion for a long time.

March, undated

Criticism misleads; like Bonaparte's quartermaster, if we listen to him, we shall never stir a step. The part you have to take, none but you must know. The critic can never tell you.

March, undated

The annexation of Texas looks like one of those events which retard or retrograde the civilization of ages. But the World Spirit is a good swimmer, and storms and waves cannot easily drown him. He snaps his finger at laws.

March, undated

The only use which the country people can imagine of a scholar, the only compliment they can think of to pay him, is, to ask him to deliver a Temperance Lecture, or to be a member of the School Committee.

A few foolish and cunning managers ride the conscience of this great country with their Texas, or Tariff, or Democracy, or other mumbo-jumbo, and all give in and are verily persuaded that that is great, — all else is trifling. And why? Because there is really no great life, and one demonstration in all the broad land of that which is the heart and the soul of every rational American man; — the mountains walking, the light incarnated, reason and virtue clothed in flesh, — he does not see.

March, undated

Does the same skepticism exist at all times which prevails at present in regard to the powers of performance of the actual population? Edmund Hosmer thinks the women have degenerated in strength. He can find no matron for the else possible community. The men think the men are less, a puny race. And George Minot thinks the cows are smaller.

March, undated

Poetry must be as new as foam, and as old as the rock.

March, undated

The puny race of Scholars in this country have no counsel to give, and are not felt. Every wretched partisan, every village brawler, every man with talents for contention, every clamorous place-hunter makes known what he calls his opinion, all over the country, that is, as loud as he can scream. Really, no opinions are given; only the wishes of each side are expressed, of the spoils party, that is, and of the malcontents. But the voice of the intelligent and the honest, of the unconnected and independent, the voice of truth and equity, is suppressed. In England, it is not so. You can always find in their journals and newspapers a better and a best sense, as well as the low, coarse party cries.

March, undated

What argument, what eloquence can avail against the power of that one word *niggers?* The man of the world annihilates the whole combined force of all the anti-slavery societies of the world by pronouncing it.

May, undated

Life is a game between God and man. The one disparts himself and feigns to divide into individuals. He puts part in a pomegranate, part in a king's crown, part in a person. Instantly man sees the beautiful things and goes to procure them. As he takes down each one the Lord smiles and says, It is yourself; and when he has them all, it will be *yourself*. We live and die for a beauty which we wronged ourselves in thinking alien.

May, undated

Our virtue runs in a narrow rill: we have never a freshet. We ought to be subject to enthusiasms. One would like to see Boston and Massachusetts agitated like a wave with some generosity, mad for learning, for music, for philosophy, for association, for freedom, for art; but now it goes like a pedlar with its hand ever on its pocket, cautious, calculating.

May, undated

There is not the slightest probability that the college will foster an eminent talent in any youth. If he refuse prayers and recitations, they will torment and traduce and expel him, though he were Newton or Dante.

May, undated

I avoid the Stygian anniversaries at Cambridge, those hurrahs among the ghosts, those yellow, bald, toothless meetings in memory of red cheeks, black hair, and departed health.

June, undated

One who wishes to refresh himself by contact with the bone and sinew of society must avoid what is called the respectable portion of his city or neighborhood with as much care as in Europe a good traveller avoids American and English people.

June, undated

Even for those whom I really love I have not animal spirits.

August 19

We are the children of many sires, and every drop of blood in us in its turn betrays its ancestor. We are of the party of war and of the peace party alternately; to both very sincerely.

August 25

I heard last night with some sensibility that the question of slavery has never been presented to the South with a kind and thoroughly scientific treatment, as a question of pure political economy in the largest sense.

August, undated

B. A. [Alcott] told me that when he saw Cruikshank's drawings, he thought him a fancy caricaturist, but when he went to London he saw that he drew from nature, without any exaggeration.

September, undated

Garrison is a virile speaker; he lacks the feminine element which we find in men of genius.

October 27

As for King Swedenborg, I object to his cardinal position in morals that evils should be shunned as sins. I hate preaching. I shun evils as evils. Does he not know — Charles Lamb did — that every poetic mind is a pagan, and to this day prefers Olympian Jove, Apollo and the Muses and the Fates, to all the barbarous indigestion of Calvin and the Middle Ages?

November, undated

Far the best part, I repeat, of every mind is not that which he knows, but that which hovers in gleams, suggestions, tantalizing, unpossessed, before him. His firm recorded knowledge soon loses all interest for him. But this dancing chorus of thoughts and hopes is the quarry of his future, is his possibility, and teaches him that his man's life is of a ridiculous brevity and meanness, but that it is his first age and trial only of his young wings, but that vast revolutions, migrations, and gyres on gyres in the celestial societies invite him.

March 24, 1846

God builds his temple in the heart on the ruins of churches and religions.

March 24

The fault of Alcott's community is that it has only room for one.

March, undated

What a discovery I made one day, that the more I spent the more I grew, that it was as easy to occupy a

large place and do much work as an obscure place to do
little; and that in the winter in which I communicated
all my results to classes, I was full of new thoughts.

March, undated

I like man, but not men.

May 1

I was at Cambridge yesterday to see Everett inaugu-
rated. His political brothers came as if to bring him to
the convent door, and to grace with a sort of bitter courtesy his taking of the cowl. . . . Well, this Webster must
needs come into the house just at the moment when Everett was rising to make his Inaugural Speech. Of course,
the whole genial current of feeling flowing towards him
was arrested, and the old Titanic Earth-Son was alone
seen. The house shook with new and prolonged applause,
and Everett sat down, to give free course to the sentiment. He saved himself by immediately saying, 'I wish
it were in my power to use the authority vested in me
and to say, " *Expectatur oratio in lingua vernacula*," from
my illustrious friend who has just taken his seat.'

Everett's grace and propriety were admirable through
the day. Nature finished this man. He seems beautifully
built, perfectly sound and whole; and eye, voice, hand
exactly obey his thought. His quotations are a little
trite, but saved by the beautiful modulation and falls
of the recitation.

The satisfaction of men in this appointment is complete. Boston is contented because he is so creditable,
safe, and prudent, and the scholars because he is a

scholar, and understands the business. Old Quincy,
with all his worth and a sort of violent service he did
the College, was a lubber and a grenadier among our
clerks.

Quincy made an excellent speech, so stupid good, now
running his head against a post, now making a capital
point; he has mother wit, and great fund of honour and
faithful serving, and the faults of his speech increased my
respect for his character. . . .

The close of Everett's Inaugural Discourse was chilling
and melancholy. With a coolness indicating absolute
skepticism and despair, he deliberately gave himself over
to the corpse-cold Unitarianism and Immortality of
Brattle Street and Boston.

May, undated

When summer opens, I see how fast it matures, and
fear it will be short; but after the heats of July and
August, I am reconciled, like one who has had his swing,
to the cool of autumn. So will it be with the coming of
death.

May, undated

Alcott and Edward Taylor resemble each other in the
incredibility of their statement of facts. One is the fool of
his idea, the other of his fancy. When Alcott wrote from
England that he was bringing home Wright and Lane, I
wrote him a letter, which I required him to show them,
saying, that they might safely trust his theories, but that
they should put no trust whatever in his statement of
facts. When they all arrived here, — he and his victims,

— I asked them if he showed them that letter; they answered that he did: so I was clear.

May, undated

America. John Randolph is somebody: and Andrew
Jackson; and John Quincy Adams, and Daniel Webster.

May, undated

Criticism. The next generation will thank Dickens for
showing so many mischiefs which parliaments and Chris-
tianities had not been strong enough to remove. *Punch,*
too, has done great service.

May, undated

Hawthorne invites his readers too much into his study,
opens the process before them. As if the confectioner
should say to his customers, 'Now, let us make the cake.'

May, undated

If I were a member of the Massachusetts legislature, I
should propose to exempt all colored citizens from taxa-
tion because of the inability of the government to protect
them by passport out of its territory. It does not give the
value for which they pay the tax.

May 23

Boston or Brattle Street Christianity is a compound of
force, or the best Diagonal line that can be drawn between Jesus Christ and Abbott Lawrence.

May 23

Cotton thread holds the Union together; unites John
C. Calhoun and Abbott Lawrence. Patriotism for holi-

days and summer evenings, with music and rockets, but cotton thread is the Union.

June, undated

Is not America more than ever wanting in the male principle? A good many village attorneys we have, saucy village talents, preferred to Congress, and the Cabinet, — Marcys, Buchanans, Walkers, etc., — but no great Captains. Webster is a man by himself of the great mould, but he also underlies the American blight, and wants the power of the initiative, the affirmative talent, and remains, like the literary class, only a commentator, his great proportions only exposing his defect. America seems to have immense resources, land, men, milk, butter, cheese, timber, and iron, but it is a village littleness; — village squabble and rapacity characterize its policy. It is a great strength on a basis of weakness.

June, undated

These — rabble — at Washington are really better than the snivelling opposition. They have a sort of genius of a bold and manly cast, though Satanic. They see, against the unanimous expression of the people, how much a little well-directed effrontery can achieve, how much crime the people will bear, and they proceed from step to step, and it seems they have calculated but too justly upon your Excellency, O Governor Briggs. Mr. Webster told them how much the war cost, that was his protest, but voted the war, and sends his son to it. They calculated rightly on Mr. Webster. My friend Mr. Thoreau has gone to jail rather than pay his tax. On him they could not calculate. The Abolitionists denounce the war and give much time to it, but they pay the tax.

January 10, 1847

Machiavelli. I have tried to read Machiavelli's histories, but find it not easy. The Florentine factions are as tiresome as the history of the Philadelphia fire-companies.

February, undated

What is the oldest thing? A dimple or whirlpool in water. That is Genesis, Exodus, and all.

February, undated

Health, South wind, books, old trees, a boat, a friend.

April, undated

Here am I with so much all ready to be revealed to me, as to others, if only I could be set aglow. I have wished for a professorship. Much as I hate the church, I have wished the pulpit that I might have the stimulus of a stated task. N. P. Rogers spoke more truly than he knew, perchance, when he recommended an Abolition Campaign to me. I doubt not, a course of mobs would do me much good. . . .

I think I have material enough to serve my countrymen with thought and music, if only it was not scraps. But men do not want handfuls of gold-dust, but ingots.

April, undated

We live in Lilliput. The Americans are free-willers, fussy, self-asserting, buzzing all round creation. But the

Asiatics believe it is writ on the iron leaf, and will not turn on their heel to save them from famine, plague, or sword. That is great, gives a great air to the people.

April, undated

Scholar, Centrality. 'Your reading is irrelevant.' Yes, for you, but not for me. It makes no difference what I read. If it is irrelevant, I read it deeper. I read it until it is pertinent to me and mine, to Nature, and to the hour that now passes. A good scholar will find Aristophanes and Hafiz and Rabelais full of American history.

April, undated

I believe in Omnipresence and find footsteps in grammar rules, in oyster shops, in church liturgies, in mathematics, and in solitudes and in galaxies. I am shamed out of my declamations against churches by the wonderful beauty of the English liturgy, an anthology of the piety of ages and nations.

April, undated

What you have learned and done is safe and fruitful. Work and learn in evil days, in insulted days, in days of debt and depression and calamity. Fight best in the shade of the cloud of arrows.

May 5

Transcendentalism says, the Man is all. The world can be reeled off any stick indifferently. Franklin says, the tools: riches, old age, land, health; the tools. . . . A master *and* tools, — is the lesson I read in every shop and farm and library. There must be both. . . .

May 24

The days come and go like muffled and veiled figures
sent from a distant friendly party, but they say nothing,
and if we do not use the gifts they bring, they carry them
as silently away. [Compare the poem 'Days.']

June, undated

Alas for America, as I must so often say, the ungirt, the
diffuse, the profuse, procumbent, — one wide ground
juniper, out of which no cedar, no oak will rear up a mast
to the clouds! It all runs to leaves, to suckers, to tendrils,
to miscellany. The air is loaded with poppy, with imbecility, with dispersion and sloth.

Eager, solicitous, hungry, rabid, busy-bodied America
attempting many things, vain, ambitious to feel thy own
existence, and convince others of thy talent, by attempting and hastily accomplishing much; yes, catch thy
breath and correct thyself, and failing here, prosper out
there; speed and fever are never greatness; but reliance
and serenity and waiting.

America is formless, has no terrible and no beautiful
condensation.

June, undated

Criticism should not be querulous and wasting, all
knife and root-puller, but guiding, instructive, inspiring, a
south wind, not an east wind.

June 27

Irresistibility of the American; no conscience; his
motto, like Nature's, is, 'Our country, right or wrong.'

He builds shingle palaces and shingle cities; yes, but in
any altered mood, perhaps this afternoon, he will build
stone ones, with equal celerity; tall, restless Kentucky
strength; great race, but though an admirable fruit, you
shall not find one good, sound, well-developed apple on
the tree. Nature herself was in a hurry with these hasters
and never finished one.

July 10

Goethe in this third volume Autobiography, which I
read now in new translation, seems to know altogether
too much about himself.

August, undated

The Superstitions of our Age:
The fear of Catholicism;
The fear of pauperism;
The fear of immigration;
The fear of manufacturing interests;
The fear of radicalism or democracy;
And faith in the steam engine.

August, undated

Life consists in what a man is thinking of all day.

London, October, undated

I found at Liverpool, after a couple of days, a letter
which had been seeking me, from Carlyle, addressed to
'R. W. E. on the instant when he lands in England,' con-
veying the heartiest welcome and urgent invitation to
house and hearth. And finding that I should not be

wanted for a week in the lecture rooms, I came down to
London, on Monday, and at ten at night the door was
opened to me by Jane Carlyle, and the man himself was
behind her with a lamp in the hall. They were very little
changed from their old selves of fourteen years ago (in
August) when I left them at Craigenputtock. 'Well,'
said Carlyle, 'here we are, shovelled together again!'
The floodgates of his talk are quickly opened, and the
river is a plentiful stream. We had a wide talk that night
until nearly one o'clock, and at breakfast next morning
again. At noon or later we walked forth to Hyde Park,
and the palaces, about two miles from here, to the National Gallery, and to the Strand, Carlyle melting all
Westminster and London into his talk and laughter, as he
goes. Here in his house, we breakfast about nine, and
Carlyle is very prone, his wife says, to sleep till ten or
eleven, if he has no company. An immense talker, and,
altogether, as extraordinary in that as in his writing; I
think even more so. You will never discover his real
vigor and range, or how much more he might do than he
has ever done, without seeing him. My few hours' discourse with him, long ago, in Scotland, gave me not
enough knowledge of him; and I have now, at last, been
taken by surprise by him.

He is not mainly a scholar, like the most of my acquaintances, but a very practical Scotchman, such as
you would find in any saddler's or iron-dealer's shop, and
then only accidentally and by a surprising addition the
admirable scholar and writer he is. . . .

Carlyle and his wife live on beautiful terms. Their ways
are very engaging, and in her bookcase all his books are

inscribed to her, as they come from year to year, each
with some significant lines. . . .

I had a good talk with Carlyle last night. He says over
and over, for months, for years, the same thing, yet his
guiding genius is his moral sense, his perception of the sole
importance of truth and justice; and he, too, says that
there is properly no religion in England.

Birmingham, December 24

No dissenter rides in his coach for three generations; he
infallibly falls into the Establishment.

Edinburgh, February 13 [1848]

Thomas De Quincey. At Edinburgh, I dined at Mrs.
Crowe's with De Quincey, David Scott, and Dr. Brown.
De Quincey is a small old man of seventy years, with a
very handsome face, — a face marked by great refinement, — a very gentle old man, speaking with the utmost deliberation and softness, and so refined in speech
and manners as to make quite indifferent his extremely
plain and poor dress. For the old man, summoned by
message on Saturday by Mrs. Crowe to this dinner, had
walked on this rainy, muddy Sunday ten miles from his
house at Lasswade and was not yet dry, and though Mrs.
Crowe's hospitality is comprehensive and minute, yet she
had no pantaloons in her house. He was so simply drest,
that ten miles could not spoil him. It seemed, too, that
he had lately *walked home*, at night, in the rain, from one
of Mrs. Crowe's dinners. 'But why did you not ride?'
said Mrs. C.; 'you were in time for the coach.' Because,
he could not find money to ride; he had met two street

girls; one of them took his eight shillings out of his waist-
coat pocket, and the other his umbrella. He told this sad
story with the utmost simplicity, as if he had been a
child of seven, instead of seventy.

London, March, undated

Since the new French Revolution, Carlyle has taken in
the *Times* newspaper, the first time he has ever had a
daily paper.

If such a person as Cromwell should come now it
would be of no use; he could not get the ear of the House
of Commons. You might as well go into Chelsea graveyard yonder, and say, *Shoulder Arms!* and expect the old
dead church-wardens to arise.

It is droll to hear this talker talking against talkers,
and this writer writing against writing.

London, March, undated

Stand at the door of the House of Commons, and see
the members go in and out, and you will say these men
are all men of humanity, of good sense.

London, March, undated

They told me, that now, since February, Paris was not
Paris, nor France France, everything was *triste* and grim.
All the members of the Provincial Government had be-
come aged since February, except only Arago.

London, March, undated

At Lady Harriet Baring's dinner, Carlyle and Milnes
introduced me to Charles Buller, 'reckoned,' they said

aloud, 'the cleverest man in England' — 'until,' added
Milnes, — 'until he meddled with affairs.' For Buller
was now Poor-Laws Commissioner, and had really post-
poned hitherto to make good the extraordinary expectation which his speeches in Parliament had created.

London, March, undated

Englishwomen wear their grey hair. In the rain, they
tuck up their gown about the waist and expose their
skirt.

London, March 9

I attended a Chartist meeting in National Hall, Hol-
born. It was called to hear the report of the Deputation
who had returned after carrying congratulations to the
French Republic. The *Marseillaise* was sung by a party
of men and women on the platform, and chorused by the
whole assembly: then the *Girondins*. The leaders appeared to be grave men, intent on keeping a character for
order and moral tone in their proceedings, but the great
body of the meeting liked best the sentiment, 'Every
man a ballot and every man a musket.' Much was whispered of the soldiers, — that 'they would catch it,' i. e.,
the contagion of Chartism and rebellion.

London, March 14

It is a proof of the abundance of literary talent here that
no one knows, or, I think, asks the name of the writers of
paragraphs and articles of great ability. It seems strange
that literary power sufficient to get up twenty such reputations as Quinet or Michelet, and a hundred Prescotts or

Sparkses, is here wasted in some short-lived paper in the *Christian Remembrancer* or the *Foreign Quarterly*, or even in a few leaders in the *Times* newspaper.

London, March 14

Englishman talks of politics and institutions, but the real thing which he values is his home, and that which belongs to it, — that general culture and high polish which in his experience no man but the Englishman possesses, and which he naturally believes have some essential connection with his throne and laws. That is what he does not believe resides in America, and therefore his contempt of America only half concealed. This English tenacity in strong contrast with our facility. The facile American sheds his Puritanism when he leaves Cape Cod, runs into all English and French vices with great zest, and is neither Unitarian, nor Calvinist, nor Catholic, nor stands for any known thought or thing; which is very distasteful to English honour. It is a bad sign that I have met with many Americans who flattered themselves that they pass for English. Levity, levity. I do not wish to be mistaken for an Englishman, more than I wish Monadnock or Nahant or Nantucket to be mistaken for Wales or the Isle of Wight.

London, March, undated

Dined at Lord Ashburton's, at Lady Harriet Baring's, attended Lady Palmerston's *soirée;* saw fine people at Lady Morgan's and at Lady Molesworth's, Lord Lovelace's, and other houses. But a very little is enough for me, and I find that all the old deoxygenation and asphyxia that have in town or in village existed for me in that word 'a party,' exist unchanged in London palaces. Of course the fault is wholly mine, but I shall at least know how to save a great deal of time and temper henceforward.

London, March, undated

When I find in people narrow religion, I find narrow reading.

London [*last week in March*]

Richard Owen. Mr. Richard Owen was kind enough to give me a card to his Course of Lectures before the Royal College of Surgeons, and I heard as many of the lectures as I could. He is an excellent lecturer. His vinous face is a powerful weapon. He has a surgical smile, and an air of virility, that penetrates his audience, a perfect self-command and temperance, master of his wide nomenclature, and stepping securely from stone to stone.

Oxford, March 31

At Oxford, in the Bodleian Library Dr. Bandinel showed me the manuscript Plato of the date of A.D. 896, brought by Dr. Clarke from Egypt. . . .

London, April, undated

If I should believe the Reviews, and I am always of their opinion, I have never written anything good. And yet, against all criticism, the books survive until this day.

London, April, undated

People here expect a revolution. There will be no revolution, none that deserves to be called so. There may be a scramble for money. But as all the people we see want the things we now have, and not better things, it is very certain that they will, under whatever change of forms, keep the old system. When I see changed men, I shall look for a changed world. Whoever is skilful in heaping money now will be skilful in heaping money again.

London, April, undated

It is certain that more people speak English correctly in the United States than in Britain.

London, April 19

Sydney Smith said of Whewell, that Science was his forte and Omniscience was his foible.

London, April 19

Happy is he who looks only into his work to know if it will succeed, never into the times or the public opinion; and who writes from the love of imparting certain thoughts and not from the necessity of sale — who writes always to *the unknown friend.*

London, [May 6?]

I saw Tennyson, first, at the house of Coventry Patmore, where we dined together. His friend Brookfield was also of the party. I was contented with him, at once. He is tall, scholastic-looking, no dandy, but a great deal

of plain strength about him, and though cultivated, quite
unaffected; quiet, sluggish sense and strength, refined, as
all English are, and good-humoured. The print of his
head in Horne's book is too rounded and handsome.
There is in him an air of general superiority, that is very
satisfactory. He lives very much with his college set, —
Spedding, Brookfield, Hallam, Rice, and the rest, — and
has the air of one who is accustomed to be petted and indulged by those he lives with, like George Bradford.
Take away Hawthorne's bashfulness, and let him talk
easily and fast, and you would have a pretty good
Tennyson. . . .

Tennyson talked of Carlyle, and said, 'If Carlyle
thinks the Christian religion has lost all vitality, he is
wholly mistaken.' Tennyson and all Carlyle's friends feel
the caprice and incongruity of his opinions. . . .

After dinner, Brookfield insisted that we should go to
his house, so we stopped an omnibus, and, not finding
room inside for all three, Tennyson rode on the box, and
B. and I within. Brookfield, knowing that I was going to
France, told me that, if I wanted him, Tennyson would
go. 'That is the way we do with him,' he said. 'We tell
him he must go and he goes. But you will find him heavy
to carry.' At Brookfield's house we found young Hallam,
with Mrs. Brookfield, a very pleasing woman. I told
Tennyson that I heard from his friends very good accounts of him, and I and they were persuaded that it was
important to his health, an instant visit to Paris; and
that I was to go on Monday, if he was ready. He was
very good-humoured, and affected to think that I should
never come back alive from France, it was death to go.

But he had been looking for two years for somebody to go
to Italy with, and was ready to set out at once, if I would
go there. I was tempted, of course, to pronounce for
Italy; but now I had agreed to give my course in London.
He gave me a cordial invitation to his lodgings (in Buck-
ingham Place), where I promised to visit him before I
went away.

On [the next day?] I found him at home in his lodgings,
but with him was a Church clergyman, whose name I did
not know, and there was no conversation. He was sure,
again, that he was taking a final farewell of me, as I was
going among the French bullets, but promised to be in
the same lodgings, if I should escape alive after my three
weeks in Paris. So we parted. I spent a month in Paris,
and, when I returned, he had left London. . . .

Tennyson was in plain black suit and wears glasses.
Carlyle thinks him the best man in England to smoke a
pipe with, and used to see him much; had a place in his
little garden, on the wall, where Tennyson's pipe was
laid up.

Paris, May 6

In Paris, my furnished lodgings, a very comfortable
suite of rooms (15 *Rue des petits Augustins*) on the second
floor, cost me ninety francs a month, or three francs a
day. . . . The expenses of living for a day, at my rate, are
six francs fifteen sous, or seven francs. . . .

I looked in all the shop windows for toys this afternoon
and they are very many and gay, but the only one of all
which I really wish to buy is very cheap; yet I cannot
buy it, namely, their speech.

Paris, May 6

The boulevards have lost their fine trees, which were all cut down for barricades in February. At the end of a year we shall take account, and see if the Revolution was worth the trees.

Paris, May, undated

I went to hear Michelet lecture on philosophy, but the sublime creed of the Indian Buddhists was not meant for a Frenchman to analyze and crack his joke and make his grimace upon. But I came out hither to see my contemporaries, and I have seen Leverrier to-day working out algebraic formulas on his blackboard to his class, quite heedless of politics and revolutions. I have seen Rachel in *Phèdre* and heard her chant the *Marseillaise*. I have seen Barbès rule in his *Club de la Révolution*, and Blanqui in his *Club des droits de l'homme*, and to-day they are both in the dungeon of Vincennes.

Paris, May, undated

I have been exaggerating the English merits all winter, and disparaging the French. Now I am correcting my judgment of both, and the French have risen very fast.

Paris, May, undated

I have seen Rachel in *Phèdre*, in *Mithridate*, and now last night in *Lucrèce* (of Ponsard), in which play she took two parts, that of Lucrèce and that of Tullia. The best part of her performance is the terror and energy she can throw into passages of defiance or denunciation. Her manners and carriage are throughout pleasing by their highly intellectual cast. And her expression of the character is not lost by your losing some word or look, but is continuous and is sure to be conveyed. She is extremely youthful and innocent in her appearance, and when she appeared after the curtain fell to acknowledge the acclamations of the house and the heaps of flowers that were flung to her, her smile had a perfect good nature and a kind of universal intelligence.

London, June, undated

In England every man you meet is some man's son; in America, he may be some man's father.

London, June 27

By the kind offices of Mr. Milnes, Mr. Milman, Lord Morpeth, and I know not what other gentlemen, I found myself elected into the 'Athenæum' Club, 'during my temporary residence in England'; a privilege one must prize, not because only ten foreigners are eligible, at any one time, but because it gives all the rights of a member in the library and reading-room, a home to sit in, and see the best company, and a coffee-room, if you like it, where you eat at cost. Milnes, Milman, Crabbe Robinson, and many good men are always to be found there. Milnes is the most good-natured man in England, made of sugar; he is everywhere, and knows everything; has the largest range of acquaintances, from the Chartist to the Lord Chancellor; fat, easy, affable, and obliging; a little careless and sloven in his dress. His speeches in Parliament are always unlucky, and a signal for emptying the House, — a topic of great mirth to himself and all his friends, who frankly twit him with it. He is so entirely at home everywhere, and takes life so quietly, that Sydney Smith called him 'the cool of the evening.' . . .

For my part, I found him uniformly kind and useful to me both in London and in Paris. He procured me cards to Lady Palmerston's *soirée*, introduced me there, and took pains to show me all the remarkable persons there, the Crown Prince of Prussia; the Prince of Syracuse; Rothschild, a round, young, comfortable-looking man; Mr. Hope, reputed the richest commoner in England; the Turkish Ambassador; Lord Lincoln, head of the 'Young England' party; and princely foreigners, whose names I have forgotten.

Milnes took pains to make me acquainted with Chevalier Bunsen and Lady Bunsen, whom I had already met at Mr. Bancroft's; with young Mr. Cowper, son of Lady Palmerston; with Disraeli; and with Macaulay, whom I here met for the second time. I had a few words with both Lord and Lady Palmerston. He is frank (at least, in manner; — Bancroft says, far from frank in business), affable, of a strong but cheerful and ringing speech.

But I soon had enough of this fine spectacle and escaped. Milnes sent me again another card from Lady Palmerston, but I did not go.

London, June, undated

People eat the same dinner at every house in England. 1, soup; 2, fish; 3, beef, mutton, or hare; 4, birds; 5, pudding and pastry and jellies; 6, cheese; 7, grapes, nuts, and wine. During dinner, hock and champagne are offered you by the servant, and sherry stands at the corners of the table. Healths are not much drunk in fashionable houses. After the cloth is removed, three bottles, namely, port, sherry, and claret, invariably circulate. What rivers of wine are drunk in all England daily! One would say, every guest drinks six glasses.

London, June, undated

I stayed in London till I had become acquainted with all the styles of face in the street, and till I had found the suburbs and then straggling houses on each end of the city. Then I took a cab, left my farewell cards, and came home.

I saw Alison, Thackeray, Cobden, Tennyson, Bailey, Marston, Macaulay, Hallam, Disraeli, Milnes, Wilson, Jeffrey, Wordsworth, Carlyle, Dickens, Lockhart, Procter, Montgomery, Collyer, Kenyon, Stephenson, Buckland, Sedgwick, Lyell, Edward Forbes, Richard Owen, Robert Owen, Cruikshank, Jenny Lind, Grisi, William Allingham, David Scott, William B. Scott, Kinglake, De Tocqueville, Lamartine, Leverrier, Rachel, Barbès, Eastlake, Spence, Wilkinson, Duke of Wellington, Brougham, Joanna Baillie, De Quincey, Sir C. Fellows, Sir Henry De la Bèche, John Forster.

At Sea, July 19 (?)

The road from Liverpool to New York is long, crooked, rough, rainy, and windy. Even good company will hardly make it agreeable. Four meals a day is the usual expedient, four and five (and the extreme remedy shows the exasperation of the case), and much wine and porter

are the amusements of wise men in this sad place. Never
was a well-appointed dinner with all scientific belongings
so philosophic a thing as at sea. Even the restless American finds himself, at last, at leisure.

At Sea, July 23

The English habit of betting makes them much more
accurate than we are in their knowledge of particulars. —
'Which is the longest river, the Mississippi or the
Missouri?' — They are about the same length. —
'About! that won't do, — I've a bet upon it.'

August, undated

Henry Thoreau is like the wood-god who solicits the
wandering poet and draws him into antres vast and
desarts idle, and bereaves him of his memory, and leaves
him naked, plaiting vines and with twigs in his hand. . . .

I spoke of friendship, but my friends and I are fishes in
our habit. As for taking Thoreau's arm, I should as soon
take the arm of an elm tree.

August, undated

I observe that all the bookish men have a tendency to
believe that they are unpopular. Parker gravely informs
me by word and by letter that he is precisely the most unpopular of all men in New England. Alcott believed the
same thing of himself, and I, no doubt, if they had not
anticipated me in claiming this distinction, should have
claimed it for myself.

September **10**

George Sand is a great genius, and yet owes to her birth in France her entire freedom from the cant and snuffle of our dead Christianity.

[*Last days of September.*]

I go twice a week over Concord with Ellery, and, as we sit on the steep park at Conantum, we still have the same regret as oft before. Is all this beauty to perish? Shall none remake this sun and wind, the sky-blue river, the river-blue sky; the yellow meadow spotted with sacks and sheets of cranberry-pickers; the red bushes; the iron-gray house with just the color of the granite rock; the paths of the thicket, in which the only engineers are the cattle grazing on yonder hill; the wide, straggling wild orchard in which Nature has deposited every possible flavor in the apples of different trees? Whole zones and climates she has concentrated into apples. We think of the old bene-factors who have conquered these fields; of the old man Moore, who is just dying in these days, who has absorbed such volumes of sunshine like a huge melon or pumpkin in the sun, — who has owned in every part of Concord a woodlot, until he could not find the boundaries of these, and never saw their interiors. But we say, where is he who is to save the present moment, and cause that this beauty be not lost? Shakspeare saw no better heaven or earth, but had the power and need to sing, and seized the dull ugly England, ugly to this, and made it amicable and enviable to all reading men, and now we are fooled into likening this to that; whilst, if one of us had the chanting constitution, that land would no more be heard of.

October, undated

The salvation of America and of the human race depends on the next election, if we believe the newspapers. But so it was last year, and so it was the year before, and our fathers believed the same thing forty years ago.

October, undated

Every poem must be made up of lines that are poems.

October, undated

Alcott is a man of unquestionable genius, yet no doctrine or sentence or word or action of his which is excellent can be detached and quoted.

He is like [Ellery] Channing, who possesses a painter's eye, an appreciation of form and especially of color, that is admirable, but who, when he bought pigments and brushes and painted a landscape on a barrel head could not draw a tree so that his wife could know it was a tree. So Alcott the philosopher has not an opinion or an apothegm to produce.

I shall write on his tomb, *Here lies Plato's reader.* Read he can with joy and *naïveté* inimitable, and the more the style rises, the more natural and current it seems to him. And yet his appetite is so various that the last book always seems to him the best. *Here lies the Amateur.*

October, undated

American Literature. We have not had since ten years a pamphlet which I have saved to bind! and here at last is Bushnell's; and now, Henry Thoreau's *Ascent of Katahdin.*

October, undated

Love is necessary to the righting the estate of woman in this world. Otherwise nature itself seems to be in conspiracy against her dignity and welfare; for the cultivated, high-thoughted, beauty-loving, saintly woman finds herself unconsciously desired for her sex, and even enhancing the appetite of her savage pursuers by these fine ornaments she has piously laid on herself. She finds with indignation that she is herself a snare, and was made such. I do not wonder at her occasional protest, violent protest against nature, in fleeing to nunneries, and taking black veils. Love rights all this deep wrong.

October, undated

I find out in an instant if my companion does not want me; I cannot comprehend how my visitor does not perceive that I do not want him. It is his business to find out that I, of course, must be civil. It is for him to offer to go.

November, undated

My friends begin to value each other, now that Alcott is to go; and Ellery declares, 'that he never saw that man without being cheered,' and Henry says, 'He is the best natured man I ever met. The rats and mice make their nests in him.'

December 10

T. W. Higginson at Newburyport urged the establishment of such a journal as the *Dial* for the comfort and encouragement of young men, who, but for that paper, had felt themselves lonely and unsupported in the world.

December 22

Tests. Have you given any words to be the current coin of the country? Carlyle has.

What all men think, he thinks better.

Carlyle is thought a bad writer. Is he? Wherever you find good writing in Dorian or Rabelaisian, or Norse Sagas, or English Bible, or Cromwell himself, 'tis odd, you find resemblance to his style.

1849–1855

[MUCH refreshed by his European tour, Emerson began the year 1849 with the usual lecturing. This was the year of the 'gold rush' to California. Emerson reprinted in September his essay on *Nature* together with other *Addresses* and *Lectures*, in a single volume.

On January 1, 1850, appeared his *Representative Men*. In June he made the first of many long journeys to the West, visiting the Mammoth Cave in Kentucky, journeying down the Ohio and up the Mississippi to St. Louis, crossing Illinois by stage and Michigan by the new railroads, and returning home by way of Niagara Falls. His friend Margaret Fuller Ossoli perished by shipwreck on Fire Island on July 19. This was the year of *The Scarlet Letter* and of *In Memoriam*.

The Fugitive Slave Law occasioned many entries in the journal for 1851, and Emerson's sorrow and anger at Webster were intense. Everett and Choate are condemned with equal scorn.

Emerson's subject for his Boston lectures in the winter of 1851–1852 was the 'Conduct of Life,' later to be made the title of a book. He visited Canada in April. This was the year of *Uncle Tom's Cabin* and of Webster's death.

Emerson lectured in Ohio and Illinois early in 1853. In the autumn he was visited by Arthur Hugh Clough. Emerson's mother, who had been an inmate of his household ever since his second marriage, died on November 16.

During the early months of 1854 Emerson lectured in

New York, Philadelphia, and the West. He made a bitter
attack on Webster's memory at a meeting of the Anti-
Slavery Society of New York, on March 7. In August he
made an address at the Commencement season of Wil-
liams College.

The first months of 1855, the year of Walt Whitman's
Leaves of Grass, were spent in lecturing in New England
and in the Middle States. The journal was neglected. In
October he published *English Traits*. As the year closed
he was lecturing in towns on the Mississippi River, and
amusing himself with new types of behavior and of men.]

January, undated, 1849

Suddenly the Californian soil is spangled with a little
gold-dust here and there in a mill-race in a mountain cleft;
an Indian picks up a little, a farmer, and a hunter, and a
soldier, each a little; the news flies here and there, to New
York, to Maine, to London, and an army of a hundred
thousand picked volunteers, the ablest and keenest and
boldest that could be collected, instantly organize and
embark for this desart, bringing tools, instruments, books,
and framed houses, with them.

March 24

It is much wanted by the country scholars, a *café* or
reading-room in the city, where, for a moderate subscrip-
tion, they can find a place to sit in and find their friends,
when in town, and to write a letter in, or read a paper.
Better still, if you can add certain days of meeting when
important questions can be debated, communications
read, etc., etc. It was proposed by Hale and others, some

time since, to form in Boston a 'Graduates' Club.' This would be that.

April 1

England. The striking difference between English and our gentlemen is their thorough drill; they are all Etonians, they know prosody, and tread securely through all the humanities. The University is felt.

May, undated

Immortality. I notice that as soon as writers broach this question they begin to quote. I hate quotations. Tell me what you know.

July 13

I think, if I were professor of Rhetoric, — teacher of the art of writing well to young men, — I should use Dante for my text-book. Come hither, youth, and learn how the brook that flows at the bottom of your garden, or the farmer who ploughs the adjacent field, your father and mother, your debts and credits, and your web of habits are the very best basis of poetry, and the material which you must work up. Dante knew how to throw the weight of his body into each act, and is, like Byron, Burke, and Carlyle, the Rhetorician. I find him full of the *nobil volgare eloquenza;* that he knows 'God damn,' and can be rowdy if he please, and he does please.

July, undated

A feature of the times is, that when I was born, private and family prayer was in the use of all well-bred people, and now it is not known.

September, undated

Life. Some of the sweetest hours of life, on retrospect, will be found to have been spent with books. Yes; but the sweetness was your own. Had you walked, or hoed, or swum, or sailed, or kept school, in the same hours, it would have endeared those employments and conditions.

September, undated

Macaulay again. Macaulay's History is full of low merits: it is like English manufactures of all kinds, neat, convenient, portable, saleable, made on purpose for the Harpers to print a hundred thousand copies of. So far can Birmingham go.

October, undated

Alcott is like a slate pencil which has a sponge tied to the other end, and, as the point of the pencil draws lines, the sponge follows as fast, and erases them. He talks high and wide, and expresses himself very happily, and forgets all he has said. If a skilful operator could introduce a lancet and sever the sponge, Alcott would be the prince of writers.

December 14

Like the New England soil, my talent is good only whilst I work it. If I cease to task myself, I have no thoughts. This is a poor sterile Yankeeism. What I admire and love is the generous and spontaneous soil which flowers and fruits at all seasons.

December 14

Natural Aristocracy. It is a vulgar error to suppose that **a** gentleman must be ready to fight. The utmost that can

be demanded of the gentleman is that he be incapable of a
lie. There is a man who has good sense, is well informed,
well read, obliging, cultivated, capable, and has an absolute devotion to truth. He always means what he says,
and says what he means, however courteously. You may
spit upon him; — nothing could induce him to spit upon
you, — no praises, and no possessions, no compulsion of
public opinion. You may kick him; — he will think it the
kick of a brute: but he is not a brute, and will not kick
you in return. But neither your knife and pistol, nor your
gifts and courting will ever make the smallest impression
on his vote or word; for he is the truth's man, and will
speak and act the truth until he dies.

Jan. 13, 1850

Every man finds room in his face for all his ancestors.
Every face an *Atrium*.

January, undated

Love is temporary and ends with marriage. Marriage
is the perfection which love aimed at, ignorant of what it
sought. Marriage is a good known only to the parties, —
a relation of perfect understanding, aid, contentment,
possession of themselves and of the world, — which
dwarfs love to green fruit.

January, undated

The English journals snub my new book [*Representative
Men*]; as, indeed, they have all its foregoers. Only now
they say that this has less vigor and originality than the
others. Where, then, was the degree of merit that en-

titled my books to their notice? They have never admitted the claims of either of them. The fate of my books
is like the impression of my face. My acquaintances, as
long back as I can remember, have always said, 'Seems
to me you look a little thinner than when I saw you
last.'

February, undated

Seven years in the vat. Ellery Channing thinks the merit
of Irving's *Life of Goldsmith* is that he has not had the
egotism to put in a single new sentence. It is nothing but
an agreeable repetition of Boswell, Johnson, and Company. And so Montaigne is good, because there is nothing that has not already been in books, a good book being a Damascus blade made by the welding of old nails
and horse-shoes. Everything has seen service, and been
proved by wear and tear in the world for centuries, and
yet now the article is brand-new. So Pope had but one
good line, and that he got from Dryden, and therefore
Pope is the best and only readable English poet.

Philadelphia, April 6

I have made no note of these long weary absences at
New York and Philadelphia. I am a bad traveller, and the
hotels are mortifications to all sense of well-being in me.
The people who fill them oppress me with their excessive
virility, and would soon become intolerable if it were not
for a few friends, who, like women, tempered the acrid
mass. Henry James was true comfort, — wise, gentle,
polished, with heroic manners, and a serenity like the
sun.

May 4

Thackeray's *Vanity Fair* is pathetic in its name, and in his use of the name; an admission it is from a man of fashion in the London of 1850 that poor old Puritan Bunyan was right in his perception of the London of 1650. And yet now in Thackeray is the added wisdom or skepticism, that, though this be really so, he must yet live in tolerance of, and practically in homage and obedience, to these illusions.

July 21 [?]

On Friday, July 19, Margaret [Fuller Ossoli] dies on rocks of Fire Island Beach within sight of and within sixty rods of the shore. To the last her country proves inhospitable to her; brave, eloquent, subtle, accomplished, devoted, constant soul! . . .

She had a wonderful power of inspiring confidence and drawing out of people their last secret. The timorous said, 'What shall we do? How shall she be received, now that she brings a husband and child home?' But she had only to open her mouth and a triumphant success awaited her. She would fast enough have disposed of the circumstances and the bystanders. . . .

I have lost in her my audience. I hurry now to my work admonished that I have few days left. There should be a gathering of her friends and some Beethoven should play the dirge.

July, undated

Every glance at society — pale, withered people with gold-filled teeth, ghastly, and with minds in the same dilapidated condition, drugged with books for want of wisdom — suggests at once the German thought of the progressive god, who has got thus far with his experiment, but will get out yet a triumphant and faultless race.

September 1

I have often observed the priority of music to thought in young writers, and last night remembered what fools a few sounding sentences made of me and my mates at Cambridge, as in Lee's and John Everett's orations. How long we lived on 'Licoö'; on Moore's 'Go where glory waits thee'; and *Lalla Rookh;* and 'When shall the swan his deathnote singing.'

I still remember a sentence in Carter Lee's oration,'And there was a band of heroes, and round their mountain was a wreath of light, and in the midst, on the mountain-top, stood Liberty, feeding her eagle.'

October, undated

Old Age. The world wears well. These autumn afternoons and well-marbled landscapes of green and gold and russet, and steel-blue river, and smoke-blue New Hampshire mountains, are and remain as bright and perfect pencilling as ever.

October, undated

Fame. It is long before Tennyson writes a poem, but the morning after he sends it to the *Times* it is reprinted in all the newspapers, and, in the course of a week or two, is as well known all over the world as the meeting of Hector and Andromache in Homer.

December 18

X complained that life had lost its interest. 'Tis very funny, to be sure, to hear this. For most of us the world is all too interesting, — *l'embarras de richesses.*

We are wasted with our versatility; with the eagerness to grasp on every possible side, we all run to nothing. I cannot open an agricultural paper without finding objects enough for Methusalem. I jilt twenty books whenever I fix on one. I stay away from Boston, only because I cannot begin there to see those whom I should wish, the men and the things. I wish to know France. I wish to study art. I wish to read laws.

January, undated, 1851

Tennyson's *In Memoriam* is the commonplaces of condolence among good Unitarians in the first week of mourning. The consummate skill of the versification is the sole merit.

January, undated

I found when I had finished my new lecture that it was a very good house, only the architect had unfortunately omitted the stairs.

February, undated

Some persons are thrown off their balance when in society; others are thrown on to balance; the excitement of company and the observation of other characters correct their biases. Margaret Fuller always appeared to unexpected advantage in conversation with a circle of persons, with more common sense and sanity than any other, — though her habitual vision was through coloured lenses.

May, undated

Bad Times. [The Fugitive Slave Law] We wake up with painful auguring, and, after exploring a little to know the cause, find it is the odious news in each day's paper, the infamy that has fallen on Massachusetts, that clouds the daylight and takes away the comfort out of every hour. We shall never feel well again until that detestable law is nullified in Massachusetts and until the Government is assured that once for all it cannot and shall not be executed here. All I have and all I can do shall be given and done in opposition to the execution of the law. . . . The word *liberty* in the mouth of Mr. Webster sounds like the word *love* in the mouth of a courtezan. . . . Mr. Choate, whose talent consists in a fine choice of words which he can hang indiscriminately on any offender, has pushed the privilege of his profession so far as to ask, 'What would the Puritans of 1620 say to the trashy sentimentalism of modern reformers?' And thus the stern old fathers of Massachusetts who, Mr. Choate knows, would have died at the stake before soiling themselves with this damnation, are made to repudiate the 'trashy sentimentalism' of the Ten Commandments. The joke is too impudent. . . . Mr. Webster has deliberately taken out his name from all the files of honour in which he had enrolled it, — from all association with liberal, virtuous, and philanthropic men, and read his recantation on his knees at Richmond and Charleston. . . .

The Union! Oh, yes, I prized that, other things being

equal; but what is the Union to a man self-condemned,
with all sense of self-respect and chance of fair fame cut
off, — with the names of conscience and religion become
bitter ironies, and liberty the ghastly nothing which Mr.
Webster means by that word? The worst mischiefs that
could follow from Secession and new combination of the
smallest fragments of the wreck were slight and medica-
ble to the calamity your Union has brought us. Another
year, and a standing army, officered by Southern gentlemen to protect the Commissioners and to hunt the fugi-
tives, will be illustrating the new sweets of Union in Boston, Worcester, and Springfield. . . . Could Mr. Webster
obtain now a vote in the State of Massachusetts for the
poorest municipal office? Well, is not this a loss inevita-
ble to a bad law? — a law which no man can countenance
or abet the execution of, without loss of all self-respect,
and forfeiting forever the name of a gentleman? . . . The
fact that a criminal statute is illegal is admitted by law-
yers, and, that fact once admitted by the people, the
whole structure of this new tyranny falls to the
ground. . . .

Mr. Everett, a man supposed aware of his own meaning, advises pathetically a reverence for the Union. Yes,
but hides the other horn under this velvet? Does he
mean that we shall lay hands on a man who has escaped
from slavery to the soil of Massachusetts, and so has done
more for freedom than ten thousand orations, and tie him
up and call in the marshal, and say, 'I am an orator for
freedom; a great many fine sentences have I turned, —
none has turned finer, except Mr. Webster, — in favor of
plebeian strength against aristocracy; and, as my last and

finest sentence of all, to show the young men of the land who have bought my book and clapped my sentences and copied them in their memory, how much I mean by them, Mr. Marshal, here is a black man of my own age, and who does not know a great deal of Demosthenes, but who means what he says, whom we will now handcuff and commit to the custody of this very worthy gentleman who has come on from Georgia in search of him; I have no doubt he has much to say to him that is interesting, as the way is long. I don't care if I give them — here are copies of my Concord and Lexington and Plymouth and Bunker Hill addresses to beguile their journey from Boston to the plantation whipping-post.' Does Mr. Everett really mean this? — that he and I shall do this? Mr. Everett understands English, as few men do who speak it. Does he mean this? Union is a delectable thing, and so is wealth, and so is life, but they may all cost too much, if they cost honour.

May, undated

What a moment was lost when Judge Shaw declined to affirm the unconstitutionality of the Fugitive Slave Law!

May, undated

There can never be peace whilst this devilish seed of war is in our soil. Root it out, burn it up, pay for the damage, and let us have done with it. It costs a hundred millions. Twice so much were cheap for it. Boston is a little city, and yet is worth near two hundred millions. Boston itself would pay a large fraction of the sum, to be clean of it. I would pay a little of my estate with joy; for

this calamity darkens my days. It is a local, accidental
distemper, and the vast interests of a continent cannot
be sacrificed for it.

May, undated

George Minot thinks that it is of no use balloting, for it
will not stay, but what you do with the gun will stay so.

June, undated

It will hereafter be noted that the events of culture in
the Nineteenth Century were, the new importance of the
genius of Dante, Michel Angelo, and Raffaele to Americans; the reading of Shakspeare; and, above all, the reading of Goethe. Goethe was the cow from which all their
milk was drawn.

They all took the 'European complaint' and went to
Italy. Then there was an uprise of Natural History, and
in London, if you would see the fashionable and literary
celebrities, you must go to the *soirées* of the Marquis of
Northampton, President of the Royal Society, or to the
Geological Club at Somerset House.

It seems, however, as if all the young gentlemen and
gentlewomen of America spent several years in lying on
the grass and watching 'the grand movements of the
clouds in the summer sky' during this century.

June, undated

America. Emigration. In the distinctions of the genius
of the American race it is to be considered that it is not in-
discriminate masses of Europe that are shipped hither-
ward, but the Atlantic is a sieve through which only or

chiefly the liberal, adventurous, sensitive, *America-loving* part of each city, clan, family are brought. It is the light complexion, the blue eyes of Europe that come: the black eyes, the black drop, the Europe of Europe, is left.

June, undated

Thoreau wants a little ambition in his mixture. Fault of this, instead of being the head of American engineers, he is captain of huckleberry party.

July, undated

This filthy enactment [The Fugitive Slave Law] was made in the nineteenth century, by people who could read and write. I will not obey it, by God.

July, undated

Tools. The Age. The Age is marked by this wondrous nature philosophy as well as by its better chisels and roads and steamers. But the attention of mankind is now fixed on ruddering the balloon, and probably the next war — the war of principles — is to be fought in the air.

July, undated

Alcott thinks the American mind a little superior to English, German, Greek, or any other. It is a very amiable opinion and deserves encouragement; and certainly that is best which recommends his home and the present hour to every man. Shall I say it has the confirmation of having been held of his own country by every son of Adam?

July, undated

Goethe is the pivotal man of the old and new times with us. He shuts up the old, he opens the new. No matter that you were born since Goethe died, — if you have not read Goethe, or the Goetheans, you are an old fogy, and belong with the antediluvians.

October 14

To-day is holden at Worcester the 'Woman's Convention.' I think that as long as they have not equal rights of property and right of voting they are not on the right footing.

October 27

It would be hard to recall the rambles of last night's talk with Henry Thoreau. But we stated over again, to sadness almost, the eternal loneliness. . . . But how insular and pathetically solitary are all the people we know! . . .

October, undated

In reading Carlyle's *Life of Sterling*, I still feel, as of old, that the best service Carlyle has rendered is to Rhetoric or the art of writing. Now here is a book in which the vicious conventions of writing are all dropped; you have no board interposed between you and the writer's mind, but he talks flexibly, now high, now low, in loud, hard emphasis, then in undertones, then laughs outright, then calmly narrates, then hints or raises an eyebrow, and all this living narration is daguerreotyped for you in his page. He has gone nigher to the wind than any other craft. No book can any longer be tolerable in the old husky Neal-on-the-Puritans model. But he does not, for all that, very much uncover his secret mind.

October, undated

Undoubtedly if a Concord man of 1750 could come back in our street to-day, and walk from the meeting-house to the Depot, he would recognize all the people as if they were his own contemporaries. Yes, that is a Buttrick; and that a Flint; and that Barrett or Minot. . . .

November 1

I think that a man should compare advantageously with a river, with an oak, with a mountain, endless flow, expansion, and grit.

January, undated, 1852

I find one state of mind does not remember or conceive of another state. Thus I have written within a twelve-month verses ('Days') which I do not remember the composition or correction of, and could not write the like to-day, and have only, for proof of their being mine, various external evidences, as the MS. in which I find them, and the circumstance that I have sent copies of them to friends, etc., etc.

January, undated

[Tom Appleton said at the dinner the other day,] 'Canvasback ducks eat the wild celery, and the common black duck, if it eats the wild celery, is just as good — only, damn them, they won't eat it.'

January, undated

Jeremiah Mason said to Richard H. Dana: 'Law school! A man must read law in the court house.'

March, undated

Beauty. Little things are often filled with great beauty. The cigar makes visible the respiration of the body, an universal fact, of which the ebb and flow of the sea-tide is only one example.

May, undated

To what base uses we put this ineffable intellect! To reading all day murders and railroad accidents, to choosing patterns for waistcoats and scarfs.

June 13

Yesterday a walk with Ellery to the Lincoln Mill Brook, to Nine-Acre Corner, and Conantum. It was the first right day of summer. Air, cloud, river, meadow, upland, mountain, all were in their best. We took a swim at the outlet of the little brook at Baker Farm. Ellery is grown an accomplished Professor of the art of Walking, and leads like an Indian. . . . Since he knew Thoreau, he carries a little pocket-book, in which he affects to write down the name of each new plant or the first day on which he finds the flower.

June 13

Miss B——, a mantuamaker in Concord, became a 'Medium,' and gave up her old trade for this new one; and is to charge a pistareen a spasm, and nine dollars for a fit.

This is the Rat-revelation, the gospel that comes by taps
in the wall, and thumps in the table-drawer.

July 6

The head of Washington hangs in my dining-room for
a few days past, and I cannot keep my eyes off of it. It
has a certain Appalachian strength, as if it were truly the
first-fruits of America, and expressed the Country. The
heavy, leaden eyes turn on you, as the eyes of an ox in a
pasture. And the mouth has gravity and depth of quiet, as
if this MAN had absorbed all the serenity of America, and
left none for his restless, rickety, hysterical countrymen.

July, undated

I am my own man more than most men, yet the loss of
a few persons would be most impoverishing; — a few
persons who give flesh to what were, else, mere thoughts,
and which now I am not at liberty to slight, or in any
manner treat as fictions. It were too much to say that the
Platonic world I might have learned to treat as cloud-
land, had I not known Alcott, who is a native of that
country, yet I will say that he makes it as solid as Massachusetts to me; and Thoreau gives me, in flesh and
blood and pertinacious Saxon belief, my own ethics. He is
far more real, and daily practically obeying them, than I.

October, undated

The shoemakers and fishermen say in their shops,
'Damn learning! it spoils the boy; as soon as he gets a
little, he won't work.' 'Yes,' answers Lemuel, 'but there
is learning somewhere, and somebody will have it, and

who has it will have the power, and will rule you: knowledge is power. Why not, then, let your son get it, as well as another?'

If I have a message to send, I prefer the telegraph to the wheelbarrow.

October, undated

Last Sunday I was at Plymouth on the beach, and looked across the hazy water — whose spray was blowing on to the hills and orchards — to Marshfield. I supposed Webster must have passed, as indeed he had died at three in the morning. [Oct. 24] The sea, the rocks, the woods, gave no sign that America and the world had lost the completest man. Nature had not in our days, or not since Napoleon, cut out such a masterpiece. He brought the strength of a savage into the height of culture. He was a man *in equilibrio;* a man within and without, the strong and perfect body of the first ages, with the civility and thought of the last. '*Os, oculosque Jovi par.*' And what he brought, he kept. Cities had not hurt him; he held undiminished the power and terror of his strength, the majesty of his demeanour.

October, undated

To write a history of Massachusetts, I confess, is not inviting to an expansive thinker. . . . Since, from 1790 to 1820, there was not a book, a speech, a conversation, or a thought, in the State. About 1820, the Channing, Webster, and Everett era begun, and we have been bookish and poetical and cogitative since.

Edwards on the Will was printed in 1754.

October, undated

I saw in the cars a broad-featured, unctuous man, fat and plenteous as some successful politician, and pretty soon divined it must be the foreign Professor, who has had so marked a success in all our scientific and social circles, having established unquestionable leadership in them all; — and it was Agassiz.

November (?) undated

It is the distinction of *Uncle Tom's Cabin* that it is read equally in the parlour and the kitchen and the nursery of every house. What the lady read in the drawing-room in a few hours is retailed to her in the kitchen by the cook and the chambermaid, week by week; they master one scene and character after another.

December, undated

Wordsworth, Coleridge, Tennyson, Carlyle, and Macaulay cannot be matched in America.

January (?) undated, 1853

Certainly I go for culture, and not for multitudes. . . .

January (?) undated

The sea-serpent may have an instinct to retire into the depths of the sea when about to die, and so leave no bones on the shore for naturalists. The sea-serpent is afraid of Mr. Owen; but his heart sunk within him when, at last, he heard that Barnum was born.

June 14

I went to McKay's shipyard, and saw the *King of the Clippers* on the stocks: length of the keel, 285 feet, breadth of the beam 50 feet, carries 1500 tons more than the *Sovereign of the Seas*. Will be finished in August.

June, undated

Henry [Thoreau] is military. He seemed stubborn and implacable; always manly and wise, but rarely sweet. One would say that, as Webster could never speak without an antagonist, so Henry does not feel himself except in opposition. He wants a fallacy to expose, a blunder to pillory, requires a little sense of victory, a roll of the drums, to call his powers into full exercise.

June, undated

I admire answers to which no answer can be made.

July, undated

'Tis curious that Christianity, which is idealism, is sturdily defended by the brokers, and steadily attacked by the idealists.

August, undated

In New York, Henry James quoted Thackeray's speeches in society, 'He liked to go to Westminster Abbey to say his prayers,' etc. 'It gave him the comfort, — blest feeling.' . . . He thought Thackeray could not see beyond his eyes, and has no ideas, and merely is a sounding-board against which his experiences thump and resound: he is the merest boy.

August, undated

If Socrates were here, we could go and talk with him; but Longfellow, we cannot go and talk with; there is a palace, and servants, and a row of bottles of different coloured wines, and wine glasses, and fine coats.

Cape Cod, September 5

Went to Yarmouth Sunday, 5th; to Orleans Monday, 6th; to Nauset Light on the back side of Cape Cod. Collins, the keeper, told us he found obstinate resistance on Cape Cod to the project of building a lighthouse on this coast, as it would injure the wrecking business. He had to go to Boston, and obtain the strong recommendation of the Port Society.

September (?) undated

Rest on your humanity, and it will supply you with strength and hope and vision for the day. Solitude and the country, books, and openness, will feed you; but go into the city — I am afraid there is no morning in Chestnut Street, it is full of rememberers, they shun each other's eyes, they are all wrinkled with memory of the tricks they have played, or mean to play, each other, of petty arts and aims all contracting and lowering their aspect and character.

September (?) undated

Wendell Holmes, when I offered to go to his lecture on Wordsworth, said, 'I entreat you not to go. I am forced to study effects. You and others may be able to combine popular effect with the exhibition of truths. I cannot. I am compelled to study effects.'

October (?) undated

When some one offered Agassiz a glass of water, he said that he did not know whether he had ever drank a glass of that liquid before he came to this country.

December, undated

The first discovery I made of Phillips was, that while I admired his eloquence, I had not the faintest wish to meet the man. He had only a *platform*-existence, and no personality.

Jackson, Michigan, January, 1854

At Jackson, Michigan, Mr. Davis, I believe, a lawyer of Detroit, said to me, on coming out of the lecture-room, 'Mr. Emerson, I see that you never learned to write from any book.'

Jackson, January, undated

There is nobody in Washington who can explain this Nebraska business to the people, — nobody of weight. And nobody of any importance on the bad side. It is only done by Douglas and his accomplices by calculation on the brutal ignorance of the people, upon the wretched masses of Pennsylvania, Indiana, Illinois, Kentucky, and so on, people who can't read or know anything beyond what the village democrat tells them. But what effrontery it required to fly in the face of what was supposed settled law, and how it shows that we have no guards whatever, that there is no proposition whatever, that is too audacious to be offered us by the Southerner.

March (?) *undated*

Metres. I amuse myself often, as I walk, with humming
the rhythm of the decasyllabic quatrain, ... or other
rhythms, ... I find a wonderful charm, heroic, and
especially deeply pathetic or plaintive in cadences, and say
to myself, Ah, happy! if one could fill these small measures
with words approaching to the power of these beats!

March (?) *undated*

Realism. We shall pass for what we are. Do not fear to
die because you have not done your task. Whenever a
noble soul comes, the audience awaits. And he is not
judged by his performance, but by the spirit of his performance. . . .

March 14

The lesson of these days is the vulgarity of wealth. We
know that wealth will vote for the same thing which the
worst and meanest of the people vote for. Wealth will
vote for rum, will vote for tyranny, will vote for slavery,
will vote against the ballot, will vote against international
copyright, will vote against schools, colleges, or any high
direction of public money.

April (?) *undated*

Browning is ingenious. Tennyson is the more public
soul, walks on the ecliptic road, the path of gods and
souls, and what he says is the expression of his contemporaries. Like Burke, or Mirabeau, he says better than all
men think. Like these men, he is content to think and
speak a sort of King's speech, embodying the sense of

well-bred successful men, and by no means of the best and
highest men: he speaks the sense of the day, and not the
sense of grand men, the sense of the first class, identical
in all ages.

April (?) *undated*

Shall we judge the country by the majority or by the
minority? Certainly, by the minority. The mass are
animal, in state of pupilage, and nearer the chimpanzee.

April (?) *undated*

Solitude. Now and then a man exquisitely made can
and must live alone; but coop up most men, and you undo
them. The King lived and eat in hall, with men, and
understood men, said Selden.

May, undated

If Minerva offered me a gift and an option, I would say
give me continuity. I am tired of scraps. I do not wish to
be a literary or intellectual chiffonier. Away with this
Jew's rag-bag of ends and tufts of brocade, velvet, and
cloth-of-gold; let me spin some yards or miles of helpful
twine, a clew to lead to one kingly truth, a cord to bind
wholesome and belonging facts.

May, undated

We affirm and affirm, but neither you nor I know the
value of what we say.

August (?) *undated*

I suppose, every one has favorite topics, which make a
sort of museum or privileged closet of whimsies in his

mind, and which he thinks is a kind of aristocracy to
know about. Thus, I like to know about lions, diamonds,
wine, and Beauty; and Martial, and Hafiz.

September 5

If I reckon up my debts by particulars to English books,
how fast they reduce themselves to a few authors, and
how conspicuous Shakspeare, Bacon, and Milton become; Locke a cipher.

September 5

All the thoughts of a turtle are turtle.

October 11

Never was a more brilliant show of coloured landscape
than yesterday afternoon — incredibly excellent topaz
and ruby at four o'clock; cold and shabby at six.

February, undated, 1855

Common Fame. I trust a good deal to common fame,
as we all must. If a man has good corn, or wood, or boards,
or pigs, to sell, or can make better chairs or knives,
crucibles or church organs, than anybody else, you will
find a broad hard-beaten road to his house, though it be
in the woods.

February, undated

Munroe seriously asked what I believed of Jesus and
prophets. I said, as so often, that it seemed to me an im-
piety to be listening to one and another, when the pure
Heaven was pouring itself into each of us, on the simple

condition of obedience. To listen to any second-hand gospel is perdition of the First Gospel. Jesus was Jesus because he refused to listen to another, and listened at home.

May (?) *undated*

Jones Very, who thought it an honour to wash his own face, seems to me less insane than men who hold themselves cheap.

May (?) *undated*

Macaulay. No person ever knew so much that was so little to the purpose.

May 20

You may chide sculpture or drawing, if you will, as you may rail at orchards and cornfields; but I find the grand style in sculpture as admonitory and provoking to good life as Marcus Antoninus. I was in the Athenæum, and looked at the Apollo, and saw that he did not drink much port wine.

May 20

The Year. There is no flower so sweet as the four-petalled flower, which science much neglects. One grey petal it has, one green, one red, and one white.

July, undated

If the women demand votes, offices, and political equality, as an Elder and Elderess are of equal power in the Shaker Families, refuse it not. 'Tis very cheap wit that finds it so funny. Certainly all my points would be sooner carried in the state if women voted.

July (?) *undated*

Sleepy Hollow. The blazing evidence of immortality is our dissatisfaction with any other solution.

July (?) *undated*

Alcott. I was struck with the late superiority he showed. The interlocutors were all better than he; he seemed childish and helpless, not apprehending or answering their remarks aright; they masters of their weapons. But by and by, when he got upon a thought, like an Indian seizing by the mane and mounting a wild horse of the desert, he overrode them all, and showed such mastery and took up Time and Nature like a boy's marble in his hand, as to vindicate himself.

August, undated

The Universities are wearisome old fogies, and very stupid with their aorists and alcaics and digammas, but they do teach what they pretend to teach, and whether by private tutor, or by lecturer or by examiner, with prizes and scholarships, they learn to read better and to write better than we do.

October 9

Sent Chapter I of *English Traits* to Phillips, Sampson & Co.

Le Claire House, Davenport, Iowa, December 31

Rules of the house. 'No gentlemen permitted to sit at the table without his coat.'

'No gambling permitted in the house.'

I have crossed the Mississippi on foot three times.

Soft coal, which comes to Rock Island from about twelve miles, sells for sixteen cents a bushel; wood at six dollars per cord. They talk 'quarter-sections.' 'I will take a quarter-section of that pie.'

December 31

In Rock Island I am advertised as 'the Celebrated Metaphysician,' in Davenport as 'the Essayist and Poet.'

1856–1863

[These Western journeys stimulated Emerson's interest in the affairs of Kansas, which had now begun to be a political issue in the North. *English Traits* was finally published in 1856, eight years after Emerson's return from his visit of 1847–1848.

In 1857 John Brown came to Concord to discuss Kansas matters and was entertained in Emerson's house. *The Atlantic Monthly* was founded in this year, with Emerson as one of its leading contributors. The financial panic in the autumn interfered somewhat with his lecturing.

Eighteen-fifty-eight was likewise a year of scanty harvests for a lecturer. In the summer Emerson made the excursion to the Adirondacks described so delightfully by W. J. Stillman, the leader of the party. In 1859 there are few entries in the journal. John Brown's raid upon Harper's Ferry and death upon the scaffold moved Emerson deeply.

There were many lecture invitations from the West as 1860 opened. This was the year of Lincoln's election to the Presidency. *The Conduct of Life* was published late in the autumn.

The stirring events of 1861 are scarcely touched upon in the journal. By the end of the year Emerson was feeling the pinch of poverty, as the war lessened the demand for his books and addresses. He lectured in Washington in January, 1862, and it is believed that Lincoln was in the audience. Emerson met him repeatedly, and records his impressions. This was the year of Thoreau's death, on May 6. Emerson was deeply stirred by the Emancipation Proclamation, made public in September. For the Boston celebration of the event, on January 1, 1863, Emerson wrote one of the finest of his political poems, the 'Boston Hymn.' He served on the Board of Visitors to the Military Academy at West Point in May and was greatly pleased with what he found there.]

Beloit, Wisconsin, January 9, 1856

Mercury varying from 20° to 30° below zero for the last week. . . .

This climate and people are a new test for the wares of a man of letters. All his thin, watery matter freezes; 'tis only the smallest portion of alcohol that remains good. At the lyceum, the stout Illinoian, after a short trial, walks out of the hall. The Committee tell you that the people want a hearty laugh, and Stark, and Saxe, and Park Benjamin, who give them that, are heard with joy. Well, I think with Governor Reynolds, the people are always right (in a sense), and that the man of letters is to say, These are the new conditions to which I must conform. The architect, who is asked to build a house to go upon the sea, must not build a Parthenon, or a square house, but a ship. And Shakspeare, or Franklin, or Æsop, coming to Illinois, would say, I must give my wisdom a comic form, instead of tragics or elegiacs, and well I know to do it, and he is no master who cannot vary his forms, and carry his own end triumphantly through the most difficult.

Adrian, Michigan, January

When I see the waves of Lake Michigan toss in the bleak snowstorm, I see how small and inadequate the common poet is.

February 29

If I knew only Thoreau, I should think coöperation of good men impossible. Must we always talk for victory, and never once for truth, for comfort, and joy? Centrality he has, and penetration, strong understanding, and the higher gifts, — the insight of the real, or from the real, and the moral rectitude that belongs to it; but all this and all his resources of wit and invention are lost to me, in every experiment, year after year, that I make, to hold intercourse with his mind. Always some weary captious paradox to fight you with, and the time and temper wasted.

April, undated

Thy voice is sweet, Musketaquid; repeats the music of the rain; but sweeter rivers silent flit through thee, as thou through Concord plain.

Thou art shut in thy banks; but the stream I love, flows in thy water, and flows through rocks and through the air, and through darkness, and through men, and women. I hear and see the inundation and eternal spending of the stream, in winter and in summer, in men and animals, in passion and thought. Happy are they who can hear it.

I see thy brimming, eddying stream, and thy enchantment. For thou changest every rock in thy bed into a

gem: all is real opal and agate, and at will thou pavest
with diamonds. Take them away from thy stream, and
they are poor shards and flints: so is it with me to-day.
[Compare the poem 'Two Rivers.']

May (?) undated

My son is coming to get his Latin lesson without me.
My son is coming to do without me. And I am coming to
do without Plato, or Goethe, or Alcott.

May (?) undated

Education. Don't let them eat their seed-corn; don't
let them anticipate, ante-date, and be young men, before
they have finished their boyhood. Let them have the
fields and woods, and learn their secret and the base- and
foot-ball, and wrestling, and brickbats, and suck all the
strength and courage that lies for them in these games;
let them ride bare-back, and catch their horse in his
pasture, let them hook and spear their fish, and shin a
post and a tall tree, and shoot their partridge and trap
the woodchuck, before they begin to dress like collegians
and sing in serenades, and make polite calls.

May 21

Yesterday to the Sawmill Brook with Henry. He was
in search of yellow violet (*pubescens*) and *menyanthes*
which he waded into the water for; and which he con-
cluded, on examination, had been out five days. Having
found his flowers, he drew out of his breast pocket his
diary and read the names of all the plants that should
bloom this day, May 20; whereof he keeps account as a

banker when his notes fall due; *Rubus triflora, Quercus, Vaccinium*, etc. The *Cypripedium* not due till to-morrow. . . . He thinks he could tell by the flowers what day of the month it is, within two days.

June 2

South Carolina is in earnest. I see the courtesy of the Carolinians, but I know meanwhile that the only reason why they do not plant a cannon before Faneuil Hall, and blow Bunker Hill Monument to fragments, as a nuisance, is because they have not the power. They are fast acquiring the power, and if they get it, they will do it.

June 14

At our Kansas relief meeting, in Concord, on June 12, $962.00 were subscribed on the spot. Yesterday, the subscription amounted to $1130.00; and it will probably reach $1200.00, or one per cent on the valuation of the town. $1360.00 I believe was the final amount.

July 23

Returned from Pigeon Cove, where we have made acquaintance with the sea, for seven days. 'Tis a noble friendly power, and seemed to say to me, 'Why so late and slow to come to me? Am I not here always thy proper summer home? Is not my voice thy needful music: my breath, thy healthful climate in the heats; my touch, thy cure? Was ever building like my terraces? was ever couch so magnificent as mine? Lie down on my warm ledges and learn that a very little hut is all you need. I have made thy architecture superfluous, and it is paltry beside mine. Here are twenty Romes and Ninevehs and Karnacs in ruins together, obelisk and pyramid and giant's causeway, — here they all are prostrate or half piled.'

And behold the sea, the opaline, plentiful and strong, yet beautiful as the rose or the rainbow, full of food, nourisher of men, purger of the world, creating a sweet climate, and, in its unchangeable ebb and flow, and in its beauty at a few furlongs, giving a hint of that which changes not, and is perfect. [Compare the poem 'Sea-Shore'.]

Chicago, Tremont House, January, 1857

'In 1838,' said Dr. Boynton, 'I came here to Waukegan and there were not so many houses as there are towns now.' He got into the train at Evansville, a town a year and a half old, where are now 600 inhabitants, a Biblical Institute, or Divinity School of the Methodists, to which a Mrs. Garrett lately gave some land in Chicago appraised at $125,000; but which, when they came to sell it, the worser half brought $160,000, and the value of the whole donation, 'tis thought, will be half a million. They had in the same town a college, — a thriving institution, which unfortunately blew down one night, — but I believe they raised it again the next day, or built another, and no doubt in a few weeks it will eclipse Cambridge and Yale!

February

Captain John Brown of Kansas gave a good account of himself in the Town Hall, last night, to a meeting of citizens.

February (?) *undated*

Most men are insolvent, or promise by their countenance, and conversation, and by their early endeavor,
much more than they ever perform. Charles Newcomb
did, and Coleridge did, and Carlyle.

April (?) *undated*

Because our education is defective, because we are
superficial and ill-read, we are forced to make the most of
that position, of ignorance. Hence America is a vast
know-nothing party, and we disparage books, and cry up
intuition. With a few clever men we have made a repu-
table thing of that, and denouncing libraries and severe
culture, and magnifying the mother-wit swagger of bright
boys from the country colleges, we have even come so far
as to deceive everybody, except ourselves, into an admiration of un-learning and inspiration, forsooth.

Thursday, May 28

We kept Agassiz's fiftieth birthday at the Club. Three
or four strangers were present, to wit, Dresel, Felton,
Holmes, and Hilliard. For the rest, we had Agassiz,
Peirce, Ward, Motley, Longfellow, Lowell, Whipple,
Dwight, Woodman, and I. Cabot was due, but did not
come. Agassiz brought what had just been sent him, the
last coloured plates to conclude the First Volume of his
Contributions, etc., which will now be published incontinently. The flower of the feast was the reading of three
poems, written by our three poets, for the occasion. The
first by Longfellow, who presided; the second, by Holmes;
the third, by Lowell; all excellent in their way.

July 28

Yesterday, the best day of the year, we spent in the afternoon on the river. A sky of Calcutta; light, air, clouds, water, banks, birds, grass, pads, lilies, were in perfection, and it was delicious to live. Ellery and I went up the South Branch, and took a bath from the bank behind Cyrus Hubbard's, where the river makes a bend.

July 28

I can count on my fingers all the sane men that ever came to me. Were I to insist on silence until I was fully met, and all my faculty called out and tasked by my companion, I should have a solitary time of it. Those who visit me are young men, imperfect persons, people with some partial thought, or local culture.

September (?)

The Atlantic Monthly. A journal is an assuming to guide the age — very proper and necessary to be done, and good news that it shall be so. — But this journal, is this it? Has Apollo spoken?

October

October 14th, the New York and Boston banks suspended specie payment.

February (?) 1858

It is impossible to be a gentleman, and not be an abolitionist. For a gentleman is one who is fulfilled with all nobleness, and imparts it; is the natural defender and raiser of the weak and oppressed, like the Cid.

February 27

Felton told of Agassiz, that when some one applied to
him to read lectures, or some other paying employment,
he answered, 'I can't waste my time in earning money.'
Dr. Holmes told a story of John Hunter, that, being
interrupted by a professional call, when he was dissecting
a tiger, he said, 'Do you think I can leave my work for
your damned guinea?'

April (?)

Many of Tennyson's poems, like 'Clara Vere de Vere,'
are only the sublime of magazine poems, — admirable
contributions for the *Atlantic Monthly* of the current
month, but not classic and eternal. Milton would have
raised his eyebrow a little at such pieces. But the 'Ulysses' he would have approved.

Adirondac, August 2

Follansbee's Pond. It should be called Stillman's
henceforward, from the good camp which this gallant
artist has built, and the good party he has led and planted
here for the present at the bottom of the little bay which
lies near the head of the lake. . . .

Wednesday morn, Agassiz, Woodman, and I left the
camp, each in a boat with his guide, for Big Tupper's
Lake; passed through the inlet into Raquette River, and
down it fourteen miles to Tupper; then up the lake six
miles to Jenkins's, near the Falls of the Bog River.

April (?) 1859

I am a natural reader, and only a writer in the absence
of natural writers. In a true time, I should never have
written.

April (?)

I have now for more than a year, I believe, ceased to write in my Journal, in which I formerly wrote almost daily. I see few intellectual persons, and even those to no purpose, and sometimes believe that I have no new thoughts, and that my life is quite at an end. But the magnet that lies in my drawer, for years, may believe it has no magnetism, and, on touching it with steel, it knows the old virtue; and, this morning, came by a man with knowledge and interests like mine, in his head, and suddenly I had thoughts again.

April (?)

Secondary men and primary men. These travellers to Europe, these readers of books, these youths rushing into counting-rooms of successful merchants, are all imitators, and we get only the same product weaker. But the man who never so slowly and patiently works out his native thought, is a primary person.

April (?)

I have been writing and speaking what were once called novelties, for twenty-five or thirty years, and have not now one disciple. Why? Not that what I said was not true; not that it has not found intelligent receivers; but because it did not go from any wish in me to bring men to me, but to themselves. I delight in driving them from me. What could I do, if they came to me? — they would interrupt and encumber me. This is my boast that I have no school follower. I should account it a measure of the impurity of insight, if it did not create independence.

May (?)

Here dies the amiable and worthy Prescott amid a chorus of eulogies, and, if you believe the American and almost the English newspapers for a year or two back, he is the very Muse of History. And meantime here has come into the country three months ago a book of Carlyle, *History of Frederick*, infinitely the wittiest book that ever was written. . . .

And this book makes no noise: I have hardly seen a notice of it in any newspaper or journal, and you would think there was no such book.

May 25

Dante. Dante cannot utter a few lines, but I am informed what transcendent eyes he had, as, for example, —

'un fuoco
Ch' emisferio di tenebre vincia.'

How many millions would have looked at candles, lamps, and fires, and planets, all their days, and never noticed this measure of their illuminating force, 'of conquering a hemisphere of the darkness.' Yet he says nothing about his own eyes.

June (?)

Very little reliance must be put on the common stories of Mr. Webster's or of Mr. Choate's learning, their Greek, or their varied literature. That ice won't bear. Reading! to what purpose did they read?

August (?)

One wrong Step. On Wachusett, I sprained my foot. It was slow to heal, and I went to the doctors. Dr. Henry

Bigelow said, 'Splint and absolute rest.' Dr. Russell said, 'Rest, yes; but a splint, no.' Dr. Bartlett said, 'Neither splint nor rest, but go and walk.' Dr. Russell said, 'Pour water on the foot, but it must be warm.' Dr. Jackson said, 'Stand in a trout brook all day.'

September (?)

I think wealth has lost much of its value, if it have not wine. I abstain from wine only on account of the expense.

September (?)

There are men whose opinion of a book is final. If Ellery Channing tells me, 'Here is a good book,' I know I have a day longer to live. But there are plenty of able men whose report in that kind is not to be trusted.

October (?)

The Resistance to Slavery. It is the old mistake of the slaveholder to impute the resistance to Clarkson or Pitt, to Channing or Garrison, or to some John Brown whom he has just captured, and to make a personal affair of it; and he believes, whilst he chains and chops him, that he is getting rid of his tormentor; and does not see that the air which this man breathed is liberty, and is breathed by thousands and millions.

October (?)

We talk of Sparta and Rome, we *dilettanti* of liberty. But the last thing a brave man thinks of is Sparta or Scythia or the Gauls. He is up to the top of his boots in his own meadow, and can't be bothered with histories. That will do for a winter evening with schoolboys. As soon as a man talks Washington and Putnam and General Jackson to me, I detect the coxcomb and charlatan. He is a frivolous nobody who has no duties of his own.

'Mount Vernon'; I never heard a brave man talk of Mount Vernon, or a religious man of Mount Sinai. They leave that to hypocrites.

October (?)

The believing we do something when we do nothing is the first illusion of tobacco.

Michigan, February, 1860. [*From a letter home*]

'At Kalamazoo a good visit, and made intimate acquaintance with a college wherein I found many personal friends, though unknown to me, and one Emerson was an established authority. Even a professor or two came along with me to Marshall to hear another lecture. My chief adventure was the necessity of riding in a buggy forty-eight miles to Grand Rapids; then, after lecture, twenty more on the return; and the next morning getting back to Kalamazoo in time for the train hither at twelve. So I saw Michigan and its forests and Wolverines pretty thoroughly.'

June

Theodore Parker [died at Florence in May] has filled up all his years and days and hours; a son of the energy of New England, restless, eager, manly, brave, early old,

contumacious, clever. I can well praise him at a spectator's distance, for our minds and methods were unlike, —
few people more unlike. . . .

He was willing to perish in the using. He sacrificed the
future to the present, was willing to spend and be spent;
felt himself to belong to the day he lived in, and had too
much to do than that he should be careful for fame. He
used every day, hour, and minute; he lived to the latest
moment, and his character appeared in the last moments
with the same firm control as in the day of strength.

June

Advantages of old age. I reached the other day the end
of my fifty-seventh year, and am easier in my mind than
hitherto. I could never give much reality to evil and
pain. But now when my wife says perhaps this tumor on
your shoulder is a cancer, I say, What if it is?

November 15

The news of last Wednesday morning (7th) [The Election of Lincoln] was sublime, the pronunciation of the
masses of America against Slavery. And now on Tuesday, the 13th, I attended the Dedication of the Zoölog-
ical Museum at Cambridge, an auspicious and happy
event, most honourable to Agassiz and to the State. On
Wednesday, 7th, we had Charles Sumner here at Concord and my house.

January 4, 1861

I hear this morning, whilst it is snowing fast, the
chickadee singing.

January

Immortality. All the comfort I have found shall teach me to confide that I shall not have less in times and places that I do not yet know.

January

Do thy duty of the day. Just now, the supreme public duty of all thinking men is to assert freedom. Go where it is threatened, and say, 'I am for it, and do not wish to live in the world a moment longer than it exists.' Phillips has the supreme merit in this time, that he and he alone stands in the gap and breach against the assailants. Hold up his hands. He did me the honour to ask me to come to the meeting [of the Massachusetts Anti-Slavery Society, January 24] at Tremont Temple, and, esteeming such invitation a command, though sorely against my inclination and habit, I went, and, though I had nothing to say, showed myself. If I were dumb, yet I would have gone and mowed and muttered or made signs. The mob roared whenever I attempted to speak, and after several beginnings, I withdrew.

January

I read many friendly and many hostile paragraphs in the journals about my new book, [*The Conduct of Life*] but seldom or never a just criticism. . . . I often think I could write a criticism on Emerson that would hit the white.

February

Sects are stoves, but fire keeps its old properties through them all.

February

What came over me with delight as I sat on the ledge in the warm light of last Sunday was the memory of young days at College, the delicious sensibility of youth, how the air rings to it! how all light is festal to it! how it at any moment extemporizes a holiday! I remember how boys riding out together on a fine day looked to me! ah, there was a romance! How sufficing was mere melody! The thought, the meaning, was insignificant; the whole joy was in the melody. For that I read poetry, and wrote it; and in the light of that memory I ought to understand the doctrine of musicians, that the words are nothing, the air is all. What a joy I found, and still can find, in the Æolian harp! What a youth find I still in Collins's 'Ode to Evening,' and in Gray's 'Eton College'! What delight I owed to Moore's insignificant but melodious poetry.

That is the merit of Clough's 'Bothie,' that the joy of youth is in it. Oh the power of the spring! and, ah, the voice of the bluebird! And the witchcraft of the Mount Auburn dell, in those days! I shall be a Squire Slender for a week.

April 5

One capital advantage of old age is the absolute insignificance of a success more or less. I went to town and read a lecture yesterday. Thirty years ago it had really been a matter of importance to me whether it was good and effective. Now it is of none in relation to me. It is long already fixed what I can and what I cannot do.

May

The country is cheerful and jocund in the belief that it has a government at last. The men in search of a party, parties in search of a principle, interests and dispositions that could not fuse for want of some base, — all joyfully unite in this great Northern party, on the basis of Freedom. What a healthy tone exists! I suppose when we come to fighting, and many of our people are killed, it will yet be found that the bills of mortality in the country will show a better result of this year than the last, on account of the general health; no dyspepsia, no consumption, no fevers, where there is so much electricity, and conquering heart and mind.

August 5

The war goes on educating us to a trust in the simplicities, and to see the bankruptcy of all narrow views.

August

If we Americans should need presently to remove the capitol to Harrisburg, or to Chicago, there is almost nothing of rich association with Washington City to deter us. More's the pity. But excepting Webster's earlier eloquence, as against Hayne, and John Quincy Adams's sublime behaviour in the House of Representatives, and the fine military energy of Jackson in his presidency, I find little or nothing to remember.

August

The British nation is like old Josiah Quincy, always blundering into some good thing.

October

Lately I find myself oft recurring to the experience of
the partiality of each mind I know. I so readily imputed
symmetry to my fine geniuses, on perceiving their excellence in some insight. How could I doubt that Thoreau,
that Charles Newcomb, that Alcott, or that Henry James,
as I successively met them, was the master-mind, which,
in some act, he appeared. No, he was only master-mind
in that particular act. He could repeat the like stroke a
million times, but, in new conditions, he was inexpert, and
in new company, he was dumb.

December

I ought to have added to my list of benefits of age the
general views of life we get at sixty when we penetrate
show and look at facts.

January, 1862. [From a letter to his brother William]
'The 1st of January has found me in quite as poor a
plight as the rest of the Americans. Not a penny from my
books since last June, which usually yield five or six
hundred a year. No dividends from the banks, . . . almost
all income from lectures has quite ceased. Meantime we
are trying to be as unconsuming as candles under an ex-
tinguisher. . . . But far better that this grinding should
go on, bad and worse, than we be driven by any impa-
tience into a hasty peace, or any peace restoring the old
rottenness.'

January

Sources of Inspiration. Solitary converse with Nature
is . . . perhaps the first, and there are ejaculated sweet

and dreadful words never uttered in libraries. Ah, the spring days, summer dawns, and October woods!

January 17

We will not again disparage America, now that we have seen what men it will bear. What a certificate of good elements in the soil, climate, and institutions is Lowell, whose admirable verses I have just read! [*The Biglow Papers*, 2d Series, *Atlantic Monthly*, January, 1862.]

January

For, how can the people censure the Government as dilatory and cold, — the people, which has been so cold and slow itself at home? I say it were happier, if Genius should appear in the Government, but if it do not, we have got the first essential element, namely, honesty.

February

VISIT TO WASHINGTON, 31 JANUARY, 1862

At Washington, January 31, February 1, 2, and 3. Saw Sumner, who, on the 2d, carried me to Mr. Chase, Mr. Bates, Mr. Stanton, Mr. Welles, Mr. Seward, Lord Lyons, and President Lincoln. The President impressed me more favourably than I had hoped. A frank, sincere, well-meaning man, with a lawyer's habit of mind, good clear statement of his fact; correct enough, not vulgar, as described, but with a sort of boyish cheerfulness, or that kind of sincerity and jolly good meaning that our class meetings on Commencement Days show, in telling our old stories over. When he has made his remark, he looks up at you with great satisfaction, and shows all his white teeth, and laughs. . . .

When I was introduced to him, he said, 'Oh, Mr. Emerson, I once heard you say in a lecture, that a Kentuckian seems to say by his air and manners, "Here am I; if you don't like me, the worse for you."' . . . In the Congressional Library I found Spofford, assistant librarian. He told me that, for the last twelve (?) years, it had been under Southern domination, and as under dead men. Thus the Medical Department was very large, and the Theological very large, whilst of modern literature very imperfect. There was no copy of the *Atlantic Monthly*, or of the *Knickerbocker*, none of the *Tribune* or *Times*, or any New York journal. There was no copy of the London *Saturday Review* taken, or any other live journal, but the London *Court Journal*, in a hundred volumes, duly bound. Nor was it possible to mend matters, because no money could they get from Congress, though an appropriation had been voted.

February

Thoreau. Perhaps his fancy for Walt Whitman grew out of his taste for wild nature, for an otter, a woodchuck, or a loon.

February

Holmes came out late in life with a strong sustained growth for two or three years, like old pear trees which have done nothing for ten years, and at last begin and grow great. The Lowells come forward slowly, and Henry Thoreau remarks that men may have two growths like pears.

March

War, the searcher of character, the test of men, has tried already so many reputations, has pricked so many bladders. 'Tis like the financial crises, which, once in ten or twenty years, come to try the men and institutions of trade; using, like them, no ceremony, but plain laws of gravity and force to try tension and resistance. Scott, McDowell, McClellan, Frémont, Banks, Butler, and I know not how many more, are brought up, each in turn, dragged up irresistibly to the anthropometer, measured and weighed, and the result proclaimed to the Universe.

March

Why has never the poorest country college offered me a professorship of rhetoric? I think I could have taught an orator, though I am none.

March 24

Sam Staples yesterday had been to see Henry Thoreau. 'Never spent an hour with more satisfaction. Never saw a man dying with so much pleasure and peace.' Thinks that very few men in Concord know Mr. Thoreau; finds him serene and happy. [Thoreau died on May 6.]

May 25

Resources or feats. I like people who can do things. When Edward and I struggled in vain to drag our big calf into the barn, the Irish girl put her finger into the calf's mouth, and led her in directly.

June

The man McClellan ebbed like a sea.

June

Henry Thoreau remains erect, calm, self-subsistent, before me, and I read him not only truly in his Journal, but he is not long out of mind when I walk, and, as to-day, row upon the pond. He chose wisely no doubt for himself to be the bachelor of thought and nature that he was, — how near to the old monks in their ascetic religion!

June

I see many generals without a command, besides Henry.

June

If we should ever print Henry's journals, you may look for a plentiful crop of naturalists. Young men of sensibility must fall an easy prey to the charming of Pan's pipe.

July

Why are people so sensitive about the reputation of General McClellan? There is always something rotten about a sensitive reputation. Besides, is not General McClellan an American citizen? And is it not the first attribute and distinction of an American to be abused and slandered as long as he is heard of?

August

When I compare my experience with that of my own family and coevals, I think that, in spite of the checks, I have had a triumphant health.

August

I believe in the perseverance of the saints. I believe in effectual calling. I believe in life everlasting.

August

How shallow seemed to me yesterday in the woods the speech one often hears from tired citizens who have spent their brief enthusiasm for the country, that Nature is tedious, and they have had enough of green leaves. Nature and the green leaves are a million fathoms deep, and it is these eyes that are superficial.

August

I grieve to see that the Government is governed by the hurrahs of the soldiers or the citizens. It does not lead opinion, but follows it.

September (?)

Resources. If Cabot, if Lowell, if Agassiz, if Alcott come to me to be messmates in some ship, or partners in the same colony, what they chiefly bring, all they bring, is their thoughts, their ways of classifying and seeing things; and how a sweet temper can cheer, how a fool can dishearten the days!

September (?)

When I bought my farm, I did not know what a bargain I had in the bluebirds, bobolinks, and thrushes; as little did I know what sublime mornings and sunsets I was buying.

September

How partial, like mutilated eunuchs, the musical artists appear to me in society! Politics, bankruptcy, frost, famine, war, — nothing concerns them but a scrap-

ing on a catgut, or tooting on a bass French horn. The
crickets in the grass chirp their national song at all hours,
quite heedless who conquers, Federals or rebels, in the
war, and so do these.

October

Great is the virtue of the Proclamation. [Of Emancipation, promulgated Sept. 22.] It works when men are
sleeping, when the army goes into winter quarters, when
generals are treacherous or imbecile.

October

George Francis Train said in a public speech in New
York, 'Slavery is a divine institution.' 'So is hell,' ex-
claimed an old man in the crowd.

November 29

What a convivial talent is that of Wendell Holmes! He
is still at his Club, when he travels in search of his
wounded son [Capt. O. W. Holmes, Jr., now (1926)
Justice of the U. S. Supreme Court]; has the same delight
in his perceptions, in his wit, in its effect, which he watches
as a belle the effect of her beauty; would still hold each
companion fast by his spritely, sparkling, widely-allusive
talk, as at the Club table; tastes all his own talent, cal-
culates every stroke, and yet the fountain is unfailing,
the wit excellent, the *savoir vivre* and *savoir parler* admirable.

November 29

Isaac Hecker, the Catholic Priest, came to see me and
desired to read lectures on the Catholic Church in Con-

cord. I told him that nobody would come to hear him, such was the aversation of people, at present, to theological questions; and not only so, but the drifting of the human mind was now quite in another direction than to any churches. Nor could I possibly affect the smallest interest in anything that regarded his church.

December

A Lyceum needs three things, a great deal of light, of heat, and of people. At Pittsburgh we wanted all three, and usually we lack one or the other.

Indianapolis, January 26, 1863

Titan [By Jean Paul Richter] I have read on this journey, and, for its noble wisdom and insight, forgive, what still annoys me, its excessive efflorescence and German superlative. How like to Goethe's *Wilhelm Meister* is its culture, manners, and wisdom! Rome is the best part of it, and therein it resembles Goethe the more.

February (?)

The human mind cannot be burned nor bayonetted, nor wounded, nor missing.

April 17

Of me, Alcott said, 'Some of the organs were free, some fated; the voice was entirely liberated; and my poems or essays were not rightly published, until I read them!'

April 28

I have never recorded a fact, which perhaps ought to have gone into my sketch of 'Thoreau,' that, on the 1st August, 1844, when I read my Discourse on Emancipation [in the British West Indies], in the Town Hall, in Concord, and the selectmen would not direct the sexton to ring the meeting-house bell, Henry went himself, and rung the bell at the appointed hour.

May 4

On Friday morning, May 1st, at 3 o'clock, died Mary Moody Emerson, at Williamsburg, New York, aged 88 years, 8 months.

June

West Point Academy makes a very agreeable impression on me. The innocence of the cadets, the air of probity, of veracity, and of loyalty to each other struck me, and the anecdotes told us confirmed this impression. I think it excellent that such tender youths should be made so manly and masterly in rough exercises of horse and gun and cannon and muster; so accurate in French, in mathematics, geology, and engineering; should learn to draw, to dance, and to swim. I think their ambition should be concentrated on their superiority in science, — being taught, that whoever knows the most must command *of right*, and must command *in fact*, if just to himself.

June

At West Point, I saw a civilization built on powder. It is not quite creditable to our invention that all the instruction in engineering, infantry, cavalry, artillery, rigidly rests on this one accident of our chemistry, gunpowder. A new invention to-morrow would change all the art of war. Just as our commerce and civilization are so built on cotton as to have deceived the Southern States and many other States into neglect of all other possibility, and of morality. But cotton is only one of two hundred thousand plants known to our botany; and powder is but one of a million combinations that are to be tried in turn.

June

Take egotism out, and you would castrate the benefactors. Luther, Mirabeau, Napoleon, John Adams, Andrew Jackson; and our nearer eminent public servants, — Greeley, Theodore Parker, Ward Beecher, Horace Mann, Garrison would lose their vigour.

June 24

In reading Henry Thoreau's journal, I am very sensible of the vigour of his constitution. That oaken strength which I noted whenever he walked, or worked, or surveyed wood-lots, the same unhesitating hand with which a field-labourer accosts a piece of work, which I should shun as a waste of strength, Henry shows in his literary task. He has muscle, and ventures on and performs feats which I am forced to decline. In reading him, I find the same thought, the same spirit that is in me, but he takes a step beyond, and illustrates by excellent images that which I should have conveyed in a sleepy generality. 'Tis as if I went into a gymnasium, and saw youths leap, climb, and swing with a force unapproachable, — though their feats are only continuations of my initial grapplings and jumps.

July 24

I went to Dartmouth College, and found the same old Granny system which I met there twenty-five years ago. The President has an aversion to emulation, as injurious to the character of the pupils. He therefore forbids the election of members into the two literary societies by merit, but arranges that the first scholar alphabetically on the list shall be assigned to the Adelphi, and the second to the Mathesians, and the third to the Adelphi, and the fourth to the Mathesians; and so on. Every student belonging to the one or the other. 'Well, but there is a first scholar in the class, is there not, and he has the first oration at Commencement?' 'Oh, no, the parts are assigned by lot.' The amiable student who explained it added that it tended to remove disagreeable excitement from the societies. I answered, 'Certainly, and it would remove more if there were no college at all.' I recommended morphine in liberal doses at the College Commons.

October

Good out of evil. One must thank the genius of Brigham Young for the creation of Salt Lake City, — an inestimable hospitality to the Overland Emigrants, and an efficient example to all men in the vast desert, teaching how to subdue and turn it to a habitable garden. And one must thank Walt Whitman for service to American literature in the Appalachian enlargement of his outline and treatment.

October

When our young officers come back from the army, on a forty days' furlough, they find apathy and opposition in the cities.

October (?)

You cannot refine Mr. Lincoln's taste, extend his horizon, or clear his judgment; he will not walk dignifiedly through the traditional part of the President of America, but will pop out his head at each railroad station and make a little speech, and get into an argument with Squire A. and Judge B. He will write letters to Horace Greeley, and any editor or reporter or saucy party committee that writes to him, and cheapen himself.

But this we must be ready for, and let the clown appear, and hug ourselves that we are well off, if we have got good nature, honest meaning, and fidelity to public interest, with bad manners, — instead of an elegant *roué* and malignant self-seeker.

November (?)

Boutwell said to me the other day, 'It makes no difference whether we gain or lose a battle, except the loss of valuable lives; we gain the advantage from month to month.'

New York, December 22

Renan writes *Vie de Jésus.* Many of his contemporaries have no doubt projected the same theme. When I wrote *Representative Men*, I felt that Jesus was the 'Representative Man' whom I ought to sketch; but the task required great gifts, — steadiest insight and perfect temper; else, the consciousness of want of sympathy in the audience would make one petulant or sore, in spite of himself. Theodore Parker, of course, wished to write this book; so did Maria Child in her *Book of Religions*, and Miss Cobbe, and Alcott, and I know not how many more.

1864–1875

[THERE are few references to public events in the journals for 1864 and 1865. Indeed from the close of the Civil War a distinct decline in Emerson's general powers begins to be traceable. His poem 'Terminus,' written in 1866, is the best evidence that he realized that it was now time 'to take in sail.' Yet for another decade he continued to write a little and to speak occasionally. Many honors came to him: a degree of LL.D. from Harvard in 1866, an election as Overseer of Harvard in 1867, and also as Phi Beta Kappa orator, — his first appearance as a speaker at his university for nearly thirty years. In 1870 he lectured there regularly, on philosophy. He had published a second volume of verse, *May Day*, in 1867. In 1869 he gave in Boston a long series of readings from English poets. In 1871 he journeyed to California, and in the following year, after the partial destruction of his Concord house by fire, he visited Europe for the third time, enjoying especially the ascent of the Nile. There are a few records of these things in the journal, but after 1875 he made but a few scattered memoranda. The last entry quoted in this volume is the record of Carlyle's birthday, on December 5, 1875.

A few quiet years were still his portion, but his work was done. He died on the 27th of April, 1882.]

New York, January 13, 1864

Beecher, at breakfast, illustrated the difference between the impulsive mob in New York Cooper Institute and the organized mob in Liverpool meeting. 'In one you go by a corner where the wind sucks in, and blows your hat off, but, when you get by it, you go along comfortably to the next corner. In the other, you are on the prairie, with no escape from the irresistible northwester.'

February 28

Yesterday at the Club with Cabot, Ward, Holmes, Lowell, Judge Hoar, Appleton, Howe, Woodman, Forbes, Whipple, with General Barlow, and Mr. Howe, of Nova Scotia, for guests; but cramped for time by late dinner and early hour of the return train, — a cramp which spoils a club. For you shall not, if you wish good fortune, even take pains to secure your right and left hand men. The least design instantly makes an obligation to make their time agreeable, which I can never assume.

January 28

Captain O. W. Holmes tells me that the Army of the Potomac is acquiring a professional feeling, and that they have neither panics nor excitements, but more self-reliance.

April

The single word *Madame* in French poetry, makes it instantly prose.

April 24

Yesterday the Saturday Club met to keep the birth-night of Shakspeare, at the end of the third century. We met at the Revere House, at 4 o'clock P.M. Members of the Club present were seventeen: Agassiz, Appleton, Cabot, Dwight, Emerson, Forbes, Hedge, Hoar, Holmes, S. G. Howe, Estes Howe, Longfellow, Lowell, Norton, Peirce, Whipple, Woodman.

Guests: Governor Andrew, Rev. Dr. Frothingham, R. H. Dana, Jr., Esq., Dr. J. G. Palfrey, Richard Grant White, Esq., Robert C. Winthrop, George S. Hillard, George William Curtis, James Freeman Clarke, Francis J. Child, Dr. Asa Gray, James T. Fields, John Weiss, Martin Brimmer, George T. Davis.

We regretted much the absence of Mr. Bryant, and Whittier, Edward Everett, and William Hunt, who had at first accepted our invitations, but were prevented at last; — and of Hawthorne, Dana, Sumner, Motley, and Ward, of the Club, necessarily absent; also of Charles Sprague, and Wendell Phillips, and T. W. Parsons, and George Ticknor, who had declined our invitations. William Hunt graced our hall by sending us his full-length picture of Hamlet, a noble sketch. It was a quiet and happy evening filled with many good speeches, from Agassiz who presided (with Longfellow as *Croupier*, but silent), Dr. Frothingham, Winthrop, Palfrey, White, Curtis, Hedge, Lowell, Hillard, Clarke, Governor Andrew, Hoar, Weiss, and a fine poem by Holmes, read so admirably well that I could not tell whether in itself it were one of his best or not. The company broke up at 11.30.

April

Shakspeare should be the study of the University. In Florence, Boccaccio was appointed to lecture on Dante.

But in English Oxford, or in Harvard College, I have
never heard of a Shakspeare Professorship. Yet the students should be educated, not only in the intelligence of,
but in the sympathy with, the thought of great poets.

April

I am inquisitive of all possible knowledge concerning
Shakspeare, and of all opinions. Yet how few valuable
criticisms, how few opinions I treasure! How few besides
my own! And each thoughtful reader, doubtless, has the
like experience.

May 24

Yesterday, May 23, we buried Hawthorne in Sleepy
Hollow, in a pomp of sunshine and verdure, and gentle
winds. James Freeman Clarke read the service in the
church and at the grave. Longfellow, Lowell, Holmes,
Agassiz, Hoar, Dwight, Whipple, Norton, Alcott, Hillard,
Fields, Judge Thomas, and I attended the hearse as pall-
bearers. Franklin Pierce was with the family. The church
was copiously decorated with white flowers delicately
arranged. The corpse was unwillingly shown, — only a
few moments to this company of his friends. But it was
noble and serene in its aspect, — nothing amiss, — a
calm and powerful head. A large company filled the
church and the grounds of the cemetery. All was so
bright and quiet that pain or mourning was hardly sug-
gested, and Holmes said to me that it looked like a happy
meeting.

Clarke in the church said that Hawthorne had done
more justice than any other to the shades of life, shown a

sympathy with the crime in our nature, and, like Jesus, was the friend of sinners.

I thought there was a tragic element in the event, that might be more fully rendered, — in the painful solitude of the man, which, I suppose, could not longer be endured, and he died of it.

I have found in his death a surprise and disappointment. I thought him a greater man than any of his works betray, that there was still a great deal of work in him, and that he might one day show a purer power. Moreover, I have felt sure of him in his neighbourhood, and in his necessities of sympathy and intelligence, — that I could well wait his time, — his unwillingness and caprice, — and might one day conquer a friendship. It would have been a happiness, doubtless to both of us, to have come into habits of unreserved intercourse. It was easy to talk with him, — there were no barriers, — only, he said so little, that I talked too much, and stopped only because, as he gave no indications, I feared to exceed. He showed no egotism or self-assertion, rather a humility, and, at one time, a fear that he had written himself out. One day, when I found him on the top of his hill, in the woods, he paced back the path to his house, and said, '*This path is the only remembrance of me that will remain.*' Now it appears that I waited too long.

June

I, too, am fighting my campaign.

June

Within, I do not find wrinkles and used heart, but unspent youth.

June

'Tis bad when believers and unbelievers live in the same manner; — I distrust the religion.

July (?)

Old age brings along with its uglinesses the comfort that you will soon be out of it, — which ought to be a substantial relief to such discontented pendulums as we are. To be out of the war, out of debt, out of the drouth, out of the blues, out of the dentist's hands, out of the second thoughts, mortifications, and remorses that inflict such twinges and shooting pains, — out of the next winter, and the high prices, and company below your ambition, — surely these are soothing hints. And, harbinger of this, what an alleviator is sleep, which muzzles all these dogs for me every day?

September 21

Hon. Lyulph Stanley, Wendell Phillips, and Agassiz, Channing, and Alcott here.

Agassiz is really a man of great ability, breadth, and resources, a rare and rich nature, and always maintains himself, — in all companies, and on all occasions.

September 24

Yesterday with Ellery walked through 'Becky Stow's Hole,' dry-shod, hitherto a feat for a muskrat alone. The sky and air and autumn woods in their early best. This year, the river meadows all dry and permeable to the walker. But why should Nature always be on the gallop? Look now and instantly, or you shall never see it: not ten minutes' repose allowed. Incessant whirl. And 'tis the same with my companion's genius. You must carry a stenographic press in your pocket to save his commentaries o1. things and men, or they are irrecoverable. I tormented my memory just now in vain to restore a witty criticism of his, yesterday, on a book.

September (?)

The War at last appoints the generals, in spite of parties and Presidents. Every one of us had his pet, at the start, but none of us appointed Grant, Sherman, Sheridan, and Farragut, — none but themselves.

September (?)

Criticism. I read with delight a casual notice of Wordsworth in the *London Reader*, in which, with perfect aplomb, his highest merits were affirmed, and his unquestionable superiority to all English poets since Milton, and thought how long I travelled and talked in England, and found no person, or none but one, and that one Clough, sympathetic with him, and admiring him aright, in face of Tennyson's culminating talent, and genius in melodious verse. What struck me now was the certainty with which the best opinion comes to be the established opinion.

October 12

Returned from Naushon, whither I went on Saturday, the 8th, with Professor Goldwin Smith, of Oxford University, Mr. Charles B. Sedgwick, John Weiss, and George C. Ward.

Mr. Forbes at Naushon is the only 'Squire' in Massachusetts, and no nobleman ever understood or performed his duties better. I divided my admiration between the landscape of Naushon and him. He is an American to be proud of. Never was such force, good meaning, good sense, good action, combined with such domestic lovely behaviour, and such modesty and persistent preference of others. Wherever he moves, he is the benefactor. It is of course that he should shoot well, ride well, sail well, administer railroads well, carve well, keep house well, but he was the best talker also in the company, — with the perpetual practical wisdom, seeing always the *working* of the thing, — with the multitude and distinction of his facts (and one detects continually that he has had a hand in everything that has been done), and in the temperance with which he parries all offence, and opens the eyes of his interlocutor without contradicting him. I have been proud of many of my countrymen, but I think this is a good country that can breed such a creature as John M. Forbes. . . .

I came away from Naushon saying to myself of John Forbes, how little this man suspects, with his sympathy for men, and his respect for lettered and scientific people, that he is not likely ever to meet a man superior to himself!

New York, October 20

Bryant has learned where to hang his titles, namely, by tying his mind to autumn woods, winter mornings, rain, brooks, mountains, evening winds, and wood-birds. Who speaks of these is forced to remember Bryant.

[He is] American. Never despaired of the Republic. Dared name a jay and a gentian, crows also. His poetry is sincere.

October 25

Power of certain states of the sky. There is an astonishing magnificence even in this low town, and within a quarter of a mile of my doors, in the appearance of the Lincoln hills now drest in their coloured forest, under the lights and clouds of morning, as I saw them at eight o'clock. When I see this spectacle so near, and so surprising, I think no house should be built quite low, or should obstruct the prospect by trees.

Concord, February 13, 1865

Home from Chicago and Milwaukee. Chicago grows so fast that one ceases to respect civic growth: as if all these solid and stately squares which we are wont to see as the slow growth of a century had come to be done by machinery as cloth and hardware are made, and were therefore shoddy architecture without honour.

'Twas tedious, the squalor and obstructions of travel; the advantage of their offers at Chicago made it necessary to go; in short, this dragging of a decorous old gentleman out of home and out of position to this juvenile career was tantamount to this, — 'I'll bet you fifty dollars a day that you will not leave your library, and wade and ride and run and suffer all manner of indignities and stand up for an hour each night reading in a hall'; and I answered, 'I'll bet I will.' I do it and win the $900.

April

'Tis far the best that the rebels have been pounded instead of negociated into a peace. They must remember it, and their inveterate brag will be humbled, if not cured. George Minot used to tell me over the wall, when I urged him to go to town meeting and vote, that 'votes did no good; what was done so wouldn't last, but what was done by bullets would stay put.' General Grant's terms certainly look a little too easy. . . .

May

It should be easy to say what I have always felt, that Stanley's *Lives of the Philosophers*, or Marcus Antoninus, are agreeable and suggestive books to me, whilst St. Paul or St. John are not, and I should never think of taking up these to start me on my task, as I often have used Plato or Plutarch. It is because the Bible wears black cloth. It comes with a certain official claim against which the mind revolts. The book has its own nobilities — might well be charming, if it was left simply on its merits, as the others; but this 'you must,' — 'it is your duty,' repels. 'Tis like the introduction of martial law into Concord. If you should dot our farms with picket lines, and I could not go or come across lots without a pass, I should resist, or else emigrate. If Concord were as beautiful as Paradise, it would be detestable at once.

July

In every house and shop, an American map has been unrolled, and daily studied, and now that peace has come, every citizen finds himself a skilled student of the condition, means, and future, of this continent.

I think it a singular and marked result that the War has established a conviction in so many minds that the right will get done; has established a chronic hope for a chronic despair.

July 23

Notes for Williamstown. Returns the eternal topic, the praise of intellect. I gain my point, gain all points, whenever I can reach the young man with any statement which teaches him his own worth. Thus, if I can touch his imagination, I serve him; he will never forget it.

July 23

Miss Peabody tells me that Jones Very one day said to her, 'To the preëxistent Shakspeare wisdom was offered, but he declined it, and took only genius.'

August (?)

Beware of the Minor Key. Despair, whining, low spirits, only betray the fact that the man has been living in the low circle of the sense and the understanding. These are exhaustible, and he has exhausted them, and now looks backward and bewails them.

November 5

We hoped that in the peace, after such a war, a great expansion would follow in the mind of the Country; grand views in every direction, — true freedom in politics, in religion, in social science, in thought. But the energy of the nation seems to have expended itself in the war, and every interest is found as sectional and timorous as before. . . .

Williamstown, November 14

I saw to-night in the observatory, through Alvan
Clark's telescope, the Dumb-Bell nebula in the Fox and
Goose Constellation; the four double stars in Lyra; the
double stars of Castor; the two hundred stars of the
Pleiades; the nebula in (Perseus?). Mr. Button, Professor
Hopkins's assistant, was our star-showman, and Stan-
brough and Hutton, who have been my committee of
the 'Adelphic Union,' inviting me here, carried me
thither. I have rarely been so much gratified.

Early in the afternoon Professor Bascom carried me in a
gig to the top of the West Mountain, and showed me the
admirable view down the valley in which this town and
Adams lie, with Greylock and his attendant ranges towering in front. Then we rose to the crest, and looked down
into Rensselaer County, New York, and the multitude of
low hills that compose it, — this was the noted Anti-Rent
country, — and beyond, in the horizon, the mountain
range to the west.

Of all tools, an observatory is the most sublime. And
these mountains give an inestimable worth to Williamstown and Massachusetts. But, for the mountains, I don't
quite like the proximity of a college and its noisy students.
To enjoy the hills as poet, I prefer simple farmers as
neighbours.

December

Carlyle. I have neglected badly Carlyle, who is so
steadily good to me. Like a Catholic in Boston, he has
put himself by his violent anti-Americanism in false position, and it is not quite easy to deal with him. But his

merits are over-powering, and when I read *Friedrich*, I forget all else.

I am far from thinking it late. I do not despond at all whilst I hear the verdicts of European juries against us. Renan says so and so. That does not hurt us at all. Arnold says thus or thus: neither does that touch us. I think it safer to be so blamed, than praised. Listen to every censure in good part. It does not hit the quick since we do not wince. And if you do wince, that is best of all. Set yourself instantly to mend the fault, and thank the critic as your benefactor. And Ruskin has several rude and some ignorant things to say.

University. But be sure that scholars are secured, that the scholar is not quite left out; that the Imagination is cared for and cherished; that the money-spirit does not turn him out; that Enthusiasm is not repressed; and Professor Granny does not absorb all. Teach him Shakspeare. Teach him Plato; and see that real examiners and awards are before you.

In the college, 'tis complained, money and the vulgar respectability have the same ascendant as in the city. What remedy? There is but one, namely, the arrival of genius, which instantly takes the lead, and makes the fashion at Cambridge.

When I read a good book, say, one which opens a literary question, I wish that life were 3000 years long.

Who would not launch into this Egyptian history, as opened by Wilkinson, Champollion, Bunsen, but for the *memento mori* which he reads on all sides? Who is not provoked by the temptation of the Sanscrit literature? And, as I wrote above, the Chaldaic Oracles tempt me. But so also does Algebra, and astronomy, and chemistry, and geology, and botany. Perhaps, then, we must increase the appropriation, and write 30,000 years. And, if these years have correspondent effect with the sixty years we have experienced, some earnest scholar will have to amend by striking out the word 'years' and inserting 'centuries.'

May (?)

America should affirm and establish that in no instance should the guns go in advance of the perfect right. You shall not make *coups d'état*, and afterwards explain and pay, but shall proceed like William Penn, or whatever other Christian or humane person who treats with the Indian or foreigner on principles of honest trade and mutual advantage. Let us wait a thousand years for the Sandwich Islands before we seize them by violence.

July 2

I went with Annie Keyes and Mr. Channing on Wednesday, 27th June, to Troy, N. H., thence to the Mountain House in wagon, and, with Edward and Tom Ward who had come down to meet us, climbed the mountain. The party already encamped were Moorfield Storey, Ward, and Edward, for the men; and Una Hawthorne, Lizzie Simmons, and Ellen E. for the maidens.... Edward went up with me to the summit, up all sorts of

Giant stairs, and showed the long spur with many descending peaks on the Dublin side. The rock-work is interesting and grand; — the clean cleavage, the wonderful slabs, the quartz dikes, the rock torrents in some parts, the uniform presence on the upper surface of the glacial lines or scratches, all in one self-same direction. Then every glance below apprises you how you are projected out into stellar space, as a sailor on a ship's bowsprit out into the sea. We look down here on a hundred farms and farmhouses, but never see horse or man. For our eyes the country is depopulated. Around us the arctic sparrow, *Fringilla nivalis*, flies and peeps, the ground-robin also; but you can hear the distant song of the wood-thrushes ascending from the green belts below. I found the picture charming, and more than remunerative. Later, from the plateau, at sunset, I saw the great shadow of Monadnoc lengthen over the vast plain, until it touched the horizon. The earth and sky filled themselves with all ornaments, — haloes, rainbows, and little pendulums of cloud would hang down till they touched the top of a hill, giving it the appearance of a smoking volcano. The wind was north, the evening cold, but the camp-fire kept the party comfortable, whilst Storey, with Edward for chorus, sang a multitude of songs to their great delectation. The night was forbiddingly cold, — the tent kept the girls in vital heat, but the youths could hardly keep their blood in circulation, the rather, that they had spared too many of their blankets to the girls and to the old men. Themselves had nothing for it but to rise and cut wood and bring it to the fire, which Mr. Channing watched and fed.

July (?)

I see with joy the Irish emigrants landing at Boston, at New York, and say to myself, There they go — to school.

July (?)

The scatterbrain, Tobacco. Yet a man of no conversation should smoke.

July (?)

I find it a great and fatal difference whether I court the muse, or the muse courts me: That is the ugly disparity between age and youth.

July 30

This morn came again the exhilarating news of the landing of the Atlantic telegraph cable at Heart's Content, Newfoundland, and we repeat the old wonder and delight we found on the Adirondac, in August, 1858. We have grown more skilful, it seems, in electric machinery, and may confide better in a lasting success. Our political condition is better, and, though dashed by the treachery of our American President, can hardly go backward to slavery and civil war. Besides, the suggestion of an event so exceptional and astounding in the history of human arts is, that this instant and pitiless publicity now to be given to every public act must force on the actors a new sensibility to the opinion of mankind, and restrain folly and meanness.

August 31

Visited Agassiz by invitation, with Lidian and Ellen, and spent the day at his house and on the Nahant rocks.

He is a man to be thankful for, always cordial, full of facts, with unsleeping observation, and perfectly communicative. In Brazil he saw on a half-mile square 117 different kinds of excellent timber, — and not a saw-mill in Brazil.

August 31

I can find my biography in every fable that I read.

September (?)

Fame. I confess there is sometimes a caprice in fame, like the unnecessary eternity given to these minute shells and antediluvian fishes, leaves, ferns, yea, ripples and raindrops, which have come safe down through a vast antiquity, with all its shocks, upheavals, deluges, and volcanoes, wherein everything noble in art and humanity had perished, yet these snails, periwinkles, and worthless dead leaves come staring and perfect into our daylight. — What is Fame, if every snail or ripple or raindrop shares it?

September

My idea of a home is a house in which each member of the family can on the instant kindle a fire in his or her private room. Otherwise their society is compulsory and wasteful to the individual.

October 25

Success in your work, the finding a better method, the better understanding that insures the better performing is hat and coat, is food and wine, is fire and horse and health and holiday. At least, I find that any success in my work has the effect on my spirits of all these.

Washington, Iowa, February 13, 1867

In riding in an open sleigh, from Oshkosh to Ripon, in a fiercely cold snowstorm driving in my face, I blessed the speed and power of the horses. Their endurance makes them inestimable in this rough country. They seem left out of doors in the snow and wind all day. Around this square before the house, I counted just now twenty horses tied. Some of them seem to stand tied all day. Last night, just before going to bed, I looked out, — there stood two or three at that hour, — the farmers perhaps listening to the railroad men in the court-house, or sitting round the bar-room fire.

February (?)

I am so purely a spectator that I have absolute confidence that all pure spectators will agree with me, whenever I make a careful report. I told Alcott that every one of my expressions concerning 'God,' or the 'soul,' etc., is entitled to attention as testimony, because it is independent, not calculated, not part of any system, but spontaneous, and the nearest word I could find to the thing.

April

You complain that the Negroes are a base class. Who makes and keeps the Jew or the Negro base, who but you, who exclude them from the rights which others enjoy?

July 2

Reading. I suppose every old scholar has had the experience of reading something in a book which was significant to him, but which he could never find again. Sure he is that he read it there; but no one else ever read it, nor can he find it again, though he buy the book, and ransack every page.

October

I rarely take down Horace or Martial at home, but when reading in the Athenæum, or Union Club, if I come upon a quotation from either, I resolve on the instant to read them every day. But, — at home again, homely thoughts.

December 17

Yesterday morning in bitter cold weather I had the pleasure of crossing the Mississippi in a skiff with Mr. ——, we the sole passengers, and a man and a boy for oarsmen. I have no doubt they did their work better than the Harvard six could have done it, as much of the rowing was on the surface of fixed ice, in fault of running water. But we arrived without other accident than becoming almost fixed ice ourselves; but the long run to the Tepfer House, the volunteered rubbing of our hands by the landlord and clerks, and good fire restored us.

Undated, 1868

Revolutions. In my youth, Spinoza was a hobgoblin; now he is a saint.

May

We had a story one day of a meeting of the Atlantic Club, when the copies of the new number of the *Atlantic* being brought in, every one rose eagerly to get a copy, and then each sat down, and *read his own article.*

May

When I remember how easily and happily I think in certain company, — as, for instance, in former years, with Alcott, and Charles Newcomb, earlier with Peter Hunt, though I must look far and wide for the persons and conditions, which yet were real, — and how unfavorable my daily habits and solitude are for this success, and consider also how essential this commerce is to fruitfulness in writing, — I see that I cannot exaggerate its importance among the resources of inspiration.

Gurney seemed to me, in an hour I once spent with him, a fit companion. Holmes has some rare qualities. Horatio Greenough shone, but one only listened to him; so Carlyle. Henry Hedge, George Ward especially, and if one could ever get over the fences, and actually on even terms, Elliot Cabot.

May 30

How important an educator has Scott been!

August 16

Came home last night from Vermont with Ellen. Stopped at Middlebury on the 11th, Tuesday, and read my discourse on *Greatness, and the good work and influence of heroic scholars.* On Wednesday spent the day at Essex Junction, and traversed the banks and much of the bed of the Winooski River, much admiring the falls, and the noble mountain peaks of Mansfield and Camel's Hump (which there appears to be the highest), and the view of

the Adirondacs across the Lake. In the evening, took the
stage to Underhill Centre, and, the next morning, in un-
promising weather, strolled away with Ellen towards the
Mansfield Mountain, four miles off; and, the clouds
gradually rising and passing from the summit, we decided
to proceed towards the top, which we reached (with many
rests at the Half-Way House and at broad stones on the
path) a little before 2 o'clock, and found George Bradford
at the Mountain House. We were cold and a little wet,
but found the house warm with stoves.

After dinner, Ellen was thoroughly warmed and re-
cruited lying on a settee by the stove, and meanwhile I
went up with Mr. Bradford and a party to the top of 'the
Chin,' which is the highest land in the State, — 4400 feet.
I have later heard it stated 4389 feet. Lake Champlain
lay below us, but was a perpetual illusion, as it would appear a piece of yellow sky, until careful examination of the
islands in it and the Adirondac summits beyond brought
it to the earth for a moment; but, if we looked away an
instant, and then returned, it was in the sky again. When
we reached the summit, we looked down upon the 'Lake
of the Clouds,' and the party which reached the height a
few minutes before us had a tame cloud which floated by a
little below them.

This summer, bears and a panther have been seen on
the mountain, and we peeped into some rocky caves
which might house them. We came, on the way, to the
edge of a crag, which we approached carefully, and lying
on our bellies; and it was easy to see how dangerous a
walk this might be at night, or in a snowstorm. The
White Mountains, it was too misty to see; but 'Owl's

Head,' near Lake Memphremagog, was pointed out.
Perhaps it was a half-mile only from the House to the top
of 'the Chin,' but it was a rough and grand walk. On such
occasions, I always return to my fancy that the best use
of wealth would be to carry a good professor of geology,
and another of botany, with you.

Autumn

The only place where I feel the joy of eminent domain
is in my woodlot. My spirits rise whenever I enter it. I
can spend the entire day there with hatchet or pruning-
shears making paths, without a remorse of wasting time.
I fancy the birds know me, and even the trees make little
speeches or hint them. Then Allah does not count the
time which the Arab spends in the chase.

Autumn

Ah, what a blessing to live in a house which has on the
ground-floor one room or one cabinet in which a Worcester's Unabridged; a Liddell and Scott; an Andrews and
Stoddard; Lemprière's Classical; a '*Gradus Ad Parnas-
sum*'; a Haydn's *Dictionary of Dates;* a *Biographie
Générale;* a Spiers' French, and Flügel's German Dictionary, even if Grimm is not yet complete, — where these
and their equivalents, if equivalents can be, are always at
hand, — and yet I might add, as I often do, — ah! happier, if these or their substitutes have been in that house
for two generations or for three, — for Horace's metres
and Greek literature will not be thoroughly domesti-
cated in one life. A house, I mean, where the seniors,
who are at fault about school questions, can inquire of

the junior with some security of a right answer. This is
one of my dreams for the American house.

Autumn

In the perplexity in which the literary public now stands
with regard to university education, whether studies shall
be compulsory or elective; whether by lectures of professors, or whether by private tutors; whether the stress shall
be on Latin and Greek, or on modern sciences, — the one
safe investment which all can agree to increase is the
library.

December 9

In poetry, tone. I have been reading some of Lowell's
new poems, in which he shows unexpected advance on
himself, but perhaps most in technical skill and courage.
It is in talent rather than in poetic tone, and rather
expresses his wish, his ambition, than the uncontrollable
interior impulse which is the authentic mark of a new
poem, and which is unanalysable, and makes the merit of
an ode of Collins, or Gray, or Wordsworth, or Herbert, or
Byron, — and which is felt in the pervading tone, rather
than in brilliant parts or lines; as if the sound of a bell, or
a certain cadence expressed in a low whistle or booming, or
humming, to which the poet first timed his step, as he
looked at the sunset, or thought, was the incipient form of
the piece, and was regnant through the whole.

December

Culture is one thing, and varnish another. There can
be no high culture without pure morals. With the truly

cultivated man, — the maiden, the orphan, the poor man, and the hunted slave feel safe.

January (?) [1869]

In this proposition lately brought to me by a class, it occurs that I could by readings show the difference between good poetry and what passes for good; that I could show how much so-called poetry is only eloquence.

January (?)

The few stout and sincere persons, whom each one of us knows, recommend the country and the planet to us. 'Tis not a bad world this, as long as I know that John M. Forbes or William H. Forbes and Judge Hoar, and Agassiz, and my three children, and twenty other shining creatures whose faces I see looming through the mist, are walking in it. Is it the thirty millions of America, or is it your ten or twelve units that encourage your heart from day to day?

May

God had infinite time to give us; but how did He give it? In one immense tract of a lazy millennium? No, but He cut it up into neat succession of new mornings, and, with each, therefore, a new idea, new inventions, and new applications.

July

At present, the friends of Harvard are possessed in greater or less degree by the idea of making it a University for men, instead of a College for boys. [Charles W. Eliot had just been made President.]

July (?)

Sumner has been collecting his works. They will be the history of the Republic for the last twenty-five years, as told by a brave, perfectly honest, and well-instructed man with social culture and relation to all eminent persons. Diligent and able workman, without humour, but with persevering study while reading, excellent memory, high sense of honour, disdaining any bribe, any compliances, and incapable of falsehood. His singular advantages of person, of manners, and a statesman's conversation, impress every one favourably. He has the foible of most public men, the egotism which seems almost unavoidable at Washington.

July (?)

At my Club, I suppose I behave very ill in securing always, if I can, a place by a valued friend, and, though I suppose (though I have never heard it) that I offend by this selection, sometimes too visible, my reason is that I, who rarely see, in ordinary, select society, must make the best use of this opportunity, having, at the same time, the feeling that

> 'I could be happy with either,
> Were the other dear charmer away.'

July (?)

I am interested not only in my advantages, but in my disadvantages, that is, in my fortunes proper; that is, in watching my fate, to notice, after each act of mine, what result. Is it prosperous? Is it adverse? And thus I find a pure entertainment of the intellect, alike in what is called good or bad.

September 15

Agassiz never appeared to such advantage as in his Biographical Discourse on Humboldt, at the Music Hall in Boston, yesterday. What is unusual for him, he read a written discourse, about two hours long; yet all of it strong, nothing to spare, not a weak point, no rhetoric, no falsetto; — his personal recollections and anecdotes of their intercourse, simple, frank, and tender in the tone of voice, too, no error of egotism or of self-assertion, and far enough from French sentimentalism. He is quite as good a man as his hero, and not to be duplicated, I fear.

October 19

Carried to Fields and Company to-day the copy of the four first chapters of my so-called new book, *Society and Solitude.*

December (?)

Compensation of failing memory in age by the increased power and means of generalization.

February 3, 1870

The last proof-sheet of *Society and Solitude* comes back to me to-day for correction.

March 15

My new book sells faster, it appears, than either of its foregoers. This is not for its merit, but only shows that old age is a good advertisement. Your name has been seen so often that your book must be worth buying.

March 15

A gentleman, English, French, or American, is rare; I think I remember every one I have ever seen.

March 23

On the 31st, I received President Eliot's letter signifying the acceptance of Carlyle's bequest of the Cromwellian and Friedrich books by the Corporation of Harvard College, and enclosing the vote of the Corporation. I wrote to Carlyle the same day enclosing the President's letter to me, and the record of their vote, and mailed it yesterday morning to him.

June 9

Were I professor of rhetoric, I would urge my class to read Plutarch's *Morals* in English, and Cotton's Montaigne for their English style.

June 9

The reason of a new philosophy or philosopher is ever that a man of thought finds that he cannot read in the old books. I can't read Hegel, or Schelling, or find interest in what is told me from them, so I persist in my own idle and easy way, and write down my thoughts, and find presently that there are congenial persons who like them, so I persist, until some sort of outline or system grows. 'Tis the common course: ever a new bias. It happened to each of these, Heraclitus, or Hegel, or whosoever.

July 21

I am filling my house with books which I am bound to read, and wondering whether the new heavens which await the soul (after the fatal hour) will allow the consultation of these.

September

Very much afflicted in these days with stupor: — acute attacks when ever a visit is proposed or made.

October 6

To-day at the laying of the corner-stone of the 'Memorial Hall,' at Cambridge. All was well and wisely done. The storm ceased for us, the company was large, — the best men and the best women all there, — or all but a few; — the arrangements simple and excellent, and every speaker successful. Henry Lee, with his uniform sense and courage, the Manager; the Chaplain, Rev. Phillips Brooks, offered a prayer, in which not a word was superfluous, and every right thing was said. Henry Rogers, William Gray, Dr. Palfrey, made each his proper Report. Luther's Hymn in Dr. Hedge's translation was sung by a great choir, the corner-stone was laid, and then Rockwood Hoar read a discourse of perfect sense, taste, and feeling, — full of virtue and of tenderness. After this, an original song by Wendell Holmes was given by the Choir. Every part in all these performances was in such true feeling that people praised them with broken voices, and we all proudly wept. Our Harvard soldiers of the war were in their uniforms, and heard their own praises, and the tender allusions to their dead comrades. General Meade was present, and 'adopted by the College,' as Judge Hoar said, and Governor Claflin sat by President Eliot. Our English guests, Hughes, Rawlins, Dicey, and Bryce, sat and listened

February 10 [1871]

I do not know that I should feel threatened or insulted
if a chemist should take his protoplasm or mix his hydro-
gen, oxygen, and carbon, and make an animalcule in-
contestably swimming and jumping before my eyes. I
should only feel that it indicated that the day had arrived
when the human race might be trusted with a new degree
of power, and its immense responsibility; for these steps
are not solitary or local, but only a hint of an advanced
frontier supported by an advancing race behind it.

What at first scares the Spiritualist in the experiments
of Natural Science — as if thought were only finer chyle,
fine to aroma — now redounds to the credit of matter,
which, it appears, is impregnated with thought and
heaven, and is really of God, and not of the Devil, as he
had too hastily believed.

March 5

Dr. E. B. Pusey of Oxford surprised me two or three
days ago with sending me, 'with greetings,' a book, *Lectures on Daniel and the Prophets*, with the following in-
scription written on the blank leaf, —

> To the unwise and wise
> A debtor I.
> 'Tis strange if true,
> And yet the old
> Is often new.

When in England, I did not meet him, but I remember
that, in Oxford, Froude one day, walking with me,
pointed to his window, and said, 'There is where all our
light came from.'

I ought also to have recorded that Max Müller, on last Christmas Day, surprised me with the gift of a book.

California, May

Golden Gate, named of old from its flowers. Asia at your doors and South America. Inflamed Expectation haunting men. . . .

The attraction and superiority of California are in its days. It has better days, and more of them, than any other country.

June

My Men. Thomas Carlyle, Louis Agassiz, E. Rockwood Hoar, J. Elliot Cabot, John M. Forbes, Charles K. Newcomb, Philip P. Randolph, Richard Hunt, Alvah Crocker, William B. Ogden, Samuel G. Ward, J. R. Lowell, Sampson Reed, Henry D. Thoreau, A. B. Alcott, Horatio Greenough, Oliver Wendell Holmes, John Muir.

June

In my lifetime have been wrought five miracles, — namely, 1, the Steamboat; 2, the Railroad; 3, the Electric Telegraph; 4, the application of the Spectroscope to astronomy; 5, the Photograph; — five miracles which have altered the relations of nations to each other. Add cheap postage; and the mowing-machine and the horse-rake. A corresponding power has been given to manufactures by the machine for pegging shoes, and the power-loom, and the power-press of the printers. And in dentistry and in surgery, Dr. Jackson's discovery of Anæsthesia. It only needs to add the power which, up to this hour, eludes all human ingenuity, namely, a rudder to the balloon, to give us the dominion of the air, as well as of the sea and the land. But the account is not complete until we add the discovery of Oersted, of the identity of Electricity and Magnetism, and the generalization of that conversion by its application to light, heat, and gravitation. The geologist has found the correspondence of the age of stratified remains to the ascending scale of structure in animal life. Add now, the daily predictions of the weather for the next twenty-four hours for North America, by the Observatory at Washington.

October 18

Bret Harte's visit. Bret Harte referred to my essay on Civilization, that the piano comes so quickly into the shanty, etc., and said, 'Do you know that, on the contrary, it is vice that brings them in? It is the gamblers who bring in the music to California. It is the prostitute who brings in the New York fashions of dress there, and so throughout.' I told him that I spoke also from Pilgrim experience, and knew on good grounds the resistless culture that religion effects.

October 21

Ruskin is a surprise to me. This old book, *Two Paths*, is original, acute, thoroughly informed, and religious.

October

The physicists in general repel me. I have no wish to read them, and thus do not know their names. But the anecdotes of these men of ideas wake curiosity and delight.

October

Look sharply after your thoughts. They come unlooked for, like a new bird seen on your trees, and, if you turn to your usual task, disappear; and you shall never find that perception again; never, I say, — but perhaps years, ages, and I know not what events and worlds may lie between you and its return!

October

The only limit to the praise of Tennyson as a lyric poet is, that he is alive. If he were an ancient, there would be none.

November (?)

Home again from Chicago, Quincy, Springfield, and Dubuque, which I had not believed I should see again, yet found it easier to visit than before, and the kindest reception in each city.

Undated [1872]

One thing is certain: the religions are obsolete when the reforms do not proceed from them.

May (?)

Old Age. We spend a great deal of time in waiting.

May 26, 1872

Yesterday, my sixty-ninth birthday, I found myself on my round of errands in Summer Street, and, though close on the spot where I was born, was looking into a street with some bewilderment and read on the sign *Kingston*

Street, with surprise, finding in the granite blocks no hint
of Nathaniel Goddard's pasture and long wooden fence,
and so of my nearness to my native corner of Chauncy
Place.

Wednesday, July 24

House burned.

Naushon, August 31

I thought to-day, in these rare seaside woods, that if
absolute leisure were offered me, I should run to the college or the scientific school which offered best lectures on
Geology, Chemistry, Minerals, Botany, and seek to make
the alphabets of those sciences clear to me. How could
leisure or labour be better employed? 'Tis never late to
learn them, and every secret opened goes to authorize our
æsthetics. Cato learned Greek at eighty years, but these
are older bibles and oracles than Greek.

Shepheard's Hotel, Cairo, January, 1873

Nothing has struck me more in the streets here than the
erect carriage and walking of the Copts (I suppose them);
better and nobler in figure and movement than any passengers in our cities at home.

On the Nile, January 7

On Tuesday, January 7, we sailed from Cairo for
Philæ, in the dahabeah *Aurora*, with Mahmoud Bedowa,
dragoman; a *reis* or captain, and his mate; ten oarsmen,
two cooks, a factotum boy, a head waiter named Mar-
zook, and second waiter Hassan, — in all eighteen.

Nile, January 7

Egypt is the Nile and its shores. The cultivated land is
a mere green ribbon on either shore of the river. You can
see, as you sail, its quick boundary in rocky mountains
or desart sands. Day after day and week after week of
unbroken sunshine, and though you may see clouds in the
sky, they are merely for ornament, and never rain.

The Prophet says of the Egyptians, 'It is their strength
to sit still.'

Nile, undated

All this journey is a perpetual humiliation, satirizing
and whipping our ignorance. The people despise us because we are helpless babies who cannot speak or understand a word they say; the sphinxes scorn dunces; the
obelisks, the temple walls, defy us with their histories
which we cannot spell. Every new object only makes new
questions which each traveller asks of the other, and none
of us can answer, and each sinks lower in the opinion of
his companion. The people, whether in the boat, or out
of it, are a perpetual study for the excellence and grace of
their forms and motion. No people walk so well, so up-
right as they are, and strong, and flexible; and for studying the nude, our artists should come here and not to
Paris.

Paris [*March* 16 *to April.*]

In the Hotel de Lorraine, Rue de Beaune, Paris, where
Ellen and I took rooms for some weeks during both our
visits to Paris, we lived with James R. Lowell and his
wife, and John Holmes, to our great satisfaction. There

also I received, one evening, a long and happy visit from
Mr. James Cotter Morison, who is writing the *Life of
Comte*. At the house of Mr. Laugel, I was introduced to
Ernest Renan; to Henri Taine; to Elie de Beaumont; and
to some other noted gentlemen. M. Taine sent me, the
next day, his *Littérature anglaise*, in five volumes.

London, April

In London, I saw Fergusson the architect; Browning
the poet; John Stuart Mill; Sir Henry Holland; Huxley;
Tyndall; Lord Houghton; Mr. Gladstone; Dean Stanley;
Lecky; Froude; Thomas Hughes; Lyon Playfair; Sir Arthur Helps; the Duke of Argyle; the Duke of Cleveland;
the Duke of Bedford; Sir Frederick Pollock; Charles
Reade; Mr. Dasent; — with the Amberleys I paid a visit
to Lord Russell at his house, and lunched there. . . .

Mr. Thomas Hughes introduced me to the Cosmo-
politan Club, which meets every Sunday and Wednesday
night at 10 o'clock, and there I saw on two evenings very
agreeable gentlemen, Sir Frederick Pollock, Fergusson,
Lord Houghton, William Story, and others. Professor
Tyndall procured me the privileges of the Athenæum,
which is still the best of the great London Clubs; and also
of the Royal Institution, in Albemarle Street, where he
presides since the death of Faraday.

Oxford, May

At Oxford [April 30 to May 3] I was the guest of Professor Max Müller, and was introduced to Jowett and to
Ruskin and to Mr. Dodgson, author of *Alice in Wonder-
land*, and to many of the University dignitaries. Prince

Leopold was a student, and came home from Max Müller's lecture to lunch with us, and then invited Ellen and me to go to his house, and there showed us his pictures and his album, and there we drank tea. The next day I heard Ruskin's lecture, and we then went home with Ruskin to his chambers, where he showed us his pictures, and told us his doleful opinions of modern society. In the evening we dined with Vice-Chancellor Liddell and a large company.

June (?)

Egypt. Mrs. Helen Bell, it seems, was asked, 'What do you think the Sphinx said to Mr. Emerson?' 'Why,' replied Mrs. Bell, 'the Sphinx probably said to him, "You're another."'

July

Harvard College. My new term as overseer begun at the close of Commencement Day, 1873, and ends at the close of Commencement Day, 1879.

September (?) [1874]

The death of Francis Cabot Lowell is a great loss to me. Now for fifty-seven years since we entered college together, we have been friends, meeting sometimes rarely, sometimes often; seldom living in the same town, we have always met gladly on the old simple terms. He was a conservative, I always of a speculative habit; and often in the wayward politics of former years, we had to compare our different opinions. . . . Mr. Henry Lee Higginson told me how scrupulously honest he was, how slow to avail himself of the right to take up mortgages, the terms of which had not been kept. Mr. H. thought him romantically honest. . . . He was the friend in need, silent but sure, and the character of the giver added rare value to the gift, as if an angel brought you gold. I may well say this, when I recall the fact that on the next day after my house was burned, he came to Concord to express his sympathy in my misfortune, and a few days afterward surprised me with a munificent donation from himself and his children which went far to rebuild it.

Boston, Parker House, Monday night, November

The secret of poetry is never explained, — is always new. We have not got farther than mere wonder at the delicacy of the touch, and the eternity it inherits.

December 5, 1875

Thomas Carlyle's 80th birthday.

INDEX

Palmerston, Lord and Lady, 236.
Palmistry, 182.
Paris, visited, 73–75, 232–35, 335.
Parker, Theodore, 188, 298; thought himself unpopular, 238; death, 284; character of, 284, 285; wished to write Life of Jesus, 301.
Parochial visits, 53.
Past, the, and the present, 178; saints and heroes saved in, 190, 191.
Patmore, Coventry, 231.
Patriotism, 25.
Peabody, Elizabeth, 132.
Peace, Grant's terms of, 311.
Peau d'Ane, Le, 185.
Pedigree, 28.
Penn, William, 52.
Penobscot Indians, 16.
People, the, the supposed ignorance of, 39, 40, 106; works of art never seen by, 104.
Perfection, man alone fails to attain, 46.
Perkins, Colonel, 117.
Persons, the key to, 183.
Phi Beta Kappa, the first ('The American Scholar'), 97, 117, 120, 135; the second, 302.
Phillips, Wendell, his eloquence, 209; without personality, 265.
Philosophy, the reason of a new, 328.
Physicians, 198.
Physicists, 332.
Pierce, Franklin, at Hawthorne's funeral, 305.
Piety, fragrant, 99.
Plato, 311, 314; his *Timæus*, 179; manuscript of, 230.
Plutarch, 112, 154, 155, 311; his *Morals* in English, style of, 328.
Poem, every line of, a poem, 240.
Poems, early, 146.
Poetry, high, is ethical, 126; the finest rhythms and cadences of, yet unfound, 165, 166; of man and nature, 196; must be new

and old, 213; tone in, 324; and eloquence, the difference between, 325; the secret of, 338.
Poets, survival of, 93; common, 274.
Pope, Alexander, poems of, 23; his Moral Essays, 24; his bookishness, 112; has but one good line, 248.
Poverty, not an unmixed good, 162.
Power and joy, 188.
Prayer, efficacy of, 9; public, 31; the effect of a, 94.
Prayers, family, 109, 245; answered, 134.
Preacher, should be a poet, 126.
Preachers, are cunning in proportion to their intelligence, 178; in the Puritan days, 178.
Preaching, and truth, 69; good and bad, 110; a sickly employment, 126.
Prescott, W. H., 208; death, 282.
'Present Age, The,' lectures on, 140, 149–51.
Price, Richard, on Morals, 8, 9.
Priestcraft, 15.
Primary and secondary men, 281.
Principles, the beauty and dignity of, 45.
Proclus, 179.
Progress of an individual in knowledge, 32.
Protest, a brave, 137.
Proverbs of Solomon, 23.
Public prayer, 31.
Punch, 219.
Puritans, New England, 164, 165.
Pusey, Dr. E. B., 330.
Pythologian poem, 4, 6.

Quincy, Josiah, President of Harvard College, 218.

Rabelais, François, 186, 187.
Rachel, Elisa, 234.
Railroads, 183, 194.
Randolph, John, 219.
Randolph, Philip P., a real man, 331.

INDEX

355

Shakespeare, William, his charac-
ters, 56; made England enviable,
239; conspicuousness of, 268;
keeping of his birthday, 303;
should be the study of the Uni-
versity, 304, 314; few valuable
criticisms of, 305.
Shelley, P. B., 170, 179.
Sickness, temporary, chief use of, 9.
Simmons, Lizzie, 315.
Simplicity and goodness, 117.
Sincerity, 138.
Skating, picture of, 122.
Sky, power of certain states of, 310.
Slave-auction, a, 36.
Slave trade, 30.
Slavery, 93; as a question of pure
political economy, 215; the re-
sistance to, 283.
Sleepy Hollow, 270.
Smith, Professor Goldwin, 308.
Smith, Sydney, 231, 236.
Society, nature an antidote for
the influences of, 98; the bone
and sinew of, 215; thought sug-
gested by, 249; balance in, 251.
Society and Solitude, Emerson, 327.
Socrates, Dissertation on the Char-
acter of, 6, 7.
Soldiers, a company of, an offen-
sive spectacle, 120; cause feeling
of the ridiculous, 170.
Solitude, 267.
Soul, and heart, 90; the eternal
tendency of, to become Univer-
sal, 114.
South, the, manners in, 34, 35.
South Carolina, 276.
Southern students, 115.
Southerner, what he asks concern-
ing a man, 113, 115.
Southey, Robert, 89.
Specie payment, suspended, 279.
Spider, spinning from a twig, 205.
Spinoza, Baruch, 320.
Spiritual crises, 114.
Spiritualist, the, and Science, 330.
Sprain, the, 282, 283.
Spring, the return of, 4; a day in,
82, 83.
Stanley, Lyulph, 307.

Stanley, his *Lives of the Philoso-
phers*, 311.
Staples, Sam, on Thoreau, 292.
State, the, is our neighbors, 211.
Sterling, John, 120; could not write
dialogue, 145.
Stillman, W. J., 272, 280.
Storey, Moorfield, 315.
Stowe, H. B., her *Uncle Tom's
Cabin*, 243, 262.
Straight line, in Nature, 205.
Study, a plan of, 24, 25.
Sublimity, 164.
Summer, 131.
Sumner, Charles, at Concord, 285;
at Washington, 290; his works,
326.
Sunset, 136.
Superstitions, are valid influences,
182; of the age, 224.
Supreme Being, discourses on, are
tedious, 108.
Swedenborg, Emanuel, was genu-
ine, 59; his biography, 92; a
cold and passionless man, 177;
his cardinal position in morals,
216.
Swedenborg Chapel, a sermon in,
91.
Swiss tunes, 16.
Syracuse, Temple of Minerva at,
65.
Systems, 148.

Table-talk, 126.
Taine, Henri, 336.
Taylor, Edward ('Father'), as a
preacher, 91, 92; his oratory, 107,
108; and Alcott, 218.
Taylor, Jeremy, 99.
Temperance, 206.
Tennyson, Alfred, Lord, drenched
in Shakespeare, 124, 125; got his
inspiration in gardens, 133; is a
beautiful half of a poet, 136; his
second volume of *Poems*, 181;
his *Ulysses*, 182, 280; a master
of metre, but has no wood-
notes, 205; and Emerson, 231–
33; appearance of, 231, 232; and
Carlyle, 232, 233; publication of

A CATALOG OF SELECTED
DOVER BOOKS
IN ALL FIELDS OF INTEREST

A CATALOG OF SELECTED DOVER
BOOKS IN ALL FIELDS OF INTEREST

CONCERNING THE SPIRITUAL IN ART, Wassily Kandinsky. Pioneering work by father of abstract art. Thoughts on color theory, nature of art. Analysis of earlier masters. 12 illustrations. 80pp. of text. 5⅜ × 8½. 23411-8 Pa. $3.95

ANIMALS: 1,419 Copyright-Free Illustrations of Mammals, Birds, Fish, Insects, etc., Jim Harter (ed.). Clear wood engravings present, in extremely lifelike poses, over 1,000 species of animals. One of the most extensive pictorial sourcebooks of its kind. Captions. Index. 284pp. 9 × 12. 23766-4 Pa. $12.95

CELTIC ART: The Methods of Construction, George Bain. Simple geometric techniques for making Celtic interlacements, spirals, Kells-type initials, animals, humans, etc. Over 500 illustrations. 160pp. 9 × 12. (USO) 22923-8 Pa. $9.95

AN ATLAS OF ANATOMY FOR ARTISTS, Fritz Schider. Most thorough reference work on art anatomy in the world. Hundreds of illustrations, including selections from works by Vesalius, Leonardo, Goya, Ingres, Michelangelo, others. 593 illustrations. 192pp. 7⅛ × 10¼. 20241-0 Pa. $9.95

CELTIC HAND STROKE-BY-STROKE (Irish Half-Uncial from "The Book of Kells"): An Arthur Baker Calligraphy Manual, Arthur Baker. Complete guide to creating each letter of the alphabet in distinctive Celtic manner. Covers hand position, strokes, pens, inks, paper, more. Illustrated. 48pp. 8¼ × 11. 24336-2 Pa. $3.95

EASY ORIGAMI, John Montroll. Charming collection of 32 projects (hat, cup, pelican, piano, swan, many more) specially designed for the novice origami hobbyist. Clearly illustrated easy-to-follow instructions insure that even beginning papercrafters will achieve successful results. 48pp. 8¼ × 11. 27298-2 Pa. $2.95

THE COMPLETE BOOK OF BIRDHOUSE CONSTRUCTION FOR WOOD-WORKERS, Scott D. Campbell. Detailed instructions, illustrations, tables. Also data on bird habitat and instinct patterns. Bibliography. 3 tables. 63 illustrations in 15 figures. 48pp. 5¼ × 8½. 24407-5 Pa. $1.95

BLOOMINGDALE'S ILLUSTRATED 1886 CATALOG: Fashions, Dry Goods and Housewares, Bloomingdale Brothers. Famed merchants' extremely rare catalog depicting about 1,700 products: clothing, housewares, firearms, dry goods, jewelry, more. Invaluable for dating, identifying vintage items. Also, copyright-free graphics for artists, designers. Co-published with Henry Ford Museum & Greenfield Village. 160pp. 8¼ × 11. 25780-0 Pa. $9.95

HISTORIC COSTUME IN PICTURES, Braun & Schneider. Over 1,450 costumed figures in clearly detailed engravings—from dawn of civilization to end of 19th century. Captions. Many folk costumes. 256pp. 8⅜ × 11¾. 23150-X Pa. $11.95

BRASS INSTRUMENTS: Their History and Development, Anthony Baines. Authoritative, updated survey of the evolution of trumpets, trombones, bugles, cornets, French horns, tubas and other brass wind instruments. Over 140 illustrations and 48 music examples. Corrected and updated by author. New preface. Bibliography. 320pp. 5⅜ × 8½. 27574-4 Pa. $9.95

HOLLYWOOD GLAMOR PORTRAITS, John Kobal (ed.). 145 photos from 1926–49. Harlow, Gable, Bogart, Bacall; 94 stars in all. Full background on photographers, technical aspects. 160pp. 8⅜ × 11¼. 23352-9 Pa. $11.95

MAX AND MORITZ, Wilhelm Busch. Great humor classic in both German and English. Also 10 other works: "Cat and Mouse," "Plisch and Plumm," etc. 216pp. 5⅜ × 8½. 20181-3 Pa. $5.95

THE RAVEN AND OTHER FAVORITE POEMS, Edgar Allan Poe. Over 40 of the author's most memorable poems: "The Bells," "Ulalume," "Israfel," "To Helen," "The Conqueror Worm," "Eldorado," "Annabel Lee," many more. Alphabetic lists of titles and first lines. 64pp. 5³⁄₁₆ × 8¼. 26685-0 Pa. $1.00

SEVEN SCIENCE FICTION NOVELS, H. G. Wells. The standard collection of the great novels. Complete, unabridged. First Men in the Moon, Island of Dr. Moreau, War of the Worlds, Food of the Gods, Invisible Man, Time Machine, In the Days of the Comet. Total of 1,015pp. 5⅜ × 8½. (USO) 20264-X Clothbd. $29.95

AMULETS AND SUPERSTITIONS, E. A. Wallis Budge. Comprehensive discourse on origin, powers of amulets in many ancient cultures: Arab, Persian, Babylonian, Assyrian, Egyptian, Gnostic, Hebrew, Phoenician, Syriac, etc. Covers cross, swastika, crucifix, seals, rings, stones, etc. 584pp. 5⅜ × 8½. 23573-4 Pa. $12.95

RUSSIAN STORIES/PYCCKNE PACCKA3bI: A Dual-Language Book, edited by Gleb Struve. Twelve tales by such masters as Chekhov, Tolstoy, Dostoevsky, Pushkin, others. Excellent word-for-word English translations on facing pages, plus teaching and study aids, Russian/English vocabulary, biographical/critical introductions, more. 416pp. 5⅜ × 8½. 26244-8 Pa. $8.95

PHILADELPHIA THEN AND NOW: 60 Sites Photographed in the Past and Present, Kenneth Finkel and Susan Oyama. Rare photographs of City Hall, Logan Square, Independence Hall, Betsy Ross House, other landmarks juxtaposed with contemporary views. Captures changing face of historic city. Introduction. Captions. 128pp. 8¼ × 11. 25790-8 Pa. $9.95

AIA ARCHITECTURAL GUIDE TO NASSAU AND SUFFOLK COUNTIES, LONG ISLAND, The American Institute of Architects, Long Island Chapter, and the Society for the Preservation of Long Island Antiquities. Comprehensive, well-researched and generously illustrated volume brings to life over three centuries of Long Island's great architectural heritage. More than 240 photographs with authoritative, extensively detailed captions. 176pp. 8¼ × 11. 26946-9 Pa. $14.95

NORTH AMERICAN INDIAN LIFE: Customs and Traditions of 23 Tribes, Elsie Clews Parsons (ed.). 27 fictionalized essays by noted anthropologists examine religion, customs, government, additional facets of life among the Winnebago, Crow, Zuni, Eskimo, other tribes. 480pp. 6⅛ × 9¼. 27377-6 Pa. $10.95

FRANK LLOYD WRIGHT'S HOLLYHOCK HOUSE, Donald Hoffmann. Lavishly illustrated, carefully documented study of one of Wright's most controversial residential designs. Over 120 photographs, floor plans, elevations, etc. Detailed perceptive text by noted Wright scholar. Index. 128pp. 9¼ × 10¾.
27133-1 Pa. $11.95

THE MALE AND FEMALE FIGURE IN MOTION: 60 Classic Photographic Sequences, Eadweard Muybridge. 60 true-action photographs of men and women walking, running, climbing, bending, turning, etc., reproduced from rare 19th-century masterpiece. vi + 121pp. 9 × 12.
24745-7 Pa. $10.95

1001 QUESTIONS ANSWERED ABOUT THE SEASHORE, N. J. Berrill and Jacquelyn Berrill. Queries answered about dolphins, sea snails, sponges, starfish, fishes, shore birds, many others. Covers appearance, breeding, growth, feeding, much more. 305pp. 5¼ × 8¼.
23366-9 Pa. $7.95

GUIDE TO OWL WATCHING IN NORTH AMERICA, Donald S. Heintzelman. Superb guide offers complete data and descriptions of 19 species: barn owl, screech owl, snowy owl, many more. Expert coverage of owl-watching equipment, conservation, migrations and invasions, etc. Guide to observing sites. 84 illustrations. xiii + 193pp. 5⅜ × 8½.
27344-X Pa. $8.95

MEDICINAL AND OTHER USES OF NORTH AMERICAN PLANTS: A Historical Survey with Special Reference to the Eastern Indian Tribes, Charlotte Erichsen-Brown. Chronological historical citations document 500 years of usage of plants, trees, shrubs native to eastern Canada, northeastern U.S. Also complete identifying information. 343 illustrations. 544pp. 6½ × 9¼.
25951-X Pa. $12.95

STORYBOOK MAZES, Dave Phillips. 23 stories and mazes on two-page spreads: Wizard of Oz, Treasure Island, Robin Hood, etc. Solutions. 64pp. 8¼ × 11.
23628-5 Pa. $2.95

NEGRO FOLK MUSIC, U.S.A., Harold Courlander. Noted folklorist's scholarly yet readable analysis of rich and varied musical tradition. Includes authentic versions of over 40 folk songs. Valuable bibliography and discography. xi + 324pp. 5⅜ × 8½.
27350-4 Pa. $7.95

MOVIE-STAR PORTRAITS OF THE FORTIES, John Kobal (ed.). 163 glamor, studio photos of 106 stars of the 1940s: Rita Hayworth, Ava Gardner, Marlon Brando, Clark Gable, many more. 176pp. 8⅜ × 11¼.
23546-7 Pa. $11.95

BENCHLEY LOST AND FOUND, Robert Benchley. Finest humor from early 30s, about pet peeves, child psychologists, post office and others. Mostly unavailable elsewhere. 73 illustrations by Peter Arno and others. 183pp. 5⅜ × 8½.
22410-4 Pa. $5.95

YEKL and THE IMPORTED BRIDEGROOM AND OTHER STORIES OF YIDDISH NEW YORK, Abraham Cahan. Film Hester Street based on Yekl (1896). Novel, other stories among first about Jewish immigrants on N.Y.'s East Side. 240pp. 5⅜ × 8½.
22427-9 Pa. $6.95

SELECTED POEMS, Walt Whitman. Generous sampling from *Leaves of Grass.* Twenty-four poems include "I Hear America Singing," "Song of the Open Road," "I Sing the Body Electric," "When Lilacs Last in the Dooryard Bloom'd," "O Captain! My Captain!"—all reprinted from an authoritative edition. Lists of titles and first lines. 128pp. 5³⁄₁₆ × 8¼.
26878-0 Pa. $1.00

CATALOG OF DOVER BOOKS

MY BONDAGE AND MY FREEDOM, Frederick Douglass. Born a slave, Douglass became outspoken force in antislavery movement. The best of Douglass' autobiographies. Graphic description of slave life. 464pp. 5⅜ × 8½. 22457-0 Pa. $8.95

FOLLOWING THE EQUATOR: A Journey Around the World, Mark Twain. Fascinating humorous account of 1897 voyage to Hawaii, Australia, India, New Zealand, etc. Ironic, bemused reports on peoples, customs, climate, flora and fauna, politics, much more. 197 illustrations. 720pp. 5⅜ × 8½. 26113-1 Pa. $15.95

THE PEOPLE CALLED SHAKERS, Edward D. Andrews. Definitive study of Shakers: origins, beliefs, practices, dances, social organization, furniture and crafts, etc. 33 illustrations. 351pp. 5⅜ × 8½. 21081-2 Pa. $8.95

THE MYTHS OF GREECE AND ROME, H. A. Guerber. A classic of mythology, generously illustrated, long prized for its simple, graphic, accurate retelling of the principal myths of Greece and Rome, and for its commentary on their origins and significance. With 64 illustrations by Michelangelo, Raphael, Titian, Rubens, Canova, Bernini and others. 480pp. 5⅜ × 8½. 27584-1 Pa. $9.95

PSYCHOLOGY OF MUSIC, Carl E. Seashore. Classic work discusses music as a medium from psychological viewpoint. Clear treatment of physical acoustics, auditory apparatus, sound perception, development of musical skills, nature of musical feeling, host of other topics. 88 figures. 408pp. 5⅜ × 8½. 21851-1 Pa. $9.95

THE PHILOSOPHY OF HISTORY, Georg W. Hegel. Great classic of Western thought develops concept that history is not chance but rational process, the evolution of freedom. 457pp. 5⅜ × 8½. 20112-0 Pa. $9.95

THE BOOK OF TEA, Kakuzo Okakura. Minor classic of the Orient: entertaining, charming explanation, interpretation of traditional Japanese culture in terms of tea ceremony. 94pp. 5⅜ × 8½. 20070-1 Pa. $3.95

LIFE IN ANCIENT EGYPT, Adolf Erman. Fullest, most thorough, detailed older account with much not in more recent books, domestic life, religion, magic, medicine, commerce, much more. Many illustrations reproduce tomb paintings, carvings, hieroglyphs, etc. 597pp. 5⅜ × 8½. 22632-8 Pa. $10.95

SUNDIALS, Their Theory and Construction, Albert Waugh. Far and away the best, most thorough coverage of ideas, mathematics concerned, types, construction, adjusting anywhere. Simple, nontechnical treatment allows even children to build several of these dials. Over 100 illustrations. 230pp. 5⅜ × 8½. 22947-5 Pa. $7.95

DYNAMICS OF FLUIDS IN POROUS MEDIA, Jacob Bear. For advanced students of ground water hydrology, soil mechanics and physics, drainage and irrigation engineering, and more. 335 illustrations. Exercises, with answers. 784pp. 6⅛ × 9¼. 65675-6 Pa. $19.95

SONGS OF EXPERIENCE: Facsimile Reproduction with 26 Plates in Full Color, William Blake. 26 full-color plates from a rare 1826 edition. Includes "The Tyger," "London," "Holy Thursday," and other poems. Printed text of poems. 48pp. 5¼ × 7. 24636-1 Pa. $4.95

OLD-TIME VIGNETTES IN FULL COLOR, Carol Belanger Grafton (ed.). Over 390 charming, often sentimental illustrations, selected from archives of Victorian graphics—pretty women posing, children playing, food, flowers, kittens and puppies, smiling cherubs, birds and butterflies, much more. All copyright-free. 48pp. 9¼ × 12¼. 27269-9 Pa. $5.95

PERSPECTIVE FOR ARTISTS, Rex Vicat Cole. Depth, perspective of sky and sea, shadows, much more, not usually covered. 391 diagrams, 81 reproductions of drawings and paintings. 279pp. 5⅜ × 8½. 22487-2 Pa. $6.95

DRAWING THE LIVING FIGURE, Joseph Sheppard. Innovative approach to artistic anatomy focuses on specifics of surface anatomy, rather than muscles and bones. Over 170 drawings of live models in front, back and side views, and in widely varying poses. Accompanying diagrams. 177 illustrations. Introduction. Index. 144pp. 8⅜ × 11¼. 26723-7 Pa. $8.95

GOTHIC AND OLD ENGLISH ALPHABETS: 100 Complete Fonts, Dan X. Solo. Add power, elegance to posters, signs, other graphics with 100 stunning copyright-free alphabets: Blackstone, Dolbey, Germania, 97 more—including many lower-case, numerals, punctuation marks. 104pp. 8⅛ × 11. 24695-7 Pa. $8.95

HOW TO DO BEADWORK, Mary White. Fundamental book on craft from simple projects to five-bead chains and woven works. 106 illustrations. 142pp. 5⅜ × 8. 20697-1 Pa. $4.95

THE BOOK OF WOOD CARVING, Charles Marshall Sayers. Finest book for beginners discusses fundamentals and offers 34 designs. "Absolutely first rate . . . well thought out and well executed."—E. J. Tangerman. 118pp. 7¾ × 10⅝. 23654-4 Pa. $5.95

ILLUSTRATED CATALOG OF CIVIL WAR MILITARY GOODS: Union Army Weapons, Insignia, Uniform Accessories, and Other Equipment, Schuyler, Hartley, and Graham. Rare, profusely illustrated 1846 catalog includes Union Army uniform and dress regulations, arms and ammunition, coats, insignia, flags, swords, rifles, etc. 226 illustrations. 160pp. 9 × 12. 24939-5 Pa. $10.95

WOMEN'S FASHIONS OF THE EARLY 1900s: An Unabridged Republication of "New York Fashions, 1909," National Cloak & Suit Co. Rare catalog of mail-order fashions documents women's and children's clothing styles shortly after the turn of the century. Captions offer full descriptions, prices. Invaluable resource for fashion, costume historians. Approximately 725 illustrations. 128pp. 8⅜ × 11¼. 27276-1 Pa. $11.95

THE 1912 AND 1915 GUSTAV STICKLEY FURNITURE CATALOGS, Gustav Stickley. With over 200 detailed illustrations and descriptions, these two catalogs are essential reading and reference materials and identification guides for Stickley furniture. Captions cite materials, dimensions and prices. 112pp. 6½ × 9¼. 26676-1 Pa. $9.95

EARLY AMERICAN LOCOMOTIVES, John H. White, Jr. Finest locomotive engravings from early 19th century: historical (1804–74), main-line (after 1870) special, foreign, etc. 147 plates. 142pp. 11⅜ × 8¼. 22772-3 Pa. $10.95

THE TALL SHIPS OF TODAY IN PHOTOGRAPHS, Frank O. Braynard. Lavishly illustrated tribute to nearly 100 majestic contemporary sailing vessels: Amerigo Vespucci, Clearwater, Constitution, Eagle, Mayflower, Sea Cloud, Victory, many more. Authoritative captions provide statistics, background on each ship. 190 black-and-white photographs and illustrations. Introduction. 128pp. 8⅞ × 11¾. 27163-3 Pa. $13.95

EARLY NINETEENTH-CENTURY CRAFTS AND TRADES, Peter Stockham (ed.). Extremely rare 1807 volume describes to youngsters the crafts and trades of the day: brickmaker, weaver, dressmaker, bookbinder, ropemaker, saddler, many more. Quaint prose, charming illustrations for each craft. 20 black-and-white line illustrations. 192pp. 4⅝ × 6.   27293-1 Pa. $4.95

VICTORIAN FASHIONS AND COSTUMES FROM HARPER'S BAZAR, 1867–1898, Stella Blum (ed.). Day costumes, evening wear, sports clothes, shoes, hats, other accessories in over 1,000 detailed engravings. 320pp. 9⅜ × 12¼.
     22990-4 Pa. $13.95

GUSTAV STICKLEY, THE CRAFTSMAN, Mary Ann Smith. Superb study surveys broad scope of Stickley's achievement, especially in architecture. Design philosophy, rise and fall of the Craftsman empire, descriptions and floor plans for many Craftsman houses, more. 86 black-and-white halftones. 31 line illustrations. Introduction. 208pp. 6½ × 9¼.   27210-9 Pa. $9.95

THE LONG ISLAND RAIL ROAD IN EARLY PHOTOGRAPHS, Ron Ziel. Over 220 rare photos, informative text document origin (1844) and development of rail service on Long Island. Vintage views of early trains, locomotives, stations, passengers, crews, much more. Captions. 8⅞ × 11¾.   26301-0 Pa. $13.95

THE BOOK OF OLD SHIPS: From Egyptian Galleys to Clipper Ships, Henry B. Culver. Superb, authoritative history of sailing vessels, with 80 magnificent line illustrations. Galley, bark, caravel, longship, whaler, many more. Detailed, informative text on each vessel by noted naval historian. Introduction. 256pp. 5⅜ × 8½.   27332-6 Pa. $6.95

TEN BOOKS ON ARCHITECTURE, Vitruvius. The most important book ever written on architecture. Early Roman aesthetics, technology, classical orders, site selection, all other aspects. Morgan translation. 331pp. 5⅜ × 8½. 20645-9 Pa. $8.95

THE HUMAN FIGURE IN MOTION, Eadweard Muybridge. More than 4,500 stopped-action photos, in action series, showing undraped men, women, children jumping, lying down, throwing, sitting, wrestling, carrying, etc. 390pp. 7⅞ × 10⅝.
     20204-6 Clothbd. $24.95

TREES OF THE EASTERN AND CENTRAL UNITED STATES AND CANADA, William M. Harlow. Best one-volume guide to 140 trees. Full descriptions, woodlore, range, etc. Over 600 illustrations. Handy size. 288pp. 4½ × 6⅜.
     20395-6 Pa. $5.95

SONGS OF WESTERN BIRDS, Dr. Donald J. Borror. Complete song and call repertoire of 60 western species, including flycatchers, juncoes, cactus wrens, many more—includes fully illustrated booklet.   Cassette and manual 99913-0 $8.95

GROWING AND USING HERBS AND SPICES, Milo Miloradovich. Versatile handbook provides all the information needed for cultivation and use of all the herbs and spices available in North America. 4 illustrations. Index. Glossary. 236pp. 5⅜ × 8½.   25058-X Pa. $6.95

BIG BOOK OF MAZES AND LABYRINTHS, Walter Shepherd. 50 mazes and labyrinths in all—classical, solid, ripple, and more—in one great volume. Perfect inexpensive puzzler for clever youngsters. Full solutions. 112pp. 8⅛ × 11.
     22951-3 Pa. $4.95

THE WIT AND HUMOR OF OSCAR WILDE, Alvin Redman (ed.). More than 1,000 ripostes, paradoxes, wisecracks: Work is the curse of the drinking classes; I can resist everything except temptation; etc. 258pp. 5⅜ × 8½.   20602-5 Pa. $5.95

SHAKESPEARE LEXICON AND QUOTATION DICTIONARY, Alexander Schmidt. Full definitions, locations, shades of meaning in every word in plays and poems. More than 50,000 exact quotations. 1,485pp. 6½ × 9¼. 2-vol. set.
Vol. I: 22726-X Pa. $16.95
Vol. 2: 22727-8 Pa. $15.95

SELECTED POEMS, Emily Dickinson. Over 100 best-known, best-loved poems by one of America's foremost poets, reprinted from authoritative early editions. No comparable edition at this price. Index of first lines. 64pp. 5³⁄₁₆ × 8¼.
26466-1 Pa. $1.00

CELEBRATED CASES OF JUDGE DEE (DEE GOONG AN), translated by Robert van Gulik. Authentic 18th-century Chinese detective novel; Dee and associates solve three interlocked cases. Led to van Gulik's own stories with same characters. Extensive introduction. 9 illustrations. 237pp. 5⅜ × 8½.
23337-5 Pa. $6.95

THE MALLEUS MALEFICARUM OF KRAMER AND SPRENGER, translated by Montague Summers. Full text of most important witchhunter's "bible," used by both Catholics and Protestants. 278pp. 6⅝ × 10.   22802-9 Pa. $11.95

SPANISH STORIES/CUENTOS ESPAÑOLES: A Dual-Language Book, Angel Flores (ed.). Unique format offers 13 great stories in Spanish by Cervantes, Borges, others. Faithful English translations on facing pages. 352pp. 5⅜ × 8½.
25399-6 Pa. $8.95

THE CHICAGO WORLD'S FAIR OF 1893: A Photographic Record, Stanley Appelbaum (ed.). 128 rare photos show 200 buildings, Beaux-Arts architecture, Midway, original Ferris Wheel, Edison's kinetoscope, more. Architectural emphasis; full text. 116pp. 8¼ × 11.   23990-X Pa. $9.95

OLD QUEENS, N.Y., IN EARLY PHOTOGRAPHS, Vincent F. Seyfried and William Asadorian. Over 160 rare photographs of Maspeth, Jamaica, Jackson Heights, and other areas. Vintage views of DeWitt Clinton mansion, 1939 World's Fair and more. Captions. 192pp. 8⅞ × 11.   26358-4 Pa. $12.95

CAPTURED BY THE INDIANS: 15 Firsthand Accounts, 1750–1870, Frederick Drimmer. Astounding true historical accounts of grisly torture, bloody conflicts, relentless pursuits, miraculous escapes and more, by people who lived to tell the tale. 384pp. 5⅜ × 8½.   24901-8 Pa. $8.95

THE WORLD'S GREAT SPEECHES, Lewis Copeland and Lawrence W. Lamm (eds.). Vast collection of 278 speeches of Greeks to 1970. Powerful and effective models; unique look at history. 842pp. 5⅜ × 8½.   20468-5 Pa. $14.95

THE BOOK OF THE SWORD, Sir Richard F. Burton. Great Victorian scholar/adventurer's eloquent, erudite history of the "queen of weapons"—from prehistory to early Roman Empire. Evolution and development of early swords, variations (sabre, broadsword, cutlass, scimitar, etc.), much more. 336pp. 6⅛ × 9¼. 25434-8 Pa. $8.95

PHOTOGRAPHIC SKETCHBOOK OF THE CIVIL WAR, Alexander Gardner. 100 photos taken on field during the Civil War. Famous shots of Manassas, Harper's Ferry, Lincoln, Richmond, slave pens, etc. 244pp. 10⅝ × 8¼.
22731-6 Pa. $9.95

FIVE ACRES AND INDEPENDENCE, Maurice G. Kains. Great back-to-the-land classic explains basics of self-sufficient farming. The one book to get. 95 illustrations. 397pp. 5⅜ × 8½.
20974-1 Pa. $7.95

SONGS OF EASTERN BIRDS, Dr. Donald J. Borror. Songs and calls of 60 species most common to eastern U.S.: warblers, woodpeckers, flycatchers, thrushes, larks, many more in high-quality recording.
Cassette and manual 99912-2 $8.95

A MODERN HERBAL, Margaret Grieve. Much the fullest, most exact, most useful compilation of herbal material. Gigantic alphabetical encyclopedia, from aconite to zedoary, gives botanical information, medical properties, folklore, economic uses, much else. Indispensable to serious reader. 161 illustrations. 888pp. 6½ × 9¼. 2-vol. set. (USO)
Vol. I: 22798-7 Pa. $9.95
Vol. II: 22799-5 Pa. $9.95

HIDDEN TREASURE MAZE BOOK, Dave Phillips. Solve 34 challenging mazes accompanied by heroic tales of adventure. Evil dragons, people-eating plants, bloodthirsty giants, many more dangerous adversaries lurk at every twist and turn. 34 mazes, stories, solutions. 48pp. 8¼ × 11.
24566-7 Pa. $2.95

LETTERS OF W. A. MOZART, Wolfgang A. Mozart. Remarkable letters show bawdy wit, humor, imagination, musical insights, contemporary musical world; includes some letters from Leopold Mozart. 276pp. 5⅜ × 8½.
22859-2 Pa. $7.95

BASIC PRINCIPLES OF CLASSICAL BALLET, Agrippina Vaganova. Great Russian theoretician, teacher explains methods for teaching classical ballet. 118 illustrations. 175pp. 5⅜ × 8½.
22036-2 Pa. $4.95

THE JUMPING FROG, Mark Twain. Revenge edition. The original story of The Celebrated Jumping Frog of Calaveras County, a hapless French translation, and Twain's hilarious "retranslation" from the French. 12 illustrations. 66pp. 5⅜ × 8½.
22686-7 Pa. $3.95

BEST REMEMBERED POEMS, Martin Gardner (ed.). The 126 poems in this superb collection of 19th- and 20th-century British and American verse range from Shelley's "To a Skylark" to the impassioned "Renascence" of Edna St. Vincent Millay and to Edward Lear's whimsical "The Owl and the Pussycat." 224pp. 5⅜ × 8½.
27165-X Pa. $4.95

COMPLETE SONNETS, William Shakespeare. Over 150 exquisite poems deal with love, friendship, the tyranny of time, beauty's evanescence, death and other themes in language of remarkable power, precision and beauty. Glossary of archaic terms. 80pp. 5³⁄₁₆ × 8¼.
26686-9 Pa. $1.00

BODIES IN A BOOKSHOP, R. T. Campbell. Challenging mystery of blackmail and murder with ingenious plot and superbly drawn characters. In the best tradition of British suspense fiction. 192pp. 5⅜ × 8½.
24720-1 Pa. $5.95

CATALOG OF DOVER BOOKS

PIANO TUNING, J. Cree Fischer. Clearest, best book for beginner, amateur. Simple repairs, raising dropped notes, tuning by easy method of flattened fifths. No previous skills needed. 4 illustrations. 201pp. 5⅜ × 8½. 23267-0 Pa. $5.95

A SOURCE BOOK IN THEATRICAL HISTORY, A. M. Nagler. Contemporary observers on acting, directing, make-up, costuming, stage props, machinery, scene design, from Ancient Greece to Chekhov. 611pp. 5⅜ × 8½. 20515-0 Pa. $11.95

THE COMPLETE NONSENSE OF EDWARD LEAR, Edward Lear. All nonsense limericks, zany alphabets, Owl and Pussycat, songs, nonsense botany, etc., illustrated by Lear. Total of 320pp. 5⅜ × 8½. (USO) 20167-8 Pa. $6.95

VICTORIAN PARLOUR POETRY: An Annotated Anthology, Michael R. Turner. 117 gems by Longfellow, Tennyson, Browning, many lesser-known poets. "The Village Blacksmith," "Curfew Must Not Ring Tonight," "Only a Baby Small," dozens more, often difficult to find elsewhere. Index of poets, titles, first lines. xxiii + 325pp. 5⅜ × 8¼. 27044-0 Pa. $8.95

DUBLINERS, James Joyce. Fifteen stories offer vivid, tightly focused observations of the lives of Dublin's poorer classes. At least one, "The Dead," is considered a masterpiece. Reprinted complete and unabridged from standard edition. 160pp. 5³⁄₁₆ × 8¼. 26870-5 Pa. $1.00

THE HAUNTED MONASTERY and THE CHINESE MAZE MURDERS, Robert van Gulik. Two full novels by van Gulik, set in 7th-century China, continue adventures of Judge Dee and his companions. An evil Taoist monastery, seemingly supernatural events; overgrown topiary maze hides strange crimes. 27 illustrations. 328pp. 5⅜ × 8½. 23502-5 Pa. $7.95

THE BOOK OF THE SACRED MAGIC OF ABRAMELIN THE MAGE, translated by S. MacGregor Mathers. Medieval manuscript of ceremonial magic. Basic document in Aleister Crowley, Golden Dawn groups. 268pp. 5⅜ × 8½. 23211-5 Pa. $8.95

NEW RUSSIAN-ENGLISH AND ENGLISH-RUSSIAN DICTIONARY, M. A. O'Brien. This is a remarkably handy Russian dictionary, containing a surprising amount of information, including over 70,000 entries. 366pp. 4½ × 6⅛. 20208-9 Pa. $9.95

HISTORIC HOMES OF THE AMERICAN PRESIDENTS, Second, Revised Edition, Irvin Haas. A traveler's guide to American Presidential homes, most open to the public, depicting and describing homes occupied by every American President from George Washington to George Bush. With visiting hours, admission charges, travel routes. 175 photographs. Index. 160pp. 8¼ × 11. 26751-2 Pa. $10.95

NEW YORK IN THE FORTIES, Andreas Feininger. 162 brilliant photographs by the well-known photographer, formerly with *Life* magazine. Commuters, shoppers, Times Square at night, much else from city at its peak. Captions by John von Hartz. 181pp. 9¼ × 10¾. 23585-8 Pa. $12.95

INDIAN SIGN LANGUAGE, William Tomkins. Over 525 signs developed by Sioux and other tribes. Written instructions and diagrams. Also 290 pictographs. 111pp. 6⅛ × 9¼. 22029-X Pa. $3.50

CATALOG OF DOVER BOOKS

THE INFLUENCE OF SEA POWER UPON HISTORY, 1660–1783, A. T. Mahan. Influential classic of naval history and tactics still used as text in war colleges. First paperback edition. 4 maps. 24 battle plans. 640pp. 5⅜ × 8½.
25509-3 Pa. $12.95

THE STORY OF THE TITANIC AS TOLD BY ITS SURVIVORS, Jack Winocour (ed.). What it was really like. Panic, despair, shocking inefficiency, and a little heroism. More thrilling than any fictional account. 26 illustrations. 320pp. 5⅜ × 8½.
20610-6 Pa. $8.95

FAIRY AND FOLK TALES OF THE IRISH PEASANTRY, William Butler Yeats (ed.). Treasury of 64 tales from the twilight world of Celtic myth and legend: "The Soul Cages," "The Kildare Pooka," "King O'Toole and his Goose," many more. Introduction and Notes by W. B. Yeats. 352pp. 5⅜ × 8½.
26941-8 Pa. $8.95

BUDDHIST MAHAYANA TEXTS, E. B. Cowell and Others (eds.). Superb, accurate translations of basic documents in Mahayana Buddhism, highly important in history of religions. The Buddha-karita of Asvaghosha, Larger Sukhavativyuha, more. 448pp. 5⅜ × 8½.
25552-2 Pa. $9.95

ONE TWO THREE . . . INFINITY: Facts and Speculations of Science, George Gamow. Great physicist's fascinating, readable overview of contemporary science: number theory, relativity, fourth dimension, entropy, genes, atomic structure, much more. 128 illustrations. Index. 352pp. 5⅜ × 8½.
25664-2 Pa. $8.95

ENGINEERING IN HISTORY, Richard Shelton Kirby, et al. Broad, nontechnical survey of history's major technological advances: birth of Greek science, industrial revolution, electricity and applied science, 20th-century automation, much more. 181 illustrations. ". . . excellent . . ."—Isis. Bibliography. vii + 530pp. 5⅜ × 8¼.
26412-2 Pa. $14.95

Prices subject to change without notice.

Available at your book dealer or write for free catalog to Dept. GI, Dover Publications, Inc., 31 East 2nd St., Mineola, N.Y. 11501. Dover publishes more than 500 books each year on science, elementary and advanced mathematics, biology, music, art, literary history, social sciences and other areas.